To Elise John
from
Anna C. Dietz

Jan. 1-39

ALLURING WISCONSIN

THE HISTORIC GLAMOR AND NATURAL LOVELINESS OF AN AMERICAN COMMONWEALTH

ALLURING WISCONSIN

THE HISTORIC GLAMOR
AND NATURAL LOVELINESS
OF AN AMERICAN COMMONWEALTH

By
FRED L. HOLMES
Author
"Abraham Lincoln Traveled This Way"
"George Washington Traveled This Way"

With Map and Plates
from Original Photographs

Milwaukee
E. M. HALE and COMPANY
1937

First Printing, November 1937
Second Printing, February 1938

HE THAT WOULD BRING HOME THE WEALTH OF THE INDIES
MUST CARRY THE WEALTH OF THE INDIES WITH HIM.
SO IT IS IN TRAVELLING: A MAN MUST CARRY KNOWLEDGE
WITH HIM IF HE WOULD BRING HOME KNOWLEDGE.

Statement on facade of Union Station at
Washington, D. C.

TO

HELEN AND MARGARET

WHO ACCOMPANIED
ME ON MANY OF
THESE LITTLE JOURNEYS
IN WISCONSIN
THIS VOLUME IS DEDICATED

PREFACE

THERE is health in leisurely journeys taken in Wisconsin. The bold headlands left by the glaciers, the hundreds of talkative streams, little and big, along the way, the bluish eyelets of water peeking from beneath green plumed pines in northern Wisconsin, all give inspiration to life and compensation for any discomforts. Beauty abounds in Wisconsin.

Early in the nineteenth century, the Rev. Jedediah Morse, father of the inventor of the telegraph, suggested to John C. Calhoun, Secretary of War, that Wisconsin be kept as an Indian domain. He gave this advice because the country was such a wilderness of silent shade, gemmed with lakes and carpeted with wild flowers. Instead, a land-hungry people took it for home and playground.

On the rocks in southwestern Wisconsin is written with the finger of a bold hand a story of ages before there was life. In the hills of Baraboo and around Wausau geologists read on the pages of hardened stone, scarred by millenial storms, the record of the time when majestic peaks, higher than the Rockies, towered on the landscape. Within the land of a thousand shining lakes and a dozen spray-tossed waterfalls in the northern section the retreating icesheet did a piece of artistic landscaping thirty thousand years ago that has been a spiritual and temporal blessing to the people. And, oh! what a pleasure there is in a day of sunshine in the big woods of northern Wisconsin!

These journeys to Wisconsin's scenic spots were taken over a period of several years. Many were on days stolen from office work; some were week-end visits; while others were vacation jaunts. Each tour relieved the grim and dullness of quotidian life; each furnished hours of rich idleness. The stories presented are the roadside wonders glimpsed and the awakened voices heard on these journeys. No one can love Wisconsin deeply until a visit has been made to some of her nature shrines. The accolade of beauty has touched many of these wayside spots. Like houses of prayer they bid one to return again and again for soul nutriment.

For years I have been under a heavy personal debt to Mr. Louis W. Bridgman, Mr. Albert O. Barton, Prof. E. F. Bean, State Geologist, and Dr. Glenn Frank, former President of the University of Wisconsin, for encouragement each has given to my vacation hobbies. Both Mr. Bridgman and Mr. Barton have read the manuscript and offered many valuable suggestions.

My debt to Mr. Bronte H. Leicht, editor for the Wisconsin Department of Agriculture and Markets, is heavy. He has co-operated with me in the selection of pictures to make the illustrations for this volume representative of Wisconsin's beauty. Many of the scenes appearing were photographed by the author; a large number were selected from the extensive collection maintained by the Department of Agriculture and Markets; a few were furnished by the University Bureau of Visual Instruction, the Wisconsin Conservation Commission, the Milwaukee Association of Commerce and the Milwaukee Journal. These camera glimpses speak a faithful language.

Loitering along the way, I have met hundreds of people who by personal assistance and suggestions have intensified with color the days of my wanderings. Mrs. Eleanore Droster has been of great assistance in the preparation of this book for the public.

With many reservations I send this little volume forth. No doubt some secluded spot has escaped my deserved attention. To those skeptical of what is here put down, I only ask that they join the pilgrimage of four million tourists who annually visit Wisconsin and be convinced.

FRED L. HOLMES

MADISON, WISCONSIN

Areas of Wisconsin's Alluring Scenery Designated by Chapter Number and Title

FOREWORD

WISCONSIN'S OUTDOOR LIVING ROOM

WITH the passing years much will be said of the glories of Wisconsin's outdoors. Volumes are still to be written on our lands, our waters, our forests, our fish, our birds, our animals.

I venture the prediction that in the library still to be made, this book, "Alluring Wisconsin," by Fred L. Holmes, because of its basic nature and excellence, will hold a secure and valuable place. Here are the things we have—the facts on which our conservation program is being built. Here is a story of unpathed waters; undreamed vistas; undedicated grandeur of nature.

Years ago, Wisconsin was designated as the "Playground of the Middle West." In this interesting account Mr. Holmes not only lists our assets but tells us why we have them. To him every cloud coloring, every shady glen, every tumbling waterfall has a message for the visitor who follows his paths by the lakes, through the cool pine forests, and up the hilltops where once blazed the Indian signal fires.

No one reading this volume can help but be impressed that millions of our acres of land and water have a value of more than financial consideration. Mr. Holmes gives us a spiritual appraisal necessary to judge this state's full contribution to society. The achievements of transplanted old world civilizations and their touch of quaintness on life today are identified. Legend and story, fact and history, and the subdued tints of clear waters, rich sunshine and the deep immensity of still summer nights were on his palette when he painted this portrait of his native state.

Wisconsin is fortunate to have Mr. Holmes, a curator of the Wisconsin Historical Society, a veteran Wisconsin newspaper man, a painstaking student of Wisconsin and its history, record this biography of the beauties of the commonwealth.

Philip F. La Follette

MADISON, WISCONSIN
July 12, 1937

CONTENTS

LIST OF ILLUSTRATIONS

Group I

DEVILS LAKE COUNTRY AND AZTALAN

Group II

GREEN BAY REGION

Group III

APOSTLE ISLANDS

Group IV

MISSISSIPPI RIVER

Group V

OUTSIDE THE GLACIAL PATH

Group VI

THE KICKAPOO VALLEY

Group VII

GREEN COUNTY

Group VIII

THE DELLS

Group IX

DURWARD'S GLEN

Group XII

CHAIN O' LAKES, WAUPACA

Group XIII

WASHINGTON ISLAND AND THE KETTLE MORAINE

Group XIV

MILWAUKEE

Group XV

LAND O' LAKES

Group XVI

SUPERIOR WATERSHED

Group XVII

NORTH COUNTRY AND RIB HILL

Group XVIII

MADISON

CLEOPATRA'S NEEDLE SENTINELS DEVILS LAKE STATE PARK.

AERIAL VIEW OF BATHING BEACH AT DEVILS LAKE

ABOVE DEVI
LAKE YAWN
DEVIL'S DOO
WAY.

GLIMPSE OF DEVILS LAKE THROUGH A CLEFT IN THE ROCKS.

THIS TERMINAL MORAINE MADE DEVILS LAKE

TURK'S HEAD, DEVILS LAKE STATE PARK.

MOTHER EARTH'S CRADLE

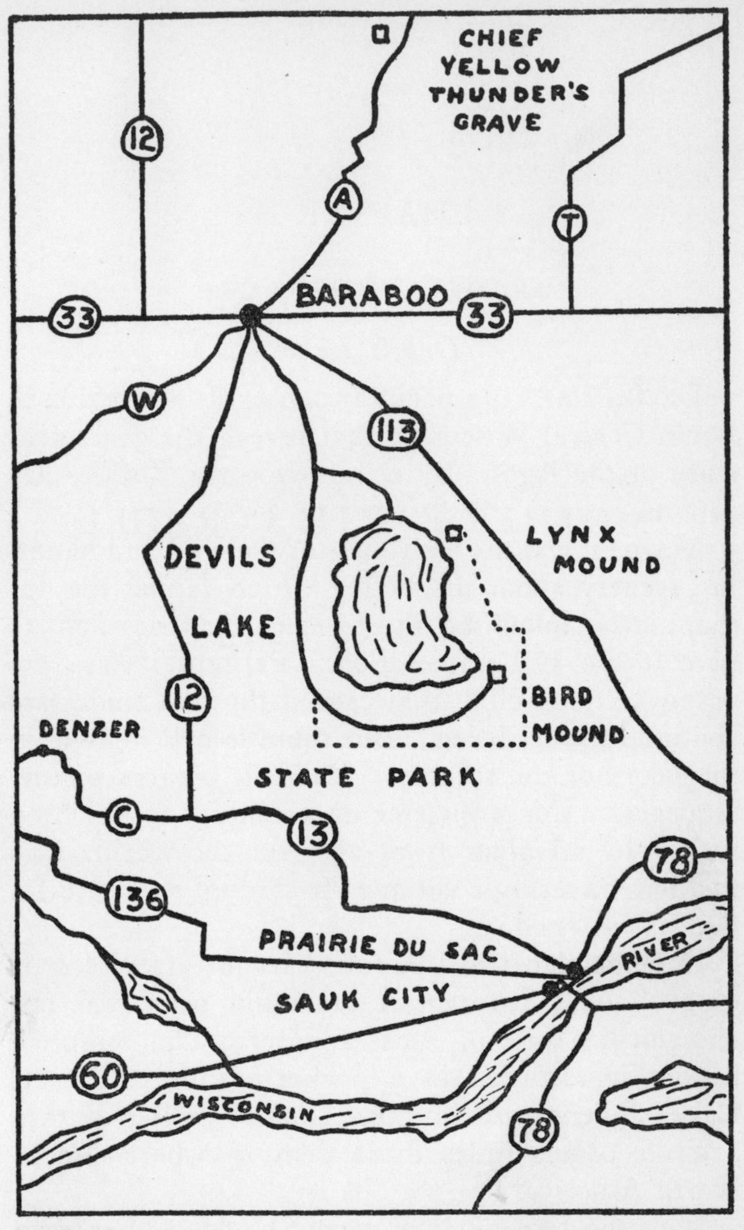

Chapter I

MOTHER EARTH'S CRADLE
DEVILS LAKE

CHAPTER I

MOTHER EARTH'S CRADLE

Devils Lake

DEVILS LAKE is a peculiar name. It is a region in South Central Wisconsin that reveals the geological story of the Ages. By comparison the Rockies are infants.

Maybe it was the weirdness of the wild and haunting scenery about the valley which caused the Indians, who inhabited the country centuries ago, to give it the evil appellation. Perhaps it was the craggy Alpine cliffs that caused the first traders to continue the tradition. But there is evil neither in the lake nor the scenery. There is bizarre picturesqueness. For a quarter of a century it has been visited by scientists from all over the world, who find here in a single volume the story of the centuries that have passed.

In other places will be found fragmentary records of geological history. A mountain peak will tell one story; a pile of rocks another. The complete history is recorded in a pocket edition at Devils Lake. Scientists claim there is more geology within a circle of ten miles there than anywhere else in North America.

Over the face of dark, heavy boulders they read

the story of ages as if it were but yesterday. They need no keystone from the Egyptian lands. Nature has written the tome in her own language and in her own inimitable way. This region was one of the first places on the North American continent to poke its nose above the watery deep.

There are other lakes in Wisconsin more beautiful than this blue-glacial eyelet surrounded by towering pinnacles and ragged rock scenery. There are none that can surpass it for the geological history which it has been unfolding through the eons of time. Surrounding it are hillsides shattered into hundreds of craggy, fantastical shapes.

It seems that I can never grow accustomed to the life of the city. Everything will be moving along fine until some morning I look out and see the flush of green coming in the trees. Then I must go. Nothing can keep me back. Everything is forgotten in a mad rush to get out where there are hills, wave-eaten rocks and open views with not a single housetop to shut out the panorama.

Usually I have felt symptoms of this yearning coming on for weeks. The camera has been looked over, a book on geology of the state has been placed beside it with two other volumes on birds and trees. Then when the spell breaks, engulfing my every feeling, I have the sedatives to assist in effecting relief. There is no cure.

All summer I find myself planning weeks in advance for a visit to some beauty spot. With the regularity of the advance of the seasons I invade the old haunts. God gave in abundance to Wisconsin all that man could desire—trees, lakes, rivers, waterfalls, bold cliffs, cool shade, and companions.

Always we go first to Devils Lake. When one knows the place there is romance in every turn. It has had a tempestuous history for ages. It was there before life existed and now, that there is life everywhere, little change has taken place. The cradle of the continent is there.

"I know of no other region of the state which illustrates so many principles of the science of geology," declared the late Charles R. Van Hise, a distinguished geologist and for many years president of the University of Wisconsin. "Geology classes from the Universities of Wisconsin and Chicago have been making trips to this spot for a quarter of a century. By students it is looked upon as one of the geological wonders of the world."

Ages ago,—who shall say how long?—this region was a carpet of the ocean. Twice it has sunk into the ocean or sea and again risen. This is the story told by geologists to whom generations of time are but ticks of a second. In the millions of splintered rocks, towering pillars and bold outcroppings over five hundred feet above the lake on either the east and west banks is written a pageant of history which the modern day geologists can interpret.

According to their story, the Archean rocks lay, possibly fifty million years ago, at the bottom of a sea. Sand came sifting over its surfaces, which at a later time changed into sandstone, and at a still later time into the hard quartzite which now forms the ragged, sharp-edged cliffs of the bluffs on either side of the quiet, wind-protected lake.

Then some vast commotion shook the foundations of the sea. When peace was restored bleak mountains stood above the surrounding country, rivaling the Alps in their majestic sublimity. The great beds of limestone and igneous rocks were folded into twists and layers and inclined about fifteen degrees, as shown along the bluffs at the east side of the lake shore.

"The Baraboo bluffs are among the oldest formed things on the globe," declared H. E. Cole, the historian of this region, "older than the Rockies or Alleghanies, older than a pound of coal in the earth, older than any bird or beast that has ever lived."

From somewhere came a mighty river, eroding the surface of the rocks and plowing a gorge through the lower Narrows of the Baraboo River, over the present bed of Devils Lake, and then onward in an avalanche of haste to its mouth.

At some later time, through some terrible cataclysm of the earth, the lands of the mountains and valley were again doused in the waters of the ocean, and the tops of the bluffs stood as little islands to be lapped and wave-bitten by the surging waters about. Again the sea retreated and a river, flowing from the north and now known as the Wisconsin, cut a valley through the range. Geologists have read this later story from certain sandstone outcroppings in Devils Lake gap and in the vicinity around.

Perhaps ages were to wear away before the glacier came nosing down from the north. The Wisconsin River, once flowing over the bed of Devils Lake, was changed from its course by the advancing Selkirk. It was this action which changed the gorge into a lake without a visible outlet after the melting ice sheet.

"Those who visit the state park at Devils Lake may picture three strikingly different scenes," wrote Prof. Lawrence Martin, formerly of the University of Wisconsin geology staff. "The first is the region as a stream valley. The river is the Wisconsin, flowing into the Devils Lake gap from the North, turning abruptly eastward near the present site of the Kirkland Hotel and its cottages, and then flowing around the Devils Nose and southwestward toward Prairie du Sac. If you had climbed the bluffs at that time, you might have found the Devils Door, or Turks Head, or some of the other picturesque crags and pinnacles of today. If they were not there, it is certain there were others equally bizarre. You would have looked down, however, on a different scene.

"The surface of the present lake lies six hundred feet below the East Bluff, but the waters of the preglacial Wisconsin River flowed along at a level at least 280 feet lower. The gorge was then 900 or 1,000 feet deep. The scene must have been even more picturesque than that in the present gorge below Niagara Falls. The river had less volume than the Niagara, but the gorge was deeper and more beautiful. At that time there was no lake. There was no hill at the railway cut east of the station. There was no hill where the wooded ridge now extends across the valley north of Devils Lake. There was no level land where the various groups of cottages now stand. The tumbled blocks in the talus slopes looked as they do now. The bluffs were much as today, except that they overlooked a deeper valley, and, therefore, appeared much higher.

"The second scene is that of Devils Lake during the Glacial Period. East of the site of Devils Lake railway station was an ice tongue, a lobe of the continental glacier. Since its terminus lay in a narrow valley it looked much like the larger glaciers in Alaska or in the Alps. No present-day ice tongue of Glacier National Park, of Mt. Ranier, or of the Canadian Selkirks equals it in size or impressiveness. North of the lake was another ice lobe of equal beauty. They ended in sheer ice cliffs one or two hundred feet high. Between them was the glacial lake, dotted with icebergs, and at a much higher level than the present lake. This was at least 35,000 years ago, perhaps 80,000 years, perhaps more.

"The third scene is that of today, with the lake, the moraines, the bluffs, the fields, and the forests, a gem of true mountain scenery, such as cannot be seen elsewhere east of the Rockies."

The circumference of Devils Lake is three and one-fourth miles, its average depth thirty feet, and its greatest depth forty-three feet. From Prospect Point on the West Bluff, 1,450 feet above sea level, there is a commanding view of the countryside—a vista of farmsteads and cities not unlike that to be had from the top of Rib Hill, near Wausau, the highest eminence in Wisconsin.

According to Mr. Cole, the Winnebago Indians have a tradition that the shattered, rocky walls and loose rock at the lake are the result of a struggle which once took place between the thunderers (thunder birds) and the water monsters or spirits which inhabited the lake itself. The Indians thought the shattered rocks resulted or were caused by the thunderbolts hurled by the gigantic birds.

It is the scenery, the bold escarpments of rock, the curious formations to be found on the trails over the cliffs on either side of the lake which mark the spot as a "world wonder." Several of these rocks because of their grotesque forms have acquired whimsical appellations. "Cleopatra's Needle," a pointed pillar of rock standing out alone from the rocky hillside on the West Bluff trail, like the spire of a gigantic cathedral, is reached over a winding, tortuous path advancing up stony cliffs and promontories. Nearby is "Turks Head," another unique formation in tabular stone. On the East Bluffs, over a path still more precipitous, will be found the "Elephant Rock," "Balanced Rock," and the "Devils Doorway."

For boldness of its setting and scenery, overlooking a valley for miles and standing out like a protruding head at a height of over four hundred feet, the "Devils Doorway" is a wonder in shattered rock formation. When this cliff was below the sea, imperious waves of the ocean opened for their retreat arches now lifted high above the valley, through which the angry billows doubtless crashed with tremendous fury. The rocks are vivid in color —splashes of burnt orange and dark red on dark, dormant boulders. From this lookout tower, as the pink of evening spreads over the valley and the sun dips crimson behind the West Ridge, the vista below presents an everchanging diorama.

All these grounds were once below the currents of rushing waters. About are a score of pot-holes, where harder rocks had been snagged in the limestone and whirled in a pool of the mighty river, boring out circular smooth surfaced openings on the boulders. There are also to be found the hard, igneous grinders, appearing half-finished as if deserted by the gods in the middle of a day's employment for work elsewhere in the valley.

From the eminences on the cliffs one sees in the foreground huge masses of broken rock rent asunder and tossed about like the ruins of a world. A blaze of light strikes one cliff while the other rests in the deepest shadow, and on the rugged surface of each may be traced a story of the ages.

The rough topography of the park and the surrounding region prevented clearing, so the percentage of forest area is large, the native flora is extremely varied, and natural conditions will be maintained so that botanists will find not only the species, but also the ecological conditions under which they grow. River birch is found along the lake shore, mixed hardwood stands occur on the higher land, large white pines occupy the rocky slopes, and the tops of the bluffs are covered with oaks.

Down in the valley at the head of the lake are heard the shouts from the contestants of a ball game, and the whole upper lakeside presents an animated scene.

In order to preserve the natural mountainous scenery, the state has purchased 1,400 acres of land To this spot each summer more than five hundred thousand people have gone for a visit or to camp. Its proximity to the larger centers of population in southern Wisconsin has made it the state's most frequented public park.

Devils Lake is in the south central part of Wisconsin, three miles south of Baraboo. U. S. Highway 12 from Southern Wisconsin leading northwestward to St. Paul passes through Baraboo. Devils Lake is forty-two miles from Madison; one hundred twenty-four miles from Milwaukee; ninety miles from Oshkosh; one hundred eight miles from La Crosse; ninety-four miles from Prairie du Chien; one hundred forty-five miles from Eau Claire. On the same trip the Wisconsin Dells, thirteen miles north of Baraboo, should be visited.

MILLSTONES OF THE GODS

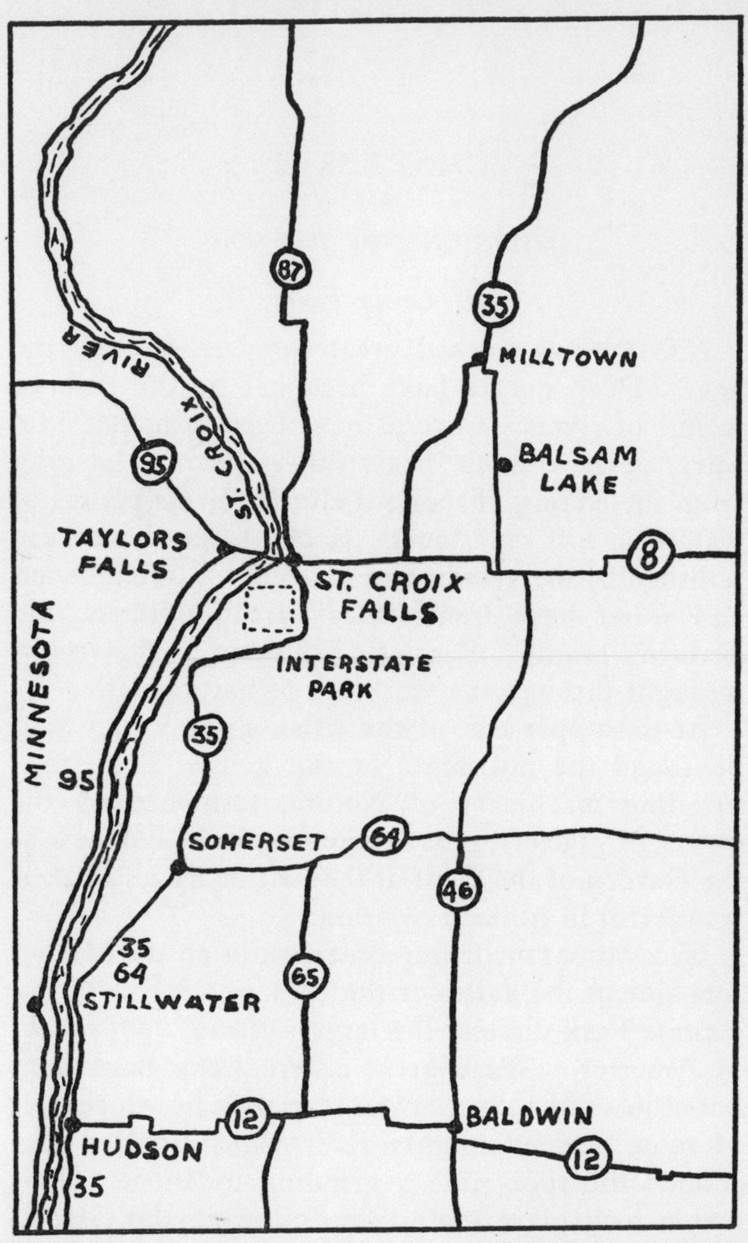

Chapter II

MILLSTONES OF THE GODS
ST. CROIX FALLS

CHAPTER II

MILLSTONES OF THE GODS

St. Croix Falls

NATURE has worked great wonders through the ages. Deep gorges have been cut by the rushing waters of rivers. Caverns have been fashioned into fairy palaces, with beautiful stalactites hanging from the ceiling, through the incessant drippings of waters on soft sandstones. Rocky ledges have been polished by the grinding of glaciers. Climate, wind and water have transformed earth's ugliness into Nature's beauty. Fantastic are some of the results wrought through the workings of natural laws.

At the upper end of the Mississippi Valley will be found the millstones of the gods. This great grinding machinery of Nature, fashioned by the power of glaciers, is as fascinating in its boldness as the Garden of the Gods at the foot of Pike's Peak is wonderful in its deep coloring.

Excavations made in recent months on the Minnesota side at the dalles of the St. Croix River in Interstate Park disclose the largest glacial "pot holes" in America. These great cistern holes have been bored in solid Keweenawan trap rock by whirlpools of some ancient, mighty river which swirled and rotated the rocks like a grinding millstone. This action took place some time following the Glacial

Period. While the presence of these enormous "pot holes" has been known for many years, their depth was not ascertained until some of the water and debris was cleaned from the cistern holes.

On the edge of one of these enormous holes, on the Minnesota side, bored out of a seamless rock, as if done by some giant carpenter's auger, the following sign has been posted:

"GLACIAL KETTLE"

"SO FAR AS IS KNOWN THIS IS THE LARGEST AND DEEPEST GLACIAL KETTLE IN AMERICA. IT HAS BEEN BORED IN SOLID ROCK BY THE ACTION OF A MIGHTY RIVER GRINDING A HARD GRANITE ROCK AGAINST THE SOFTER TRAP ROCK.

"THIS KETTLE IS TWELVE FEET IN DIAMETER AT THE MOUTH. AT A DEPTH OF FORTY-TWO FEET IT IS FIFTEEN FEET IN DIAMETER. AT ITS BASE, WHICH IS SIXTY-THREE FEET FROM ITS MOUTH, THE DIAMETER IS THREE FEET. THE BASE OF THIS KETTLE IS TWENTY-FIVE FEET BELOW THE LEVEL OF THE ST. CROIX RIVER, WHICH IS ONLY A FEW RODS AWAY."

The rock ledges at the dalles of the St. Croix River, north of Minneapolis, are ancient lava flows, according to Prof. Lawrence Martin. The lava or traps are well-jointed, so that there are vertical precipices and isolated crags along the St. Croix River.

The dalles of the St. Croix record a primer lesson in geology. Here has been left legibly the record of the glaciers when America was in the making. The interpretations of the scientist or geologist are not required. The evidence is apparent to the most casual eye. At once there is disclosed to the visitor one of the chief secrets of nature. It is a story of

WISCONSIN SIDE OF THE ST. CROIX RIVER DALLES.

ST. CROIX RIVER SCENERY AT INTERSTATE PARK.

DALLES OF THE ST. CROIX, INTERSTATE PARK.

ENTRANCE TO AZTALAN MOUND PARK NEAR LAKE MILLS.

REMAINS OF INDIAN CEREMONIAL MOUNDS, AZTALAN.

OLD MAN OF THE DALLES, INTERSTATE PARK.

ICOLET PADDLED HIS CANOE ALONG THIS SHORELINE OF PENINSULA STATE PARK, DOOR COUNTY.

EAGLE CLIFF, PENINSULA STATE PARK.

HORSESHOE ISLAND OFF PENINSULA STATE PARK.

Painting, Wisconsin State Historical Socie

LANDING OF NICOLET, THE FIRST WHITE MAN TO COME TO WISCONSIN.

GILL'S ROCK LANDING ON THE EXTREMITY OF DOOR COUNTY PENINSULA.

NICOLET FIRST MET THE WINNEBAGO INDIANS NEAR THIS POINT AT RED BANKS.

the power of rushing waters, which can only be realized by those who have seen modern engineers harness and put to the work of mankind this same force of water power.

As explained by the geologists, after this flow of lava rock had formed in this vicinity, a glacier nosed its way down from the north dragging with it large deposits of granite rock. When the glacier melted, a mighty river was formed, which carried the granite boulders along until they were snagged in some crevice of the softer trap rock formations. So powerful was the river at places that whirlpools were formed, which rotated the granite rocks, cutting deep pot holes into the softer material.

The debris from these pot holes shows great granite boulders which have been whirled in the basin so long that they have become spherical like a ball. Some of these granite boulders are three or four feet in diameter, and there are literally thousands of smaller pebbles that can be held in the hand. The grit and sand of the pot holes show that the loose gravel and earth have been produced by this mighty grinding process. They form a millstone which only the gods could operate.

There are probably forty pot holes, large and small, within the confines of the Wisconsin-Minnesota joint park area, mostly on the Minnesota side. Some of them are two or three feet in diameter and only a few feet deep. Others are ten and twelve feet in diameter. Only three or four of these pot holes have been excavated.

When it became known that these investigations and excavations were under way, the stream of visitors to the park increased. On one day 10,000 people visited the scene, and the park superintendent reports that 18,000 people visited the Interstate Park within the first ten days of one month.

Interstate Park was founded a number of years ago through the joint action of the Wisconsin and Minnesota legislatures. It contains 730 acres, of which 580 are owned by Wisconsin and 150 by Minnesota. On the Wisconsin side the city of St. Croix Falls is at the edge of the park lands, with the extensive Wisconsin State Fish Hatchery within the state park limits. The city of Taylors Falls is within the Minnesota park area.

Aside from the enormous pot holes in the park, the dells of the St. Croix are the chief feature. The river here flows through a narrow gorge in the Keweenawan trap rock, which at one point rises to a height of more than 200 feet.

Picturesque rock formations mark the landscape. It seems as if the gods at work had shoved these mighty rock ledges into a heap and then deserted the place. Interesting names have been given to some of these rock formations. "The Old Man of the Dalles" is a remarkable profile face on the Wisconsin shore, and the "Devil's Chair" is a weird-looking column of rock on the Minnesota side. Down the river is a rocky escarpment called the "Savior's Cross."

Recently the State of Wisconsin established a large

trout fish hatchery at the edge of the park on one of the steep embankments overlooking the Dalles area. Two score of fish propagating basins are fed by the numerous natural artesian springs.

Bold rock ledges mark the St. Croix dells area. The main street of the city of St. Croix Falls is on the next to the highest of these terraces. From the bridge crossing the St. Croix River, joining the two park areas and the two states, the river to the south flows turbulently through a narrow gorge. On the crests of some of these rocky escarpments, black oak trees are struggling, sending long roots down to the waterside through crevices between the split-off rocks.

The wave-cut edges on these rocks show that in ages long ago flowed a river mightier than now traverses the valley. Geologists claim that before the glacial period the St. Croix River probably lay to the west in the state of Minnesota and followed a different course all the way to the Mississippi.

A gorge through the rocks makes the high rock embankments stand out boldly, like the "Navy Yards" in the dells of the Wisconsin at Kilbourn. Through narrow passage-ways the river is angry and troubled, flecking its surface with foam. Down a mile it becomes calm and peaceful again. The boldness of the scenery gives the park a picturesque setting.

Within the park area is a large lake formed by a bayou of the St. Croix River, one of the boundaries of the state. Down the sides of the steep cliffs, pine, oak, elm, and silver maple trees abound with a heavy underbrush of blackberry.

From the lofty terraces on the Wisconsin side, looking into the amphitheatre, with its river and dells, with two cities nestled on opposite banks of the stream, with wavy, water-eaten lines in the stone ledges, the work of the century seems infinitesimal compared with the time during which Nature has been fashioning this wonderland of cliffs and rocky gorges.

The dalles of St. Croix Falls is the playground where the gods tested their strength in piling up the jagged ledges of rock for the wonder and awe of the ages of men to follow.

St. Croix Falls is in Polk County. It is fifty miles from St. Paul; forty miles from Hudson; one hundred thirty-one miles from Superior; one hundred eleven miles from Eau Claire; and three hundred eighty-seven miles from Milwaukee. It is on the state's western boundary and most easily approached by U. S. Highway No. 8 which crosses the northern part of the state, intersecting U. S. Highways 51 and 53.

AN INDIAN ACROPOLIS

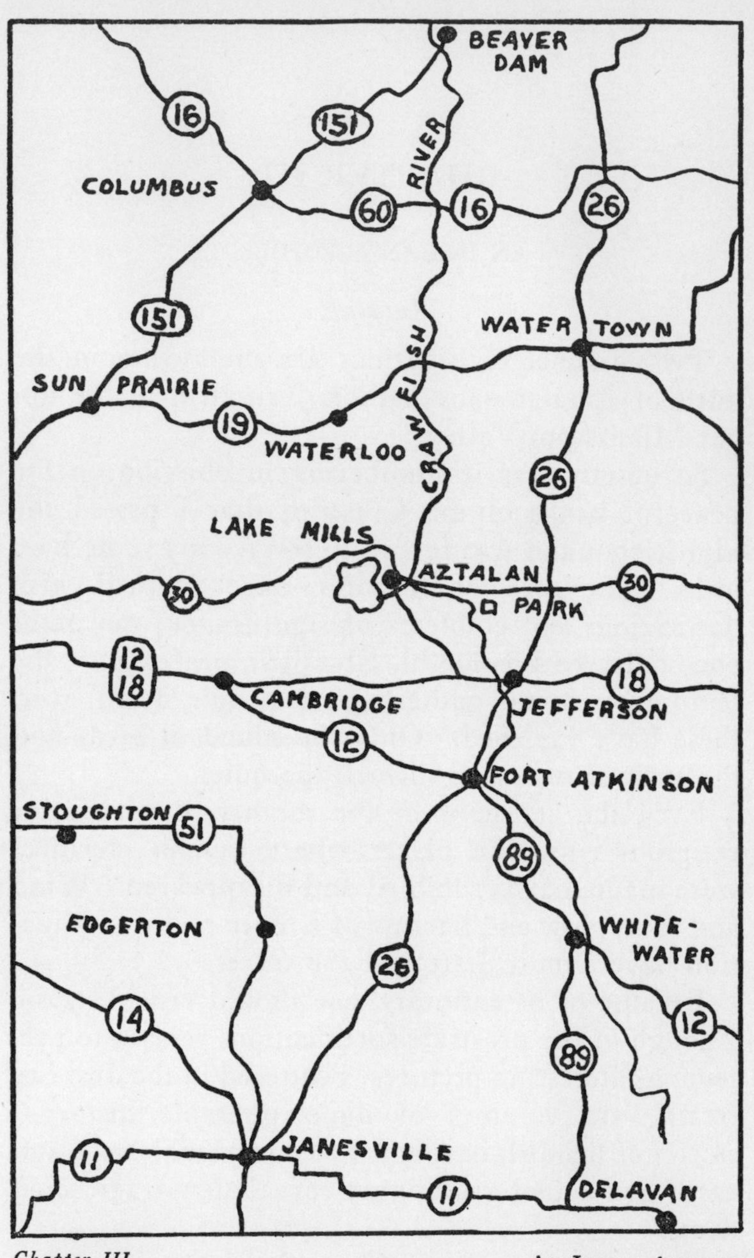

Chapter III

AN INDIAN ACROPOLIS
AZTALAN

CHAPTER III

AN INDIAN ACROPOLIS

Aztalan

TWO distinct civilizations are mellowing in the dusts of Aztalan—the Indian Jerusalem of the upper Mississippi Valley.

So quietly was it slumbering in oblivion on the peaceful banks of the Crawfish that I passed the idyllic spot and was forced to retrace my route by a mile. The ceremonial poles, once adorned with decorations and emblems of significance; the paths once noisy with colorful, ritualistic processions; the temporary home gathering of people from afar, these have vanished. Only the sound of birds and the rush of motorists disturb the quiet.

Even the acropolis of the mighty, the halls for religious rites, the places where human sacrifices were made, have crumbled and disappeared. Wind and rain, plow and harrow of a more recent civilization have almost destroyed the traces.

Because of its antiquity, one should visit Aztalan. Enough of the prostrate fortifications remain to present an interesting picture. Scattered in the dust one treads, are volumes of undecipherable history—stories of fiendish hate and revenge of which the soft earth under foot grudgingly reveals few tragic incidents.

Fifty years ago, when Dr. James D. Butler was a heralded scholar from Wisconsin, he was forced to confess: "I never set foot in Aztalan, and I was deeply mortified when I was questioned concerning the prehistoric walled enclosure by the savants of France, Germany and Italy."

After reading about the story of Aztalan in memorials to the Wisconsin legislature a few years ago asking for its preservation, I decided to visit it. Few of the motorists on the Lake Mills route between the Capital and Milwaukee know that they are traveling the old military road—the pioneer track of the old covered wagons and ox teams hauling supplies to the West. Fewer realize that on the outskirts of Lake Mills, on the west banks of the sluggish Crawfish, the oldest village in Wisconsin lies wrapped in mystery and the silence of eternity.

Aztalan was such an imaginative name that what I first saw disappointed me. Scholars have described it as "one of the wonders of the west" and "the most wonderful remains of antiquity in the state." Legend had it that the Mexican Aztecs had come from a place far to the north named "Aztalan." Because of this picture, my mind had conjured a fantastic setting. Fancy and reality were far apart. This place was only a hilly pasture-lot; there were no majestic walls nor minarets to give pomp to what had been. Aztalan is a place of memories. The visitor, without some knowledge of its past, is seriously embarrassed in restoring mentally its blurred and vandalized panorama.

Only after I had talked with the men who for two years had been making excavations in the ruins did I lose all interest in the pastoral scenery and suddenly became stirred by the revelation of its secrets. A lost page in the record of centuries was being deciphered by the aid of pick and shovel.

Nature has an inimitable way of writing her autobiography. Just as the explorations of ancient cities in the Holy Land are now unveiling the culture of Christianity's dawn, by the same methods of burrowing in these grassy Aztalan knolls was the story told of a civilization at least 1,000 years old.

Several years ago Dr. S. A. Barrett,[1] director of the Milwaukee Public Museum, and a party of scientists co-operating with the State Archeological Society began digging. Although the place had been discovered as early as 1836 and had been surveyed and reported to the federal government in 1850 as a great antiquity, nothing was known of the peoples who once lived in this esoteric village. It was as much deserted by its founders as the famous Colorado ruins of Mesa Verda.

Employing all the techniques of science, the explorers went into the mounds and the pyramids, surveyed the enclosure, examined the refuse heaps, and when all was completed, restored the external grounds so that the visitor today would never suspect a desecration.

West of the river the ruins were found to comprise

[1] Barrett, Samuel A., Bulletin of the Public Museum of the City of Milwaukee, No. xiii (April, 1933).

a rectangular enclosing "wall," two great pyramids, a large number of mounds, and the old village site, refuse heap, and field. The enclosure "wall" has a length on the west of 1,419 feet, while its north and south sections are respectively 631 feet and 700 feet. The river forms the fourth side of the enclosure, which contains in all, seventeen and two-thirds acres. Along the wall, at intervals of about seventy-five feet, are "buttresses" where the wall widens to forty feet, giving it the appearance of numerous conical mounds connected by elevated ways or ridges.

To me it seemed reasonable that if the Indians built this temple of mystery, carrying the earth in crude wooden baskets, it must have taken more toil and time than did the building of the pyramids.

Within this enclosure is the site of an extensive village and the remains of numerous mounds, rings and ridges of various kinds. The most prominent features, however, are two great pyramids. The one in the southwest corner of the enclosure was a truncated pyramid with terraced sides. Its top was level and fifty-three feet square. The pyramid in the northwest corner had a similar top about sixty feet square. What open air altars! What a place for devotion to the Sun God, if this were their belief! What a promontory for sacrificial fires!

"Fifty years ago when I was a farm boy in Aztalan these mounds were twice as high," a visitor at the old site told me as we stood on the northwest pyramid. "The road has destroyed the highest mound of them all."

"At that rate there will be nothing left in another hundred years," I suggested.

"O! yes! We plowed the place then and planted the hills with grain. Now it is a park. Whenever we had corn on these fields I would pick up a pocketful of Indian arrow heads with every harrowing of the soil."

For three-quarters of a century the agitation to preserve the grounds was sustained. As early as 1838, Edward Everett begged the President of the United States, without success, to withdraw that section of land from sale. When the state showed lack of interest, citizens of Jefferson County in 1922 raised funds and stopped further desecration by turning the lands into a park.

"Outside the enclosure were originally seventy-four mounds and a number of embankments, all located on the west bank of the river, while on the east bank were formerly two long embankments, two small enclosures, and twenty-two mounds," Dr. Barrett said in describing the excavations. "All these were apparently directly connected with the enclosure and the whole together formed one of the largest, one of the most unique, and one of the most important of the many ancient earthworks of America.

"The ancient inhabitants of Aztalan possessed a relatively high culture, as is shown especially by their pottery. Vessels of various beautiful forms ornamented with many different patterns in incised, modeled and painted decoration have been found in the old village site. Though broken and left just as these ancient people used them, they are still works of art of no mean merit and show the highest expression of the artistic sense of the former inhabitants of Aztalan. Of special importance in the present work is the fact that these potsherds show characteristic features of three widely distributed peoples, indicating that Aztalan was at one time a center of no small importance.

"The far famed 'brick' of Aztalan were irregular masses of clay mixed with grass and then burned, possibly in connection with ceremonial offerings in some instances. One instance has been found in which this clay was employed in the making of a rude fire-place.

"That cannibalism was practiced by the builders of these earthworks is clearly shown by the presence, in numerous instances, of portions of human skeletons and more especially of fragments of human bones cracked for the marrow, in the refuse heaps of the village and about the camp fires. These are found mingled with the cracked bones of various kinds of mammals and with the bones of birds and fish, and with all kinds of other kitchen refuse showing that they were undoubtedly treated in exactly the same manner as was the refuse of any other kind of food. The victims were doubtless captives of war sacrified in connection with the ceremonies which were probably the real center of the life of ancient Aztalan.

"After a careful consideration of all the facts

available from former work and of the results of the present excavations, it seems entirely unlikely that this enclosure was intended by its builders as a fortification or even that it was a palisaded town. Such an enclosure with its pyramids, embankments and mounds within, and with the large number of mounds and other earthworks without, must certainly have presented an imposing spectacle during one of its elaborate, ritualistic ceremonies with hundreds and perhaps thousands of religious devotees assembled for worship."

Nor were these an isolated people. Their visitors brought gifts from field and forest. Pottery and ornaments of a culture which belongs to the Southwest were found; other articles revealed contact with the same races that inhabited the Missouri, Tennessee and Arkansas country. One of the most interesting finds was the "Princess Burial." This was the skeleton of a young woman of importance richly bedecked with bead necklaces, with strands that were draped around her shoulders and waist and looped about her ankles.

Aztalan was a mecca. Before the coming of Columbus, people gathered from great distances to participate in its ceremonials. It may be that these same pilgrims and crusaders, returning to their homes, built the strange mounds in outlines of the bird, snake, squirrel, turtle, buffalo, and man to be found all over Wisconsin, and especially around lakes in the southern half of the State in the vicinities of Milwaukee, Madison, Beloit, Waukesha, Fort Atkinson, Sheboygan, Baraboo, Manitowoc, Koshkonong, and Prairie du Chien. On the banks opposite the fallen acropolis is a lizard mound more than six hundred feet long.

After a time Aztalan was again deserted. The story of its founders has no climax. It just ends. What happened is only supposition. Perhaps, its people were overwhelmed by enemies. Perhaps, they lost faith and deserted their temple. A sylvan quiet descended on the neighborhood. Then another race came prospecting the old site for another village. Soon the exotic gathering rivalled all cities outside of Milwaukee. It boasted four hotels, a wagon factory employing fifty men, and various industries. Day after day the rutted streets were crowded with trudging wagons to and from Milwaukee.

Love for ceremonials again stirred in the soil. The invaders grew proud of their home and hopeful of its future. The Wisconsin legislature of 1836 was urged to establish the capital there. When the final roll was called, Aztalan lost by two votes. Industries moved away. Hotels fell to decay. One by one the houses were deserted.

Memories now keep vigil with the great stone boulder by the entrance:

AZTALAN MOUND PARK

SITE OF THE FAMOUS PRE-HISTORIC INDIAN STOCKADE PROTECTED VILLAGE KNOWN AS AZTALAN. FIRST DESCRIBED BY N. F. HYER IN THE MILWAUKEE ADVERTISER IN JANUARY 1837. DESCRIBED BY DR. INCREASE A. LAPHAM IN THE ANTIQUITIES OF WISCONSIN IN 1855. EXPLORED BY THE MILWAUKEE PUBLIC MUSEUM IN 1919-21. PURCHASED BY THE

CITIZENS OF JEFFERSON COUNTY IN 1922 AND PRESENTED TO THE WISCONSIN ARCHEOLOGICAL SOCIETY. MARKED BY THE WISCONSIN ARCHEOLOGICAL SOCIETY 1927.

For me, reclining on a pyramid, night came on suddenly. Distant landmarks grew faint and then merged in the gray gloaming. The nearby mounds became sullen and dark. I waited for the ghosts of the deserted founders to relight their divine torches and chant their service. The noises of the world died away until the red moon rolled slowly up over the horizon. As it sailed away like a bubble into the skies, the whip-poor-will sang to its mate a pledge of devotion. Aztalan was wrapped in peaceful slumber.

Aztalan is in Jefferson County. It is three miles east of Lake Mills on State Highway 30 between Milwaukee and Madison. Aztalan is four and one-half miles west of Johnson Creek which is on Highway 26 between Janesville and Oshkosh. It is eighty miles from Oshkosh; fifty miles from Milwaukee; thirty-seven miles from Janesville; thirty-two miles from Madison and two hundred twenty-one miles from Eau Claire.

DOOR COUNTY IN SPRINGTIME IS A ROLLING SNOW SCENE OF CHERRY BLOSSOMS.

ROAD THROUGH VIRGIN TIMBER IN PENINSULA STATE PARK.

INDIAN TOTEM POLE IN PENINSULA STATE PARK.

BUILT IN 1776, THE TANK COTTAGE AT GREEN BAY IS THE OLDEST HOUSE IN WISCONSIN.

HOME OF ELEAZAR WILLIAMS, FIRST ROMANCE MAKER OF WISCONSIN, NEAR DE PERE

OLD FORT HOWARD, GREEN BAY.

ROCKY SHORE OF ONE OF THE APOSTLE ISLANDS.

GERMAN TRAMP FREIGHTER AT DOCK AT SUPERIOR.

COMMERCIAL FISHERY AT BAYFIELD.

OLD FRENCH CEMETERY, MADELINE ISLAND

TREE CLINGING TO A ROCK NEAR ONE OF THE APOSTLE ISLANDS.

SUMMER HOMES ON MADELINE ISLAND, LAKE SUPERIOR.

THE WINNEBAGO EDEN

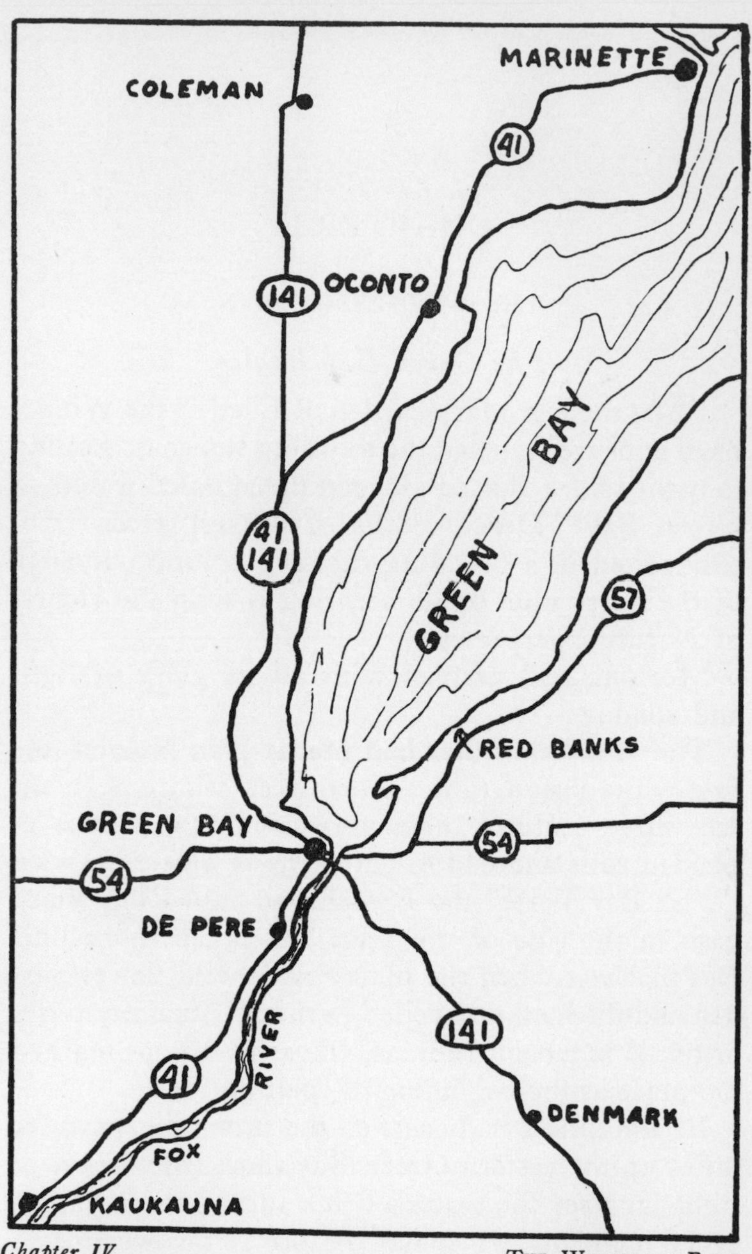

Chapter IV

THE WINNEBAGO EDEN
THE GREEN BAY REGION

CHAPTER IV

THE WINNEBAGO EDEN

The Green Bay Region

FROM the legendary garden of Eden of the Winnebago tribe we watched the morning sun come smiling to bathe with reflected glory in the agitated waters of Green Bay. Dense cedars of darkest green were silhouetted in a brooding mystery around our edge of the misty blue basin, scenting it with the richest of Nature's perfumes.

Morning had arrived with all its glory of light and shadow.

The same wind that had blown Jean Nicolet, the first white visitor to the Northwest, ashore near our feet three centuries ago, was tossing the waters in playful rolls and eddies before us in a careless way.

"La Bay Verte" the French had called this sharp gash in the side of the Lake Michigan shore line. But that was when the place was a wild flower garden and the land was veiled in the spiritual mysteries of the Winnebago Indians, whose traditions marked the place as the beginning of their nation.

By the time I had reached the promontory twelve miles up the eastern Green Bay shore, the flicker of light far over the water's brink turned more golden every moment. It chased before it the wraiths of any of the heroic Indian spirits that traditions claim once inhabited the vicinity.

In the cool air the green trees and shrubs had transformed the home of the departed Winnebagoes into an overhanging garden, one hundred feet above the glistening white beach and wave-lapped pebbles. The hoe of the summer cottager has not changed this red clay embankment since the French saw it. To the earth itself still clings the elusive odor of the stories of adventures among the spruce and the maple of this ancient throne.

"In a day of sore distress a miracle occurred on this spot," I told my companion.

"Do you expect me to believe that?" There was a tone of incredibility in the voice of response.

"Yes, I do," I rejoined, and started to open the volume in hand as proof. "I shall tell you about it."

"Once upon a time, many centuries before the coming of the white people,—"

"That's the way most fables begin," he broke in.

"These lands were occupied by the Sauk Indians," I continued, ignoring his attempted interruption, "but the Menominees living across the bay knew of the great fertility of the soil and longed to conquer the place. One spring they came with a great flotilla of canoes surrounding the entrance to the bay. With another horde of warriors on land, escape by forest was made impossible. Unable to secure water, the besieged soon choked with thirst. Strings suspending clay pots into the bay at night were cut. Their enemies now taunted them as the torment of their victims increased. Every attempt at escape resulted in death. To a young brave who had fasted for ten days there came a vision.

"'Listen! Last night there stood by me a young man clothed in white raiment, who said, 'He whom you behold was alive once like you. I died and now live forever. Trust in me and I will deliver you. At night a deep sleep will fall upon your enemies; go forth boldly and silently and you shall escape.'

"Those who believed in the revelation were saved. That night as darkness fell there followed a great silence in the camps of the foe. One by one the ambushed warriors stole away, leaving Red Banks to their enemies. When dawn arrived, those who did not leave were murdered most cruelly.

"There are many other legends, but history begins with the coming of the explorers. Encamped upon this spot were the Winnebago Indians with their gardens of corn and squash when the first white visitor to the Northwest came calling in 1634."

"So this red clay bank is the Plymouth Rock of the Upper Mississippi Valley," remarked my companion, who was listening to my reading of an account found a few years ago among the reports of the Jesuit priests.[2]

"Yes," I responded, "and it was only fourteen years after the coming of the Mayflower."

Among the most notable zealots sent out from Quebec to gather information for Champlain, the governor of New France, was Jean Nicolet. He had

[2] "The Jesuit Relations," edited by Edna Kenton, pp. 176-180.

already spent a dozen years among the Algonquins.

During the years the governor continually received reports of a strange people called "Men of the Sea." Just who they were the Indians had no definite knowledge. The description fired the imagination of the governor. Could it be that the coast of Asia was so near and that these were Chinese? He would learn!

Jean Nicolet, now thirty-six years of age, was chosen to make the discovery. Starting in July, 1634, with several Indian companions, they paddled their way up the St. Lawrence, entering Lake Michigan through the Mackinac passage,—Nicolet to be the first white man to see the surface of this great inland sea.[3]

About to enter Green Bay, and learning from some of the Indians on land that the "Strange Men of the Sea" were but a few leagues ahead, he dispatched some of his guides to notify the Celestial Empire of his coming that its people might be prepared to welcome him.

Along the western shore of the present Door County peninsula, skirting ridges that today are rolling show scenes of cherry blossoms, in sight of picturesque coves and pinnacles, Nicolet's canoes made their way. Eagle Cliff, that haughty battlement of ancient rock, now a part of scenic Peninsula State Park, must have frowned down in its dignity. Per-

[3] On August 9, 1934, President Franklin D. Roosevelt visited Green Bay to participate in the 300th anniversary of the coming of Jean Nicolet. Upwards of 100,000 people swarmed to Green Bay on that occasion.

haps Nicolet spent a night on Eagle Island, near Ephraim, then a friendly Indian camp ground,[4] for he must not hasten his reception.

It was toward the village on the precipitous heights at Red Banks that the frail bark of Nicolet slowly made its way.

The early French narrative describes how Nicolet, dressed in flowing robes, still common among the Chinese of today, his garments besprinkled with embroidered birds of bright plumage and flowers of many hues, climbed up the narrow passageway to the village accompanied by Indians. He carried in his hands pistols which he fired, frightening the Indian squaws who fled in fear before a God who carried thunder and lightning in his hands.

Then the fact became known. The "Strange People" were not the Chinese. They were only Winnebago Indians. Banquetted on beaver for many days, Nicolet passed up the Fox River to about the present site of Berlin where he visited the famous Mascoutin Indian village.

For a long time we sat on the banks watching the changing colors of the waters—light green along the shore, dark blue afar out. In the mists, little fishing boats bobbed up and down with the swell of the waves. Lake breezes rolled up in the pageantry of departed centuries. Despite all attempts to change the spirit of the past, the bay teemed rich in its memories.

[4] Holand, H. R., "Old Peninsula Days," Menasha, Wis., p. 39; For claim of other localities as first landing site, see Schafer, Joseph, "The Winnebago-Horicon Marsh," (Madison, Wis., 1937), pp. 14-24.

Men of a more romantic time were passing toward this gateway for the civilization of the Northwest. The history which they left is almost as old and as worthy of reverence as that of New England; the thrilling adventures in their pioneer lives were almost as daring as the deeds of Lexington farmers. Father Claude Allouez in 1670-71 came to establish a mission at De Pere Rapids; then followed other characters out of the past: Nicholas Perrot,[5] first governor of the region; Joliet and Father Marquette; Recollect Friar Hennepin; Henri de Tonte; Charlevoix; and many more. Priest, trader, adventurer, and wood ranger went this way into the forest shadows. Triumphant armies of three nations—France, England, and the United States—have hoisted their banners over these crumbled fortifications.

In fancy I followed in their trail. A return to the city of Green Bay failed to break the spell. As long as history keeps tryst with the past this old world spirit at the Bay will survive. The French habitant seems waiting on his cabin veranda facing the river. A statue to "The Spirit of the Northwest" on the Court House lawn, carved by Sidney Bedore, a former Green Bay resident, symbolizes in the figures of priest, trader and Indian, the religion, the industry, and the transformation which the new civilization brought. Only two cities have given me the same courtly touch with the long ago—New Orleans

[5] In the Neville Museum, Green Bay, Wisconsin, may be seen the silver ostensorium presented by Perrot to the De Pere Mission in 1686. It is the oldest and finest relic of the French Regime.

and Quebec. It is a haunting feeling that invites one to linger and reminisce; to listen at evening for sweet strains of music and the soft rustle of dancing.

Even the noise of traffic cannot smother the past. Tablets mark the home of de Langlade, the first cleared and cultivated farm in the Mississippi Valley States; the site of Fort Howard, and the old Surgeon's Headquarters. Guides point out the Tank cottage, oldest residence in Wisconsin, built in 1776; indicate the first places of worship in the state for Episcopalian, Methodist and Presbyterian; take one to the banks of La Riviere Glaise, now known as Dutchman's Creek, homesite of the first judge west of Detroit; and to the grave of the brave Ashwaubemie, the young Ottawa warrior who rescued the Indian maiden, Morning Star, when the Chippewa stole her from her own tribe. Even the centuries remember her romance. Poetry and drama have rescued the tale from oblivion and made a pathway to the resting place of the Indian Romeo on the green banks of a little creek which bears his name.

From the lands and streams tributary to Green Bay, defiant Indians went forth to battle,—first as allies of the French, and then as friends of the British. Langlade and eight hundred bedaubed warriors marshalled in 1755 to the ambush of General Braddock and the provincials under George Washington in the Pennsylvania highlands; other Wisconsin tribesmen in 1779 opposed George Rogers Clark, who was marching on Vincennes to gain the Mississippi Valley to the cause of the American Revolution; and again in 1813 at the battle of the Thames, Wisconsin Indians, surrounding their chief, shared in the defeat of the great Tecumseh, who dreamed of a Mississippi Valley Indian confederacy. There were no more courageous warriors than those from the valley of the Fox.

As the afternoon of our first day's visit advanced, we started a tour up the banks of the Fox over whose surface soldier and pioneer had made their way into the wilderness. A broad highway of cement now follows close to the river.

It was spring, and such a promise of harvest! In the streets at De Pere a boulder told of the first mission:

NEAR THIS SPOT
STOOD THE CHAPEL OF ST. FRANCIS XAVIER
BUILT IN THE WINTER OF 1671-72 BY
FATHER CLAUDE ALLOUEZ, S. J.
AS THE CENTRE OF HIS WORK
IN CHRISTIANISING THE INDIANS
OF WISCONSIN.
THIS MEMORIAL TABLET
WAS ERECTED BY THE CITIZENS OF DE PERE
AND UNVEILED BY THE
STATE HISTORICAL SOCIETY OF WISCONSIN
SEPTEMBER 6, 1899.

"Are you going by the Williams home?" asked some dignitary who might have been the mayor. He had watched me copy the wording on the memorial.

"Who's Williams, and where's his place?"

"Eleazar Williams was the 'lost dauphin' of France who was visited by the Prince de Joinville. Maybe he wasn't the dauphin after all, but he pretended he was." [6]

[6] Lawson, P. V., "Prince and Creole;" Milwaukee Journal, Feb. 11, 1923; Mary Catherwood's "Lazarre" is the fiction of this same story.

The faded home of Eleazar Williams twelve miles southwest of Green Bay is drab and shabby. He had come West to make of Wisconsin a great Indian state. Instead of becoming a ruler he was forced to content himself with preaching to the Indians. Such were the stories he told of his own achievements that he has become Wisconsin's first romance maker.

Trade and commerce have fought a winning battle for domination of the historic Fox River.[7] The trail has become the highway; the Indian village has been transformed into a city. As a high school boy I had read of the "Treaty of the Cedars," which relinquished these lands to the white invaders. On the northern rim of Appleton in an undestroyed natural amphitheater I read again the history:

NEAR THIS SITE SEPT. 3, 1836,
THE MENOMINEE INDIANS CEDED TO
THE UNITED STATES BY
THE TREATY OF THE CEDARS
FOUR MILLION ACRES BETWEEN THE
FOX, WOLF AND MENOMINEE RIVERS.
SIGNED BY
HENRY DODGE OSHKOSH
TERRITORIAL GOVERNOR. MENOMINEE HEAD CHIEF.

From the old treaty ground I looked out over the river. Once the easy flowing Fox went its way to the song of the trader and voyager. At night it heard along its banks, campfire tales of Indian adventures while the French trader smoked his pipe and dreamed of home.

Tonight I saw it in the afterglow of sunset. It was the Fox river of commerce, chained by a score

[7] For Story of the Fox Headwaters, see Chapter XII.

of dams into submission to the wealth of hydraulic power. Yet, it seemed to be lounging in its banks as carefree as of old, still humming a song of romance as it went on its way.

The Green Bay region outlined in this chapter is at the mouth of Green Bay. The city of Green Bay is one hundred thirty-five miles from Madison; sixty-six miles from Sheboygan; fifty-one miles from Oshkosh; one hundred one miles from Stevens Point; fifty-six miles from Marinette; one hundred ninety-five miles from Eau Claire; one hundred sixteen miles from Milwaukee. Persons going to Green Bay should also visit the entire Door County Peninsula.

ISLES OF ENCHANTMENT

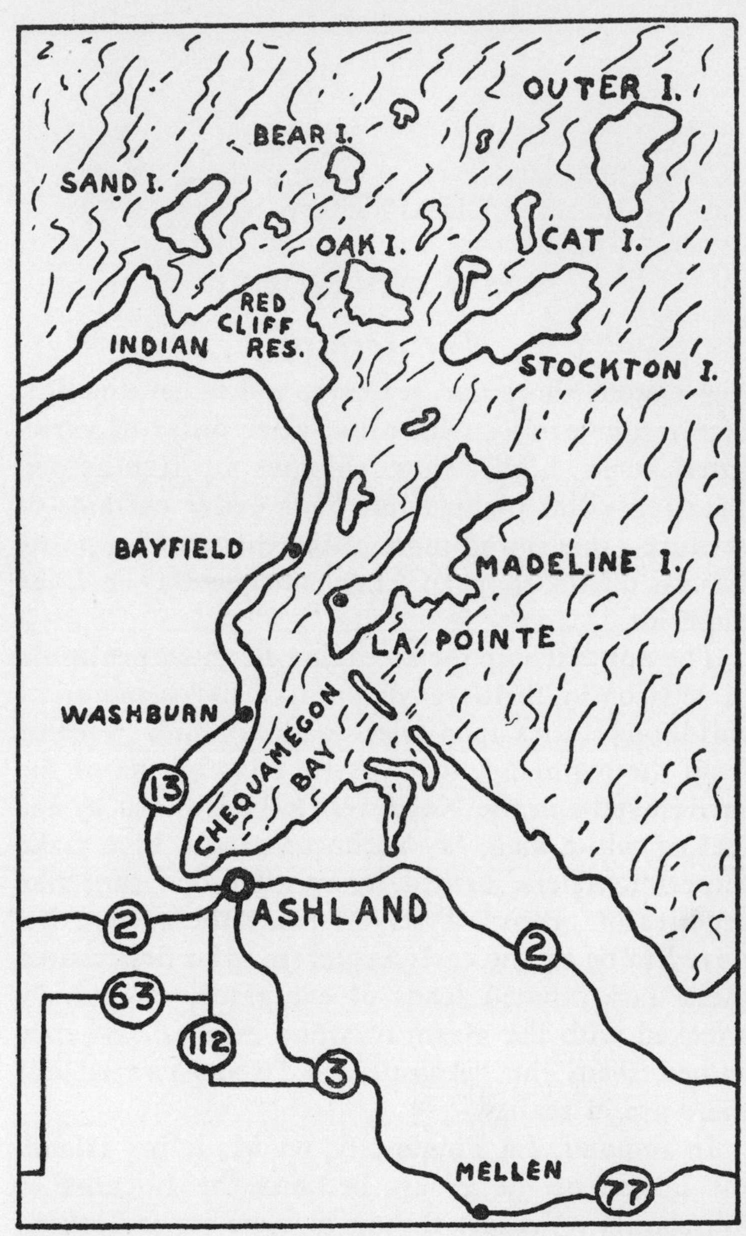

Chapter V | ISLES OF ENCHANTMENT
THE APOSTLES

CHAPTER V

ISLES OF ENCHANTMENT

The Apostles

A CRAGGY shore line, sea caves and red stone cliffs, picturesque grottos with pillar after pillar of variegated stone, high, white columns of lighthouses, dazzling villas planted like tents under curtains of verdure—this is a glimpse of the enchanted Apostle Islands off the shore of Chequamegon Bay in Lake Superior.

The approach up the ascending Bayfield peninsula of Wisconsin thrills a visitor like the glamour of childhood stories upon entering a fairyland. Viewed from the mainland, the Apostle Islands, one of the earliest spots in the Northwest to be trodden by the feet of white men, lay anchored in the blue Lake Superior waters, bathed in an afternoon sun, like argosies of green. Twelve islands there were believed to be by the early explorers, who first visited these dark-plumed lands of evergreen, irregularly streaked with the gleam of white birches. So they named them the "Apostles." Twenty-two islands there are in reality.

In summer, La Pointe city, on Madeline Island, the largest of the group, becomes the Lucerne of Wisconsin. Visitors throng to view its sculptured shores, or to seek quiet and rest far from the dust and smoke of cities and the noise of a commercial world. Sublime peace reigns in these isolated lands.

Legend and history abound in these remote places. Before Columbus discovered America, the Ojibwas had made Madeline their island home. Still later the lands became the Northwest gateway for zealous French explorers and trappers and for pious, "black-gowned" priests seeking converts in the wilds; and then as an early commercial outpost of the Astor fur company. Long since the Indians were moved to reservations after an internecine warfare for years with the tribes on the shore. But the stories of their daring and bravery, their trials and vicissitudes linger, rehearsed by old island residents on their porches during the cool summer evenings with the solemnity of a gospel reading.

The collective name of the Apostle Islands is at least two centuries old. Based on information gathered by Charlevoix, a noted Jesuit missionary, who in 1721 visited the western country as an agent for the French government, this name was placed on a 1744 map. The first English traveler to note these islands was Jonathan Carver. He coasted the shore of Lake Superior in 1767 and published a map in his "Travels," applying the name "Apostle Islands" to the group.

Governor Lewis Cass of Michigan and James D. Doty, afterwards territorial governor of Wisconsin, were probably the first Americans to make an official tour to this locality. Their visit was in 1820. At

VIEW OF LAKE SUPERIOR NEAR PAGEANT GROUNDS, BAYFIELD.

ALONG THE SHORES OF CHEQUAMEGON BAY AT WASHBURN.

LAKE SUPERIOR COASTLINE AT BAYFIELD.

ONE OF MANY PECULIAR ROCK FORMATIONS OF THE APOSTLE ISLANDS.

PASSENGER BOAT RETURNING FROM MADELINE ISLAND TO BAYFIELD.

CHURCH BUILT IN 1834 AT LA POINTE, MADELINE ISLAND.

CONFLUENCE OF THE WISCONSIN AND MISSISSIPPI RIVERS, DISCOVERED BY FATHER JAMES MARQUETTE.

TREMPEALEAU (SINKING) MOUNTAIN, PERROT STATE PARK.

A DAYLIGHT RIDE ALONG THE UPPER MISSISSIPPI IS A RARE TRAVEL TREAT.

LOOKING TOWARD PRAIRIE DU CHIEN FROM NELSON DEWEY STATE PARK.

FISH NETS AND BOATS AT GENOA.

MAIDEN ROCK, AN OLD MISSISSIPPI RIVER TOWN.

that time Henry R. Schoolcraft, later a distinguished Indian agent at Sault Sainte Marie, who accompanied them, attempted to rename the islands after several of the states in the Union. His proposal was not generally followed, although the present names of York and Michigan Island seem to remain as a part of his suggestion.

It is apparent that the early traders did not see each of the separate islands. Since the principal mission was named "Mission du Saint Esprit," the name of the twelve islands which they had counted appeared appropriate. Strange as it may seem, not a single island of the group bears the name of an apostle. The individual names of many of the islands have been taken from their outward natural characteristics. Outer Island explains itself, as do Ironwood, Oak, Basswood, Sand, Rocky, North and South, Twin, Bear, Wild Cat and Otter. Raspberry Island takes its name from the Raspberry River which empties into Lake Superior. "Devil's Island" and "Manitou Island" are the same.

Hermit Island and Stockton Island have taken their appellations from their early inhabitants. Madeline Island received its name from the wife of an early trader, Michael Cadotte. It was frequently known as St. Michael's, from the given name of Cadotte, who was the principal trader on the island for many years. Its Indian name was Moningwanekaning, supposed to mean "the place of the Golden Breasted Woodpecker." As "Woodpecker Island" it is often referred to in story and song.

There are no characters in American history more picturesque than the first adventurous fur traders to visit the Lake Superior region—Pierre d'Esprit, Sieur Raddison, and his sister's husband, Medard Chouart, Sieur des Groseilliers. In their fond desire to "travel and see countries" and to be known "with the remotest people," they roved through the country of St. James Bay and Central Wisconsin in 1655 and by many able historians are believed to have discovered the Mississippi River twelve years before Marquette. Five years later they are found exploring the Lake Superior region, skirting the shore of Chequamegon Bay, visiting the famous "Pictured Rocks" on the banks of Michigan Peninsula.

Within full view of the Apostle Islands, they made their home on the mainland, probably near the site of the present city of Washburn. Winter was setting in and the waters of the bay and about the islands were assuming the dark and sullen aspect peculiar to the season. Burying their trading supplies, doubtless on one of the islands, they spent the winter on a hunt with remnants of the starving band of Algonquin Indians in the Mille Lacs region of Minnesota.

In 1665 the first missionary, Father Claude Allouez, reached the locality. For four years he labored alone with the Indians, attaining little success amid the greatest of hardships and privations. Father James Marquette, a more youthful priest, was sent to relieve him in the fall of 1669. Here it was that he first learned from the Indians about the mighty Mississippi with which his name will be linked through the ages. Soon trouble arose among the warring Sioux and their neighbors with the result that Marquette and a band of Hurons were forced to retire to Mackinac. It was 1835 before Mass was again said on the tree-mantled shore overlooking the Apostle Islands.

During this interregnum a panorama of noted fur traders passed in an historic procession. Sieur Raudin, the personal representative of the impetuous La Salle, came cajoling the Sioux in 1673; Daniel Graysolon du Luth, after whom the city at the head of the lakes is named, followed in 1679; Le Seur in 1693, to build his stockade on Madeline Island, and other notable traders who were to leave an imprint upon the early history of this enchanted land.

After the fall of New France, an English trader, Alexander Henry, spent the winter of 1766 opposite Madeline Island and formed a partnership with the Cadotte family. About the opening of the Nineteenth century Michael Cadotte took up his abode on Madeline Island, and from that time to the present it has been permanently occupied. In 1830 Frederick Ayer of Mackinac visited the island and opened what was then the only Protestant mission on the shores of the Great Lakes. Five years later Father Frederick Baraga established a Catholic mission there, just one hundred sixty-four years after Marquette had been driven from Chequamegon Bay by war parties of the Western Sioux. The old

"Mission House" which he built in 1841 was recently destroyed by fire.

Little wonder, with all this early history dramatized by the fiery words of Parkman, that the Apostle Islands should be a place of historic remembrance. But even the romantic and fabled story of trials and disappointments, of strivings for power and control, the rise and fall of kingly domain in the Northwest, pale into comparative insignificance when the islands themselves are visited. Long ago as a school boy I had traced the line of advance of these first traders and missionaries, but it was never indelibly imprinted until, one fall afternoon, I motored over the peninsula to have the dream of a quarter of a century made a reality.

Before me the great lake was calm as a mirror, silvery in the light of an afternoon sun. First one island and then another came into view upon the blue haze of the Lake Superior background. Here was the gateway of the Northwest.

Each of the islands has some especial peculiarity, some grotesqueness of outline or sculptured shore which differentiates it from the others. Madeline Island, the largest of the group, is the only one that is settled. It is reached by a little steamboat, which makes daily trips for tourists to La Pointe, a community made prosperous by their trade.

The inhabitants of the remaining islands are lighthouse keepers and a few summer campers, several of whom have been coming to the locality for more than a quarter of a century.

Madeline, "Queen of the Apostles," is a treasure spot of romantic interest. Indian legends make it the foundation stone of Mother Earth. Among them there is a story that "Winnebozho," the first white man, had a quarrel with the "Water Spirit," who ruled the floods, and in consequence of which the Spirit determined to drown him. The waters were caused to rise so as to cover the whole earth. But supernatural powers were also possessed by "Winnebozho" and, when he saw the flood advance, he went to the pine tree, and climbing into its topmost branches, commanded it to grow as fast as the mounting tide. Finding his efforts fruitless the "Water Spirit" then allowed the waters to subside. After the twelfth sun the surface became calm and still, and "Winnebozho" descended. Around the tree trunk an otter was swimming, seeking safety. "Winnebozho" lifted him up and, after he had rested him in his arms, told him to dive down and bring up some earth that he might create land. Trial after trial was made, but the otter could not reach bottom. Just as he had failed, a mink came swimming along, but his efforts were also unsuccessful.

Still "Winnebozho" was not discouraged. Seeing a muskrat paddling about in the waters, he took him up and breathing into his nostrils told him to go down and bring up earth, or never to come back. The rat swam swiftly down and, after a terrible struggle below, floated up lifeless on his back. "Winnebozho" picked him up and found in his black claws some grains of sand. Restoring the animal to life, he took the sands and blew a strong breath upon the grains, scattering them at some distance over the surface of the waters. Every grain began to grow and multiply and soon formed islands. It was thus that the lands were created and one of them, "Madeline," became the hunting ground of "Winnebozho." Since the muskrat saved "Winnebozho" it became the favorite animal of the Ojibwas.

Several miles out from the Wisconsin shore line near the city of Bayfield, at the north end of Chequamegon Bay, lies Madeline Island—a succession of great land waves. It is a beautifully wooded island, twelve miles long and three miles wide. Fine summer homes line its western shores and a number of farmsteads have been carved out in the interior. Fall time makes it a haven for hayfever sufferers.

It is La Pointe, old and historic as a city on the island, which attracts attention. A long dock comes out from the water's edge; one long shady street traverses the town; further on is the old Indian cemetery, and then at the deep bend in Crescent Bay are the beautiful grounds of the Old Mission. The air pungent with the scent of evergreens, the paths of the village, the byways through the land—all seem to be permeated with its legends and romances of a day when the Indian, the trader and the coureurs de bois held heyday in the land.

According to tradition the Ojibways settled on the island about 1490. They had been driven westward by their ancient foes, the Iroquois. They rested for a time at Mackinac, and then moved on to the Apostle Islands. Soon they became adept in the handling of the canoe and were able to escape from their enemies on the shore. It is estimated that at one time 10,000 Indians of the Ojibway tribe made their home on Madeline Island. The waters about abounded in fish and great flocks of wild pigeons came in the early spring and fall. Here the Ojibways lived for one hundred and twenty years unhampered by their enemies, their camp fires never smothered.

Then came a sudden change. Their desertion of the island home is one of the sad, romantic chapters in the story of the islands. Among these Indians there grew up a strong group of medicine men, known as Shamans, who demanded every year the sacrifice of an Indian maid. The Indians, steeped in superstitious fear, reluctantly acceded to their demands. Once the maidens were given up, they were never seen again. It remained for a dusky Indian lover who had been robbed of his sweetheart to solve the mystery. Spying on the medicine men, he learned that they had slain his sweetheart, had taken her body to the medicine lodge and were roasting it for a feast.

Arousing the young braves, he led them against the Shamans, destroying their lodges and murdering the cannibalistic feasters. Among the Indians there grew up a superstitious fear that the spirits of the murdered maidens haunted their homes and hovered menacingly over the island. Women heard their cries in the night and warriors saw their faces in the clouds. Panic seized them. In fear they fled to the mainland. By the year 1620 the island was entirely deserted. Some migrated far north into Canada and northern Minnesota, and the Ojibways or Chippewas who are there today are the descendants of the tribes who never returned to their island homes.

Years afterward some came back. For them fear lurked in their footsteps. Whenever they passed the big stone near the cliffs where the Shamans were supposed to have murdered the maids, they would scatter tobacco on the rock and waters to appease the angry spirits. The scene of life in the Northwest was about to shift. Soon thereafter came the traders and missionaries, and again Madeline became a place of pulsing interest.

Probably the most remarkable scenery is to be seen along the shores of Outer, Devil's and Bear Islands. At Bear Island, if one cares to penetrate the shore, is seen the great brownstone bathtub hewn from the foundation of the island by the force of the waves.

Devil's Island, which according to the Ojibway legend was the prison of "Matchie-Manitou," the great spirit, has its surprises—among them being the most picturesque sea caves of the group. The island is a huge block of Postdam sandstone rising from forty to fifty feet above the water level, the land covered with a dense evergreen forest. Resisting the force of three hundred miles of sea, during the passing centuries the waves have honey-combed the solid walls into great chambers, expanding arches and fantastically carved pillars. A rowboat can pass through these connected caverns several hundred feet, the cold moist corridors narrowing and expanding from passageway to chamber.

"During the terrible storms that sweep periodically over the great chain of lakes, these caverns become seething caldrons, and the rushing waves dash into them with almost resistless power," declared an old resident of Madeline Island. "Often when the storms are at their height, the spray from the sea, beating against the rocks below, is thrown against the glass of the lighthouse lantern, forty feet above its base, while the roar of rushing waters is like deafening thunder, and the island itself is shaken to its very foundation."

Nearby is Presque Island, known on government maps as Stockton. Third in area, it stands out boldly in the watery mirror with several miles of high frowning walls, crowned with moss-seamed battlements, along its north and east shore line. Centuries of rain and storm, sunshine and frost have fashioned these stone ruins to resemble ancient castles. A rocky sentinel, known as the "Sphinx," guards the entrance to one of the dells whose walls tower from forty to fifty feet in height. Sheltered in one of the grottos is the little musical waterfall, the Silver Cascade. The wave-nibbled shore line seems like a beguiling cavern leading to a fabled fairyland.

Two miles away is "Hermit" or "Wilson's Island." Shortly after the American Fur Company had settled at La Pointe, a stranger appeared at the post. He made a few purchases, lingered about the place for a few days and then disappeared. A month later the Indians reported that the stranger was erecting a log hut and making a clearing on an island. Soon he had a large garden for cultivation. Twice a year he visited the fort, bought his supplies, paid for them in Mexican gold and silver, and then departed. His money caused comment among the inhabitants and it was whispered that he was possessed of fabulous wealth and had a hidden treasure on the shore. Seldom was he visited except by the Indians. One day they reported at La Pointe that he was dead. Investigation disclosed that he had been murdered for his money. Among his effects were found a number of books, in both French and English, indicating that he was well educated. In a clock, overlooked by the assassins, a canvas bag was found. It contained forty-four Mexican dollars and a few gold pieces, which the authorities used in defraying the expense of his funeral at La Pointe. Thereafter, the island was known as the "hermit's land."

A few miles west of Oak Island and between Raspberry and Steamboat Islands is Sand Island with its great sea arch made famous by the celebrated American landscape painter, Bierstadt, who visited here in 1878. Fable and fancy have connected them with other thrilling romances.

As we left the islands the sun was setting over the Bayfield peninsula, bathing the anchored ships of green in a flood of golden light, mirroring their trees and shore line in the deep blue of Lake Superior. Far off, a freighter was steaming past on its way towards the "Soo," a reminder that the paths of civilization are near these enchanted islands of beauty and peace.

The Apostle Islands are off the Bayfield Peninsula in far northern Wisconsin, and are reached both from Bayfield and Ashland. Bayfield is ninety-four miles from Superior; two hundred twenty-five miles from St. Paul; four hundred seven miles from Milwaukee; three hundred thirty-six miles from Madison; two hundred eighty-three miles from Green Bay, and two hundred two miles from Eau Claire.

FRINGE OF MAJESTY

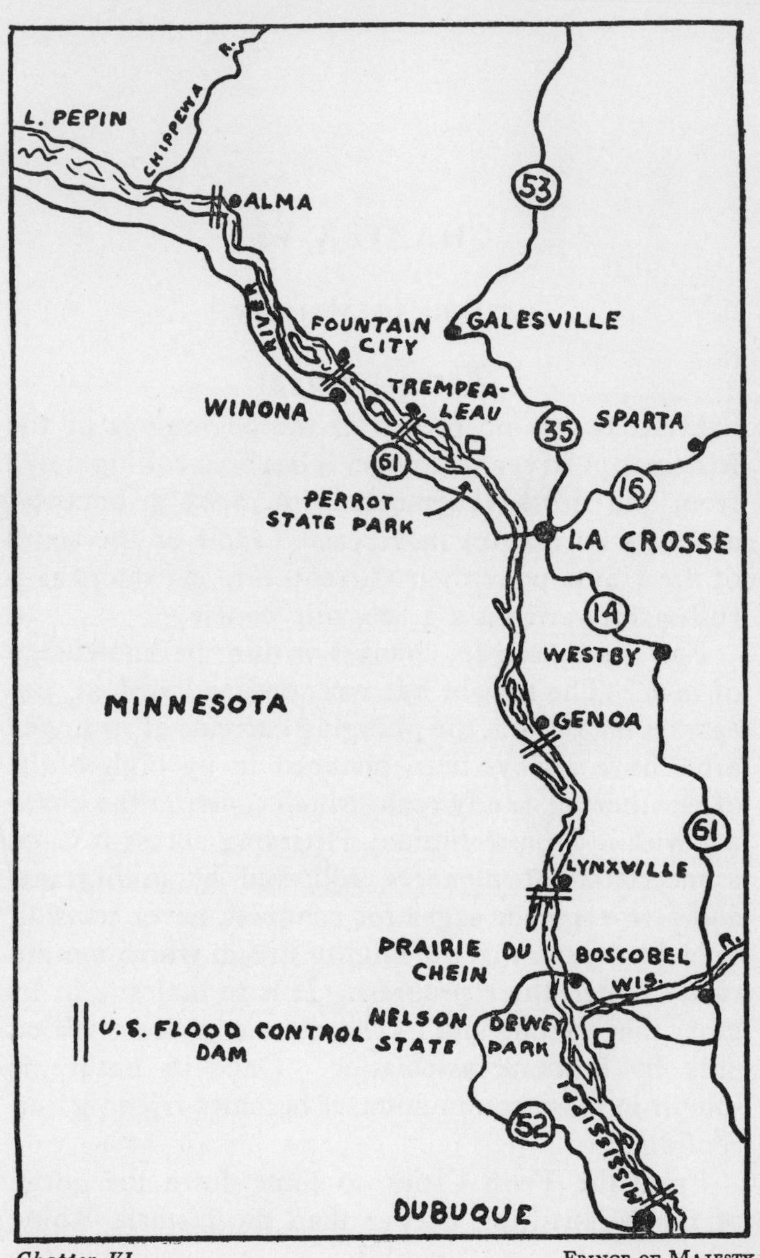

Chapter VI

FRINGE OF MAJESTY
THE MISSISSIPPI

CHAPTER VI

FRINGE OF MAJESTY

The Mississippi

HISTORY has no record of the beginnings of the Mississippi River. For ages it has been rolling down from the north, augmented by many tributaries, draining an empire in acreage. Half of the states of the Union pour their currents into its waters as it rushes forward on a 1,800-mile course.

Few have been its changes within the knowledge of man. The stream has wriggled and shifted, uneasy on its bed, but the plunging currents of its upper arms have always been hemmed in by high bluffs of weathering, sandy rock, which constrict the channel within definite limits. Hurrying across it came a succession of pioneers, followed by immigrants and farmers, ever eager for conquest, never pausing to learn the story of the mighty stream which temporarily halted their progress. It is so majestic in its glory that its song and its characteristics are revealed only by intimate association. Once its nature is sought in close communion, it becomes friendly and confiding.

From the Twin Cities, to come down the gorge of the Mississippi, deeper than the historic Rhine

Valley, is to comprehend the luring attractions of rocky cathedral domes and the serenity of surroundings which follow ages of transformation. The steep hillsides, when sunlit, are jade with green trees and foliage; in late summer the foreground is a riotous tangle of black-eyed susan and golden rod, or glowing on the higher peaks with sumac turning a flaming red. Like some old folk ballad, hidden within the river are themes that link her, decade by decade, with the past and the present. She has been the priceless subject of many a picture, song and story. Most of the many paintings reflect the tones of summer, when the trench through which the river runs is hung with a vapor of light blue and the bluffs in the morning are wrapped in a deeper purple.

It was on a June morning over two and a half centuries ago, that Marquette and Joliet, with their frail canoes, came paddling out of the mouth of the Wisconsin River upon this majestic expanse. They were the first visitors. A century and a half later the developing fur trade necessitated military garrisons. Traders, priests and soldiers with Indians in garish dress held the scene for a time. In another fifty years hamlets and rudely-built cities sprang up along its banks; a life made colorful by steamboat trade flourished before the days of the railroad. Then the picturesque activities of the valley faded into the quiet shadows of its towering hills.

Many times had I crossed and re-crossed the Mississippi up and down its route of nearly two

INDIAN HEAD BLUFFS NEAR FOUNTAIN CITY.

HIGHWAY AND RAILROAD SKIRTING LAKE PEPIN.

MISSISSIPPI FLOOD CONTROL DAM AT TREMPEALEAU.

OLD STEAMBOAT WAREHOUSE, PRAIRIE DU CHIEN.

FORT CRAWFORD (RESTORED), PRAIRIE DU CHIEN.

VILLA LOUIS, PRAIRIE DU CHIEN, HOME OF WISCONSIN'S FIRST MILLIONAIRE.

CASTLE ROCK, ON THE BEAUTIFUL MILITARY RESERVATION AT CAMP DOUGLAS.

ROCK BRIDGE SPANNING A RIVER NEAR RICHLAND CENTER.

OLD SHOT TOWER SHAFT, TOWER HILL STATE PARK.

TRIPLE PEAKS BETWEEN SPARTA AND NORWALK.

HOUSES OF THE CORNISH MINERS IN MINERAL POINT.

LITTLE NORWAY, NEAR MOUNT HOREB, LARGEST OUTDOOR NORWEGIAN MUSEUM ON CONTINENT.

thousands of miles and I did not catch its romantic story. Not until I traveled down its course on a flat-boat to the Illinois line, pausing now and then to visit with fishermen gathering in their morning haul, stopping to gossip with residents of the quaint little one-street hamlets, each with its white church set snugly on the hillside, or anchoring to watch the busy government engineers building reefs and wing dams to keep the currents within bounds—only then did I learn something of the fantastic witchery which has made men hesitate upon its banks and wonder at the omnipotence of the vanished power which made it.

Only after our boat had headed down stream for many miles did I settle back from the startling surprises wrought in its ever-changing embankments to listen to the song of the waters and glean something about the pulsing life along the river itself. What changes have come in a century!

The Mississippi days of Mark Twain are gone forever. The Civil War, with its attendant fever for railroad building, swept away the steamboat trade for which the river was long a marvel of changing wonders depicted in story and song. Guided with a fine precision by the "diamond boards" with which the government engineers now mark the course of the stream, the old river pilots of three-quarters of a century ago with no such chart before them must have been men of great knowledge and foresight. Only their intimate acquaintance with the stream and an intuition that comes to those who live for long upon the river, could have directed them safely by day and night through such a tangle of sloughs, shallows and pockets. The present day contrast is worth recording. The story of the marvelous transformation which has been wrought by the science of government engineers was told me by one who as a boy worked on the river boats after the close of the Civil War, before the commerce was finally wrested away.

"The pilot of that day," declared the late George B. Merrick, a Mississippi riverman, "was absolutely dependent upon his knowledge of and familiarity with the natural landmarks on either side of the river, for guidance in working his way through and over the innumerable sandbars and crossings. No lights on shore guided him by night, and no 'diamond boards' gave him assurance by day. No ready searchlight revealed the marks along the shore. Only a perspective of bluffs, sometimes miles away, showing dimly outlined against a leaden sky, guided the pilot in picking his way over the dangerous crossings, where there was often less than forty feet to spare on either side of the boat's hull, between safety and destruction.

"To 'know the river' under those conditions meant to know absolutely the outline of every range of bluffs and hills, as well as every isolated knob or even treetop. It meant that the man at the wheel must know these outlines absolutely, under the constantly changing point of view of a moving steamer; so that he might confidently point his steamer at a solid wall of blackness, and guided only by the shape of distant hills and by the mental picture which he had of them, know the exact moment at which to put his wheel over and steer his boat away from an impending bank.

"Today a thousand beacons are kindled every night to mark the dangerous or intricate crossings; by day great white 'diamond boards' spot the banks. At night the pilot has only to jingle a bell in the engine room, the dynamo is started, and by pulling a line at either hand the searchlight turns night into day, the big white board stands out in high relief against the leafy background, and the pilot heads for it, serene in the confidence that it is placed in line with the best water; for he knows that the government engineers have sounded every foot of the crossing within a date so recent as to make them cognizant of any change in its area or contour.

"Millions of dollars have been spent in the work, and its preservation costs hundreds of thousands of dollars annually. Sixty years ago two hundred men and a hundred boats groped their way in darkness, amid known and unknown terrors, up and down the windings of the great river, without having for their guidance a single token of man's helpful invention."

And now the Government has changed its policy of dredging the river channel to keep the Mississippi within its banks at flood time. By a series of dams, which appear like step-ladders in the long river course, the Federal Government is establishing a giant project to check the devastation by spring flood-waters. By restraining the excess flowage by means of reservoirs, the tremendous flood damage to cities far down the stream may be avoided. Launched under the administration of Franklin D. Roosevelt, this undertaking has become an engineering achievement rivaled only in possible values by the construction at Boulder Dam.

Between St. Paul and St. Louis this watery stairway will consist of twenty-six steps, costing when completed $148,000,000. The annual expense to the government for maintenance will be around $1,750,000. When finished, each step will be a lake or impounded pool of about twenty-five miles to make the drop of 347.9 feet from the waters of St. Anthony's Falls to the mouth of the Missouri.

Army engineers say that, when the dams are in, they are going to put the Father of Waters at work again as an important link in river navigation. They call the project "the canalization of the Upper Mississippi for a nine-foot navigation channel." They foresee a period of water transportation, barge lines towing the freight of industries created by cheap hauling.

Ten steps in this stairway for Father Neptune down the Mississippi are along the Wisconsin border.[8] Many a utility magnate is wondering if the "upper Mississippi navigation" project is another embryonic Muscle Shoals. So far, on the

[8] Dam sites constructed or to be built touching Wisconsin are: Dam No. 3, Red Wing; No. 4, Alma; No. 5, Fountain City; No. 5A, Winona; No. 6, Trempealeau; No. 7, Onalaska; No. 8, Genoa; No. 9, Lynxville; No. 10, Guttenberg; No. 11, Dubuque.

Mississippi only the Rock Island and Keokuk dams have power plants. But it is just like Wisconsin to make the demand as soon as the ten dams on her border are in operation. To one who sees the tremendous energy of these pent-up waters at any one of the dams, there will not long be a doubt. Some day soon "Old Man River," famous in Show Boat song, will be furnishing electrical power to light the cities and do the drudgery on the farms of the Middle West.[9]

No need to go to Boulder Dam to witness the tremendous power of restrained waters. Visit the Winona dam above La Crosse, or any other of those completed. Watch the fury when the gates are opened!

For both the occasional and commercial fisherman, the Mississippi is a paradise. On every sandbar and wing dam, whole families may be seen patiently attending to their poles. During early morning the river seems alive with Waltonians. As the heat of the day comes, their numbers decrease, but they assemble later as the sun dips behind the high, precipitous banks in the afternoon.

Of lesser importance is clamming, now strictly supervised by both the Federal and State Governments. Alternate strips five miles apart are opened for clamming for five years and then closed for another five-year period. Piled like great shipments of potatoes in northern Wisconsin warehouses may

[9] French, Lewis C., "Building a Stairway for Father Neptune," Milwaukee Journal, June 23, 1935; See National Geographic Magazine, July, 1937.

be seen the burlap bags of clam shells at the railroad stations. Along the river one meets an occasional clam fisherman with long rows of hooks suspended from a horizontal pole from both sides of his boat. The industry furnishes the button factories at La Crosse and other places along the river with a supply of raw material. Pearl fishing, which is a part of the clamming, has declined somewhat in recent years, although a lucky find is reported occasionally.

When one tires of the commerce and life of the pulsing river valley, interest can always be found in the little one-street villages, and in the bold scenery along the banks.

Bay City, with its nearby palisades that rival the Hudson; Maiden Rock, with its legend of an Indian's "lovers leap" more thrilling than the story of Hiawatha; Pepin, where the waters expand to a glistening lake; the vine-clad banks of Fountain City, often called "the Rhine of the Mississippi"; Trempealeau Mountain, "soaking" in the waters, a park of historical allurements; La Crosse, where Indian shinny was played on the plain; Genoa, a counterpart to the city that gave Christopher Columbus to the world, with its little fishing bay overlooked by Italian porticos; Victory, the final battle-ground of the last Indian war east of the Mississippi; Prairie du Chien, redolent with thrilling tales of a gay frontier; Galena Junction, once the head of steamboat traffic for the Wisconsin lead mines—each reveals a peculiar touch from its pioneer founders—

squat houses of Germany; a white-spired Italian church; severe homes of Vermont and New Hampshire farmers.

The river has its own attractions. Sometimes one will travel for miles, as from Prairie du Chien to Cassville, in a regular fairyland of islands midstream.

These secluded, wild bottom lands have become a refuge for bird life. As one descends the river, the phenomena of varied species becomes more noticeable. Crows perch in old leafless trees along the route, as if inspecting the character of the traffic. Turkey buzzards, reported by the fishermen to be equipped with telescopic eyes, seem to hang in the heavens with wings outstretched as if they were sailing helpless through the blue. Now and again the long-legged sandhill crane is surprised when some turn in the stream is rounded, and he flies clumsily away to another haven. Kingfishers patrol the stream, feasting on the minnows and smaller fish that venture into the shallows.

During the early morning and again as the brooding shadows of afternoon steal over the water surface, gregarious flocks of white-breasted swallows dip and glide over the glistening river, feasting on the whirling waterbugs that are floating down stream. Toward noonday they seem to desert their familiar feeding grounds. However, one by one, as evening approaches, they come from hiding places along the sandy banks and begin their acrobatic maneuvers. They dart and turn; they soar and glide. Sometimes they will sail swiftly for long distances a few inches above the current and then as if checked by a queer fancy they wheel abruptly, circling at times in such large numbers as to make one wonder if they do not infest the river in swarms like the bees that live in rotting tree trunks on the precipitous hillsides. Often as they tire from their flights, long lines of them seek momentary rest on telephone wires suspended across the valley. Soon they are off again on another gyrating excursion.

The pulsing power of our little boat does not carry us so rapidly but that we read the two signboards marking the place where the red man made his last stand near the present-day village of Victory. In this ravine the retreating army of Black Hawk was annihilated in July, 1832. The little signboards "Battle Hollow," and "Black Hawk War 1832" commemorate not merely the end of the red man's range in Wisconsin, but the beginning of the occupation of the white man east of the Mississippi Valley in Iowa and Minnesota. As the river "keeps rolling along" it passes spots of great interest.

The thrill of historic sentiment is bubbling over in Prairie du Chien and citizens are making efforts to mark all of the historic spots within the confines of the city. Next to Green Bay, this city has the oldest and most historic record in the state. Only four miles away, the Wisconsin River joins the Mississippi where Marquette and Joliet first beheld these lands on June 17, 1673, and on the southern heights above the confluence sits beautiful Nelson Dewey State

Park, like an overlord of the great domain. The second Fort Crawford, within the city limits of Prairie du Chien, has recently been rebuilt, a part of the old army fort being utilized.

To the memory of a young army doctor who saved a hunter from death and then conducted experiments on the digestion of food through a wound in the man's stomach, a fourteen-ton boulder has been erected at the second Fort Crawford. The inscription on the boulder's bronze tablet reads:[10]

WILLIAM BEAUMONT, M. D.
PIONEER IN PHYSIOLOGY
BORN IN LEBANON, CONN., 1785
DIED AT ST. LOUIS, MO., 1853

AT OLD FORT CRAWFORD, ONE MILE AND A HALF NORTHWEST OF THIS SPOT, 100 YEARS AGO, DR. BEAUMONT, A SURGEON IN THE UNITED STATES ARMY, PERFORMED THOSE EXPERIMENTS ON ALEXIS ST. MARTIN WHICH LAID THE FOUNDATION FOR OUR KNOWLEDGE OF DIGESTION.

The spectacular experiments performed by Dr. Beaumont, which have caused him to be known as one of the great physiologists of all time, resulted from the accidental shooting of St. Martin, a boatman. Dr. Beaumont saved the young boatman after all had despaired of his life, but the gaping abdominal wound would not heal, leaving a hole leading into St. Martin's stomach.

Dr. Beaumont's procedure was simple. He inserted a spoon through the hole in St. Martin's stomach and learned the digestive processes on vari-

[10] Beaumont marker erected August 30, 1931.

ous foods. The subject made only one objection—he refused to have liquor enter his stomach except through his mouth.

All told, Dr. Beaumont made 204 experiments on St. Martin, 54 of them while he was stationed at old Fort Crawford from December, 1829, to August, 1832.

Before the Mexican War, Zachary Taylor, later President of the United States, was commandant of Fort Crawford, and Jefferson Davis, later President of the Confederacy, was one of his young lieutenants. Still standing on the college grounds of St. Mary's Academy is a sentinel pillar, once one of the outposts of civilization in a savage wilderness.

It's worth going ashore for an hour to visit historic spots. Close to the water's edge is the old stone building which once housed the Astor Fur Trading Company, owned by John Jacob Astor, who made a fortune in pelts and a national reputation in business. Astor's Wisconsin agent was Hercules L. Dousman, who became the state's first millionaire. The romantic old Dousman home, known as Villa Louis,[11] built in 1815, overlooking a broad sweep of the Mississippi river, was bequeathed in 1935 by the Dousman heirs to the city of Prairie du Chien for a public memorial, and has been restored to the glory of a vanished epoch by a re-gathering of the scattered heirlooms. It reflects the wealth and aroma of those days when John Jacob Astor was the fur

[11] For full description of Villa Louis, Milwaukee Journal, April 30, 1936.

king of the Northwest and his agents were in every fur market.

If you have time, climb to Brisbois Point, north of the city. The view of the old Frenchtown, the green islands in the river, the pontoon railroad bridge,[12] one of the four in the world and the largest —and the far purple hills of Iowa make charming the vista and fleeting the hours. Nearby is the grave of Michael Brisbois, who loved the beautiful spot and was interred there in 1837. Even in death the business rivalry that stirred him in life lives on in tradition. He wanted to be buried here, so in death he might look down upon his rival in the fur trade, Joseph Rolette, who is buried far below in the Frenchtown cemetery.

Across the "rolling river" where we take boat again, the pioneers of the far West were ferried in "covered wagons" a century ago. Scenery scarcely attracted them. They were bent on building new homes and founding an empire of farms.

About twenty miles below Prairie du Chien, on the Iowa side, one comes upon a real surprise in community development. Unlike all of the other little towns, Guttenberg is a novelty. Its shores are rip-rapped; there is a park along the water's edge, and the whole village is modern and appears freshly painted.

After an enchanting journey through the long gorge of the upper Mississippi, one feels that this majestic river is too small for its broad, deep passage-

[12] For history of bridge, see Milwaukee Journal, May 13, 1934.

way. The embankment features are so bold and wild that they impart new sensations to the mind. It is probable that long before the glaciers, a still mightier stream traversed this route. Steep and craggy bluffs, at an elevation of from 200 to 600 feet, lend enchantment to each succeeding day of travel. Sometimes they will be close to the Minnesota or Iowa side of the river and the Wisconsin precipices will be far away. Within a few miles the route will change and the western banks will be in the distance.

Between its bluffs, at some places six miles apart or contracting further on to less than a mile, is the still narrower channel of the river. Geologists claim that the Mississippi gorge is deeper than that of Niagara, but not so narrow, and that "now and then there may be seen mural precipices nearly as steep as the Palisades of the Hudson, and continuous perhaps for two, three, or even five miles." Sometimes the bluffs are closely crowded in rows and for a score of miles the cliff wall may be broken only by narrow ravines or the constricted gorges of little streams. Again the interspaces widen and the bluffs become a line of isolated buttes, round-topped, like deserted castles on some signal point.

In the world's civilization the gorge and the far extending valley have written an illuminated page in the story of the advancement of mankind. Out of the waters of "Old Man River" the Nation is now developing one of the greatest conservation projects of history. When finished, it will have a significance upon national development more far-reaching than the digging of the Panama Canal.

The Mississippi River forms the western boundary of the state. All along the way are scenic spots—at Prescott, Maiden Rock, Alma, Fountain City, La Crosse, Genoa, Victory, De Soto, Prairie du Chien, and Cassville. From St. Paul to Cassville, Highway 35 follows closely the river route.

SIGN POSTS OF ETERNITY

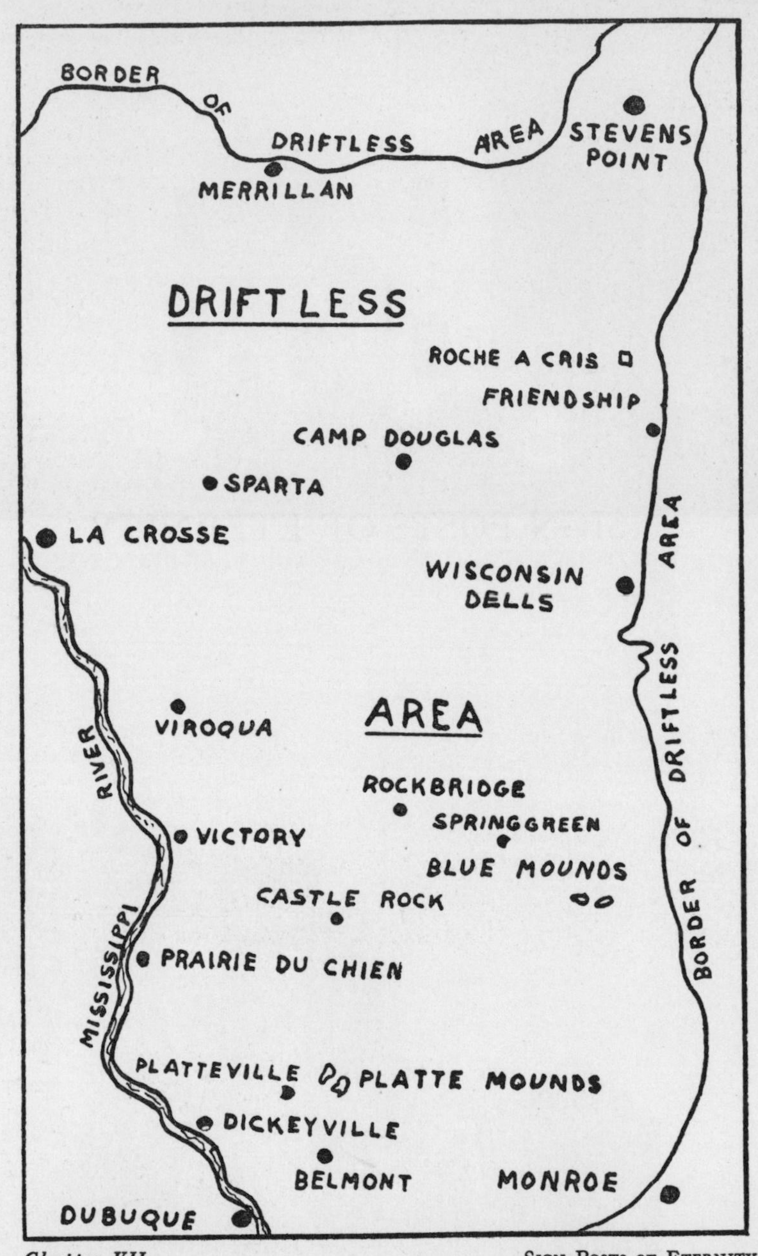

Chapter VII

SIGN POSTS OF ETERNITY OUTSIDE THE GLACIAL PATH

WISCONSIN'S TERRITORIAL CAPITOL NEAR BELMONT.

CKEY-
LLE
TTO, A
INE FOR
USANDS
VISITORS.

—Milwaukee Journal Photo.

ROCHE A CRIS, A NATURAL ROCK WONDER NEAR FRIENDSHIP.

STERN CACTI
OW WILD NEAR
SAUK CITY.

LEAD AND ZINC MINE NEAR LINDEN

TALIESIN, HOME OF FRANK LLOYD WRIGHT.

WINDING ROAD OVER WILD CAT MOUNTAIN.

A BEND IN THE KICKAPOO RIVER.

PICTURESQUE KICKAPOO VALLEY RAILWAY SCENERY.

A NATURAL PANTHEON SOUTH OF READSTOWN.

WATERS OF THE KICKAPOO ARE PEACEFUL AND CALM.

MOUNT NEBO, A FAMILIAR VIEWPOINT NEAR VIOLA.

CHAPTER VII

SIGN POSTS OF ETERNITY

Outside the Glacial Path

SCATTERED over southwestern Wisconsin are the weather-tarnished sign posts which must have guided the gods of a manless world as they fled before the destruction of the threatening glacier eons ago. Within this region the work of the divinely inspired hand of Nature as a landscape gardener may be seen in original outlines, and its sculptured art of fantastic conception can be examined. Unadvertised, these uplands are more interesting to the scientist, more fascinating to the loitering tourist, than many lakes and dells, the common possession of several states.

"The driftless area of Wisconsin is famous the world over because it is completely surrounded by glaciated territory," observed Lawrence Martin, geographer.[13] "It preserves a large sample of what the rest of Wisconsin, as well as northern and eastern United States, were like before the glacial period. Within the belts covered by the gigantic continental ice sheets of northeastern North America and northwestern Europe, there is no similar region left bare of glacial ice."

Missed by the glaciers which flattened much of

[13] Martin, Lawrence, "Physical Geography of Wisconsin," p. 74.

the rest of the state, this section remains as a remnant of the country as it existed before the ice age. It has no lakes to make youthful its countenance; no erratic-strewn rock gardens to freckle the landscape. It looks old, and it is old. The attractions of these puckered uplands are hidden in a crumpled masterpiece of the Creator's art.

Travel where you will in this unglaciated area, and always some strange wonder will be found. The outer rim between the city of Wisconsin Dells, Camp Douglas and Merrillan Junction is the border line between the east and the west. The whole landscape is transformed on this tableland as distinctly as are the trees and vegetation on a mountainside at the snow line. It is difficult to compare scenes in Nature so different. To the east is a landscape softened by rain, luxuriant with lush vegetation. To the west are arid acres, dwarf trees struggling for existence, and flowers and plants common to the west and southwest. The sands around Camp Douglas are as white and in summer as dry and hot as the wastes of Arizona.

But it is the great sandstone castles and mural escarpments that challenge notice and awaken awe. Untold centuries of wind and rain, which began their sculpturing work before the glaciers invaded the rest of the state, have washed away the surrounding earth. Left standing are grim looking, grotesque appearing banks, crags, pinnacles and chimneys that arrest attention for miles over the plain. If all these figures could be grouped in a narrow area they would rival the Garden of the Gods. They have all the weirdness of execution but lack the attractive coloring and boldness of impressive outlines of the Colorado wonderland. Their turrets and towers frown down upon the country like medieval castles. At a distance their walls are suggestive of masonry and bear marks as if the waters had been dammed and held to sustain some moat to the fortress of the ruling overlord.

The Camp Douglas country was once the bottom of a sea. Shells and fossils are found imbedded in the ripple-marked rock, and the sands crunch under foot like the cushion of a beach. Bluffs and ridges loom stolid above the landscape as sentinels.

Within this immediate vicinity are flat-topped mounds in miniature form not unlike the mesas of Utah. Of these, the Roche a Cris, north of Friendship, is not only the most beautiful with its steep sides, but from a distance resembles the pictures of old monasteries in Europe that cling on a mountainside. Similar in size and of like imposing beauty from the roadside is Gibraltar Rock, north of Lodi, capped with St. Peter's sandstone and rounded on the western side by the grinding of an ice block. This embankment has recently been converted into a park by the Society of Friends of Our Native Landscape. Such road markers provoke suggestive questions of what happened in the departed ages.

With every annual visit to the Camp Douglas country my curiosity turns to wonder and then to a strange enchantment. Those nibbled cliffs, at the entrance of the reservation, eroded by running water and sand blast, and now parched in a sea of silt, bring visions of the fleeting present compared with the immensity of time. What a gulf must eternity be!

Many years ago my interest in the picturesque forms caused by the weathering of the sandstone became so stimulated that I began a series of little pilgrimages to this southwestern Wisconsin area. As artists, the wind and sun handle delicate tools to re-create their dreams. Most of the fanciful rock creations are along the roadside. Some are inaccessible except on foot. Nature has had no fixed abode for her studios.

Because of the far distances one may vision, I like to tour the country southeast of La Crosse. Many weird rock formations near Viroqua made Vernon county a sacred place for the Indians. To come upon these relics after a tour over St. Joseph Ridge is to live a poem in auto travel. As the heights are reached, the wooded coulees lie veiled in a lavender-tinted mist, with toy farm homes and fields far down in the valley. A fleeting cloud across the sun paints changing pictures in sunlight and shade—golden, followed by dark green with light tints on hillside and somber hues in the bottom lands, which the eye catches and remembers but cannot transmit.

Then for miles the roads and country become commonplace. But a surprise awaits at the next curve. Away to the west, before Viroqua is reached, are the three chimneys—a place holy to the Indians.

Many times the Indians counseled in its shadows.

I went silently about the decaying tabernacle of spiritual glory. The ruins are of a bold, rude architecture. Afar it suggests the secluded fairyland of a Mother Goose. Legends remind us that here dwells the Great Spirit, who grew angry when Indian boys invaded the sanctuary. That night, from the highest pinnacle, the Manitou delivered a message of banishment:

"Children of the forest, you sport upon sacred ground. Nevermore must the foot of man know the castle of the Spirit. As a symbol of my power I shall make grass grow,—I shall plant trees even upon these barren rocks, and the trees and the grass shall thrive."

No longer do the Indians camp in this vicinity.

Seven miles south of Viroqua is a single shaft sixty feet high. It is the most photographed stone in western Wisconsin. This extraordinary tower emerges from a forested hillside and seems to rise with extreme abruptness. I keep from its shadow in fear that the precariously perched, top-heavy column might fall.

Monument Rock was a sign-post for the red man. No one who once passed would ever forget it. From it the Indian computed distances and days by moons. Later it served a useful purpose in guiding explorers and immigrants. How it got into that nicely balanced position will remain an enigma forever.

So stands the leaning monument that it acts as a sun dial. From the shadow I observed that it was not quite noon, and I still had hours to view new wonders. Then the idea occurred that I had never visited the rocky circumference of by-gone ages north of Richland Center. The map showed a winding road leading to Hillsboro where a highway to the south passes all these interesting points. We started without delay.

Before we realized the distance, the village bottom was reached. After leaving Hub City, phantom steamboats and battleships that appeared in distant array became great headlands on closer approach.

Rockbridge was the exclamation point on the route. For it is a real rock bridge! This formation of stone, one layer upon another, ten miles north of Richland Center, crosses the east branch of the Pine river. A solid wall of rock sixty feet high, one hundred feet thick and about a mile long is what proved to the world that at one time it constituted a part of the shore line of what was probably a large body of water. Cutting its way through this wall of rock, the Pine river, eight feet wide and no longer that deep, has built over itself a natural bridge.

Although it is sufficiently wide, it does not serve as a wagon bridge, but is used only by visitors who go on foot. Those travelers are rewarded for their climb to the top of the bridge by lovely wild flowers, pines and birch trees. It is the one spot in Richland County where trailing arbutus grows. In the fall, bittersweet may always be found there.

During the Black Hawk War, Rockbridge was not merely a creation of beauty, but was a thing to be used. High water and bad weather made the river difficult to cross, and so it was that this natural bridge was used by the Indian chief during his stay in this locality. It is generally believed that the trail which now winds around the top of the rock was the same as that used by Black Hawk in the course of his warfare.

Soon after leaving Rockbridge I rubbed my eyes to see if some war camouflage had been recreated on the landscape or whether I was witnessing a mirage. Across the fields the prow of a steamboat appeared with water glistening along its side.

"It's sure a good imitation," remarked my companion after we had approached near enough to Pine River to discover the deception in outcropping rock. Later we learned that the formation is actually known in the community as "Steamboat Rock."

"There's not enough water for one to take a good plunge," urged my companion. "Let's get back to the Wisconsin valley to see if we can get cooled off."

All morning a gray mist hung over the countryside. Heat waves danced in billows over the parched fields. But these seemed to vanish as we turned into the road near the Wisconsin river across from Muscoda. The woods that rimmed the valley hills were resting in shadows,—cool nooks that were alluring.

But the way was leading toward Sauk City and now we were passing "Riverside." Even the automobile seemed to falter for a fleeting glimpse. Such scenery of glistening river and naked sandbars in a long yellow expanse! Some pictures were taken but they mean little. They reveal no part of the soul of the stream and its playful antics in carrying away these mid-channel sandpiles over night. The road curves with the river bank, a winding turnpike that twists and is finally transformed into a long crescent.

Beside the road, like a patriarch, was Bogus Bluff. Romantic legends of hidden treasures surround this honey-combed hill with its outcropping of gray locks on the forehead. There is a tradition of a buried horde of Spanish coins, which were supposed to have been stolen as the treasure was being transported from Canada to New Orleans. Another story tells of a band of river pirates, who secreted their wealth in the caves of the old bluff, but were driven away before they could recover their loot. Old families along the way say that more recent traditions make it successively the hiding den of horse thieves, counterfeiters, and, during the period of prohibition, of bootleggers.

"It's far up to the top, my friend," commented an old man, who sat listlessly watching the waters—and watching us.

"We're not looking for adventure today," I commented, and started on, leaving to the care of the riverman the silent bluff of romantic imaginations.

Near Gotham the valley sprawls out. The hills stand impressively far back from the road and there is no river in view. A few miles beyond where the sign points the way to Spring Green, the hills again become friendly,—three sister bluffs crowd near in confidence. Their brows are decked with dark green spruces, "druid priests at their orisons, murmuring their benediction over the somber valley."

Returning to Sauk City to complete the tour a few days later we had an equally interesting experience. Twelve miles northwest of Prairie du Sac and a short distance from the village of Leland, I picnicked near a natural bridge as beautiful as that of Virginia which Thomas Jefferson so often visited. The span was created by erosion. There is no stream in the vicinity, but the curve is an open arch of about thirty-five feet. Standing out in a wooded pasture lot, it makes its presence a curiosity of Nature's pranks.

On the sunny slope outside of Sauk City, once the scene of the skirmish of Wisconsin Heights during the Black Hawk War of 1832, two University students were holding a friendly argument.

"I tell you those dwarf cactus plants are the remnants of an age when Wisconsin enjoyed a tropical climate," declared the philosopher.

"I can hardly believe that," interposed the botanist. "I have been studying these cactus plants all over southwestern Wisconsin. I think they may have been brought in from New Mexico and Arizona on the hoofs of the buffalo, who roamed all over the Mississippi valley. I have found the cactus in scraggly growth at Camp Douglas, Lone Rock, and many other places, where the arid soil is similar to that of the Southwest."

"But look at the stunted trees. This is the border land with these little evergreens suggesting the pineries of the North and the spiny plants the beginning of the West."

Away they finally went, still in disagreement.

There were sandwiches and coffee sufficient for an evening meal, so we went our way to the old Shot Tower park, forty-five miles from Madison and across the river from Spring Green. Shot Tower hill is one of the most picturesque locations in southern Wisconsin. It is also one of the most historic. Here was started the "shot" industry of southern Wisconsin, which became a potent influence in bringing many settlers into the state after the Black Hawk War; here the American troops in pursuit of Black Hawk and his band crossed the river in 1832; here was located Helena, which once rivaled Madison in desiring the location of the capital; and here from an eminence of two hundred feet of rock escarpment, now crested with an observation tower, one can see for miles down the Wisconsin River valley, a silver twisted rope in the sunlight.

Probably so prominent a spot, at such an elevation might have been the signal fire ground for the Sauk Indians, who once had their principal villages across and up the river about fifteen miles away. As the sun dips to the western horizon there rises over the Wisconsin valley, visible for miles at the eminence, a thin wraith of mist that marks the course of the stream.

Helena, the once famous, bustling little village, whose site has become a part of the park gift to the state, vanished with the coming of the Civil War and the railroads. Time and progress have left the beauty of the spot undisturbed.

In a bend in the road, not far from Tower Hill Park, is the home of the internationally famous architect, Frank Lloyd Wright, whose wide-flung spreading dwelling on a hillside blends into the natural scenery of the Wisconsin Valley. "Taliesin" is the name of Mr. Wright's estate, because in Welsh tradition the word means "Shining brow." From Taliesin on through the Wyoming Valley are pastoral scenes scarcely rivaled in any foreign country.

Perhaps it was because of the freak formations in rocks so close to my home that years had passed before I visited the Devil's Chimney in Dane County. I had often heard of the delightful creation, but it was not until an out-of-state tourist asked for directions to Mount Vernon, the nearby village, to the farm birthplace of the late Senator Robert M. La Follette, and for the site of the Devil's Chimney, that I became ashamed of my neglect.

The next day was Sunday and I made early preparations. At the quaint little village, burdened with such an historic name, has been founded a "Forest of Fame" with trees taken from the birthplaces of great men and from other noted places. One can easily locate the Chimney three miles to the south.

Partly concealed behind heavy foliage, the leaning fifty-foot tower gains in impressiveness on approach. Tapered at the base, it bulges out noticeably only to return to its smaller dimension at the top. It was years before it was scaled. The first one to reach the top could not descend and was forced, a modern Stylus, to spend the night on its head, when farmers coming to their fields in the morning made the rescue.

For an hour or more I sat around the base. I could not leave it without a trial. I knew I would have to return unless the height was conquered. At last I saw the steps. Someone had cut narrow footholds. I made a partial ascent. Many others had gone before me, for I found the soft rocks approaching the top carved with names and initials of those who had recorded their deft achievement. The feat was well worth doing, with the miles of rich harvest and green woodlands all around.

Beneath some of the rock wonders are caves which have been partly, but not fully, explored. Most of them can be entered only by exertion. They are relatively small; several of them contain stalactites, and all are more or less filled with mud. No less than six of these are located within the unglaciated region. Geologists explain their presence by the action of under-ground water aided by crevices and joints in the rocks.[14]

I became interested in these caverns because of the stories told by Charles E. Brown, secretary of the Wisconsin Archeological Society. For several years he has been making visits and explorations principally of the caves within the driftless area in an attempt to decipher the numerous pictographs on the

[14] For lists and notations of caves, see Martin, Lawrence, "Physical Geography of Wisconsin," pp. 85-88.

rocks, ledges and caverns. In a cave at West Salem, La Crosse County, he found the walls daubed with paintings and engravings. Discovery of this cave had been made, however, in 1878, by a boy, Frank Samuels, son of the owner of the land, while he was following the tracks of coon and fox, the cave being plainly a lair for such animals.

Edging his way into the crevices on the hillside, the boy found a spacious room, fifteen feet wide at its opening, sixteen feet at its greatest width, thirty feet long, and thirteen feet high, which a landslide had previously concealed.

Other caves containing rude drawings are found at Glasgow, Trempealeau county; Eagle cave, and the West Lima cave, Richland County.

"In addition to the drawings in caves there are also in the state similar carvings or paintings on rocky walls and boulders," said Mr. Brown. "One of the most noted is the so-called 'Pictograph Rock,' where Indian pictographs have been cut with rude stone implements into the south side of a sandstone bluff two miles north of the village of Friendship, Adams County."

I went to the doorway of one of the largest of the caves. Nine miles west of Highland is the pinnacle called Castle Rock which rises above a ravine in majestic sublimity. On top is a thousand-ton seat, hurled into place by some upheaval in Nature in the childhood period of the world. It must have been an altar to the sun or a settee for some Titan and his love. From this sun throne, far distant farming communities can be glimpsed, and in the ravine at its feet flows the headwaters of the Blue River, a branch of the Wisconsin, named because of the deep indigo hue of its waters.

Castle Rock is a stray little piece of mountain scenery. A nearby hillside contains a cave explored a quarter of a century ago by a man who afterwards became governor of Wisconsin.[15] He used nearly a mile of binder twine in tracing its devious passageways underground. Nothing of interest was discovered within.

Above the cave the mound scenery of southwest Wisconsin is visible. Travelers in the days when the river and the Indian trail were the only means of transportation found their directions by four mounds from ten to twenty-five miles apart but easily discernible on the sky-line except in hazy weather.

Ten miles southwest of Platteville is the little rural hamlet of Dickeyville renowned for its religious shrine and Temple of Patriotism. Returning from the World War, Father Matthias Wernerus was assigned to this inland parish. There he conceived the idea of building shrines that would teach lessons of piety and patriotism through the beautiful settings of colored glass and glistening stones. For years he labored. Appealing to friends and visitors he received gifts of rock, shells, heirlooms, and curios from all over the world which he fashioned

[15] John J. Blaine; For fuller data on Castle Rock and the lead mining counties of Iowa, Lafayette and Grant, see Schafer, Joseph, "The Wisconsin Lead Region," (Madison, Wis., 1932) pp. 19-56.

with his own hands into ropes of glass, tableaus of marble, and shrines of devotion. The conception is an out-of-door museum unlike anything elsewhere. It has no cures to offer; only lessons to teach.

Surrounded with colonnades and garlands of glass and stone, Christ, Columbus, Washington, and Lincoln are there in silent statuary in this garden of glory to inspire by the example of their noble lives. Just as the exhibition was completed, the founder died. At the entrance to the Holy Ghost Cemetery, where he lies buried, angels of Gabriel, carved in white, await with uplifted horn to blow the tidings of the resurrection morning. On holidays and Sundays during the summertime upwards of two thousand cars bearing tourists come to read the lessons of love of God and devotion to country in this priest's dreamland of precious stones.

Sinsinawa Mound, in the southwestern corner of the state, Platt Mound with its sugar loaf protruding from its side, White Oak Mound, near Darlington, and Blue Mound, twenty-five miles west of Madison, are conspicuous features in the landscape, resisting time and its elements under rock-capped crowns while the earth about erodes to the lowland.

A circular tour can be made from the capital which will pass all four. The deserted lead mine, near Wiota, worked by a son of Alexander Hamilton;[16] Wisconsin's territorial Capitol of 1836 at Belmont; the quaint stone houses of the Cornish miners

[16] See "Wau Bun," Chapter XIV, by Mrs. J. H. Kinzie, for description and the story of the early days in Wisconsin (Chicago, 1901, third edition).

who settled around Mineral Point; the first Odd Fellows Lodge erected west of the Allegheny Mountains, and the flaming lilies that bloom in the abandoned dooryard of Henry Dodge, Indian fighter and first territorial governor who lived near the city that has been named for him, are vivid history pages that unfold along the route of travel.

The trip should be planned so as to see the day close when the sun dips into the west behind the Blue Mound. As night falls the twenty-five-mile vista becomes slowly indistinct. The earth rises to meet the sky. About the old round top, which in territorial days boasted a circular race track, a shadowy veil of hazy blue descends, softening the outlines and giving them their name of Blue, or "Smoky Mounds," as the Indians used to call them.

The ascent of the west mound is gradual until within two hundred feet of the top, when it becomes very abrupt. The view is magnificent at mid-day. Away to the southward stretches a beautiful rolling prairie, dotted with farmhouses and country villages with slender church spires rising above the horizon; to the east, twenty-five miles away, the white outlines of the dome of the Capitol at Madison are plainly visible; to the west and north the eye sweeps over a strange and varied landscape, isolated mounds, high ridges, tree mantled and rock crowned, and broken into by deep, narrow valleys; away to the northward sweep the bold headlands of the Wisconsin river bluffs, an occasional gleam of silver among their dark shadows, showing where the river

WATERS OF GLACIAL LAKE, WISCONSIN, LAPPED THESE ROCKS NEAR HILLSBORO.

FARM LANDSCAPE ON KICKAPOO VALLEY UPLANDS.

THE SCENIC KICKAPOO RIVER AT VIOLA.

APPLE ORCHARDS AT GAYS MILLS.

'HREE CHIM-
NORTH OF
:ROQUA.

TOBACCO FIELD AT WESTBY, VERNON COUNTY.

MONROE, GREEN COUNTY ,"THE SWISS CHEESE CAPITAL OF THE UNITED STATES."

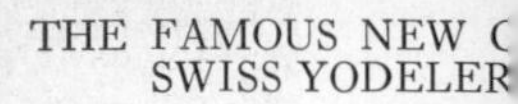
THE FAMOUS NEW G
SWISS YODELER

REPLICA IN NEW GLARUS PARK OF FIRST SWISS HOME IN GREEN COUNTY.

A SWISS FARM NEAR MONTICELLO.

THIS MONUMENT TO SWISS SETTLERS STANDS BEFORE THE SWINGLI HOUSE AT NEW GLARUS.

NEW GLARUS WOODS STATE PARK.

winds in sinuous curves. It is within the fastnesses of these wooded hills and in the deep valleys called "hollers," that a quiet people dwell.

Between Blue Mounds and Mount Horeb is a rugged farming country originally settled by people from Norway. Most of the older families still speak the Norwegian language; members of the younger group lisp their English with the soft inflexion that bespeaks their lineage.

Scenes typical of the native land abound. During fall festival time "lutfisk," "lefse" and "flat bread" are served. The bartender greets his convivial customer with the salutation, "Skoal." Norwegian fiddlers play the "halling" and "spring dance" at weddings and Christmas celebrations.

To preserve the rich life of the Norse pioneers, Isak Dahle, a neighbor's boy who made good in the city, has founded in one of the nearby secluded picturesque valleys, "Little Norway." It is a tract of hilly, ravine lands, set with a dozen sod-roofed log cabins. It is an estate common to the fjords of the old country. On the crest is the cabin of the cowgirl, who tends invisible herds; down the valley is the hunting lodge; and on the side hill is the restored Norwegian building used at the Paris Exposition and in 1893 at the World's Fair at Chicago.

Exhibits of Norwegian handicrafts, from wooden spoons to century-old Norse chests, are on display. As the pioneers reached the sundown of life, they have either sold or donated their beloved antiques to "Little Norway." It is Mr. Dahle's ambition to spend time and money to preserve Norse culture and tradition as revealed in the actual pioneer life and development of this region when it was first opened to settlement. "Little Norway" has developed into what is probably the largest outdoor Norwegian museum on this continent.

Blue Mounds Fort was an important place in the lead region during the Black Hawk war. It served as a half-way station between Fort Winnebago (Portage) and Fort Crawford (Prairie du Chien). It was a link in the topographic feature in southern Wisconsin still known as the military road, a highway built along the divide south of the Wisconsin river in 1835 to connect the military posts across the state.

As the lead industry flourished a mail route was established on the Blue Mounds road; great four-horse stage coaches lumbered by, and long ox-trains laden with ore from the mines were familiar sights on the landscape. "Pokerville," a shanty village at the foot of West mound, now a ghost town, was the Monte Carlo for the swaggering, red-shirted miners. Many men of note in the territory visited these old-time hostelries, wherein such a spirit of good fellowship reigned. That reckless, romantic, trading life has passed forever.

Still sentinels to roads eternal are the stone guide posts erected at creation's dawn and missed by the uprooting glaciers.

The southwestern part of the state is outside the glacial path. Visitors should go to Platteville, Shullsburg, Monroe. The region described in this chapter lies southwestward from Madison.

Platteville is seventy-three miles from Madison. Dickeyville (scene of the famous grotto) is eighty-five miles from Madison, on U. S. Highway 118. Mineral Point is fifty-three miles from Madison; and Monroe is forty-seven miles from Madison.

OUTSIDE MODERNISM

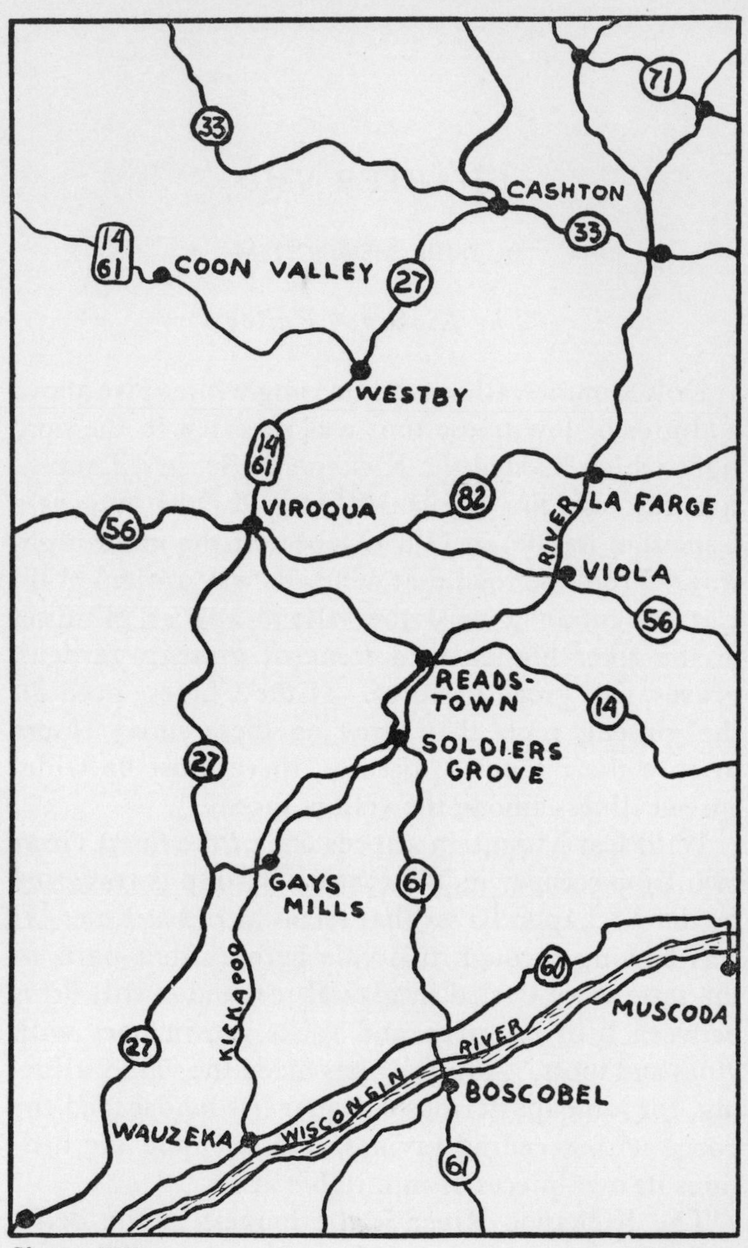

Chapter VIII

OUTSIDE MODERNISM
THE KICKAPOO VALLEY

CHAPTER VIII

OUTSIDE MODERNISM

The Kickapoo Valley

DOWN in the valley a dominating white spire above a clutter of low house tops was revealed in the opal light which flooded the Kickapoo. Set in a Laurentian fastness, the village of Ontario is as snug as a Canadian hamlet of Old Quebec off the main highway. From the road that winds its way around Wild Cat Mountain toward the village appear glimpses of the river hidden in a scene of ginseng gardens, groves, and green pastures. If the Chinese need all the ginseng roots that grow on these sunny slopes to cure their fancied diseases, there must be widespread illness among the yellow races.

Wild Cat Mountain affords one of the finest views of hilltop scenery in Wisconsin. Its lap is traversed by the Kickapoo River that seems as old as time. It was flowing through this vale before other parts of the state were buried in glacial ice, and it still flows between hills of green and rocks grown over with vines and moss. Antiquity has made the valley alluring, for some mysterious designer has landscaped the gorge with receding ravines, and set upon the hillsides its own pieces of inimitable art.

The Kickapoo River is the longest in the driftless area of Wisconsin. In its sixty-five-mile course from Wilton in Monroe County, where it rises, to Wauzeka in Crawford County where it merges with the Wisconsin river, it has a fall of three hundred and fifty feet. It moves swiftly near its source; becomes tired and sluggish in its journey before its tan-colored waters finally lose their identity forever in the silver sands and waters of the Wisconsin. The pattern of its valley looks like a tree, with spreading branches formed by the narrow ridges where it gathers its first waters from hillside springs. More railway tunnels pierce its corrugated watershed than any other river drainage in the State.

Side excursions in this country beckon at every crossroad. I took an hour's trip up the valley to Wilton, primarily to visit the sleeping ruins of ambitious hopes. At the close of the Civil War an oil craze swept western Wisconsin. Beside the road, four miles north of Ontario, a few houses, an old barn with sagging roof, the crumbling ruins of a never-painted frame hotel, and weeds growing over all, hide the scar. Locally, it still claims the ambitious name of Oil City. The site is a mournful landmark to tell of gullible investors, sunken dollars, and disappointments in Oil City on the banks of the chocolate Kickapoo. As the story is now related, an oil promoter sank a barrel of petroleum, deceiving the good people of the country and securing for himself their hoarded dollars. But, as in all oil crazes, the people of the district would not listen to the warnings of well-informed geologists.

Excitement ran high with the announcement of the discovery. News of it swept like a cyclone. Almost at once a dozen oil corporations were organized and chartered by the state legislature. Oil City became a Klondike for anticipated riches in petroleum. Would-be investors and speculators rushed to the scene. Crude buildings were erected. As soon as the stock had been sold, the bubble burst. But the deserted ghost refuses to retreat.

But the craze gave rewards to the valley people. In drilling, artesian water was struck and today along the roadside wells of clear cool water are bubbling. The wasted dollars of the oil investors of the late sixties brought health and sparkling water to the people of the upper Kickapoo.

Clouds on distant hills seemed laboring to raise a storm. The blue haze that hung in the valley softened the gorgeous scenery. Even the people who make their farms far up the retreats of numerous ravines seemed to have assimilated the somber poetry of the valley route. We decided to follow the river to its mouth.

"Here comes a team hitched to a phaeton!" cautioned my companion. "Maybe our car will frighten the horses."

The farmer and his wife had driven down from somewhere up one of the coulees and were on their way to trade at Ontario. Wooden benches have been erected in front of some of the stores.

"Those old men in front of the hardware store are called the 'Never Sweats', and congregate on those same benches every day when the weather is fine," explained a traveling man who has made the country for twenty-five years. "The lads can be found on the bench in front of the pool hall, and the belles of the town in long dresses of latest design in front of the general store."

"Country changed any since you have been making it?" I asked.

"Country hasn't changed a bit. Liked it better twenty years ago when these villages could only be reached by horse and wagon. Saw more of the scenery then. Back in those valleys are a lot of people living who used to drive oxen to town. Now they come with horses. People down in the valley are not as money-crazy as those in the highlands and plains. They like the quiet life and get a lot out of it."

It is the valley and not the towns along the river route that keep one's eyes on the horizon. Everywhere the spirit is of the past and ancient mysteries haunt the very atmosphere. The narrow road follows the river. Back and forth it shifts as the stream crowds a high perpendicular wall on one side and then turns toward the other. Thirty-four bridges must be crossed between Wilton and La Farge—nearly one every mile.

The Kickapoo valley is interesting because of its constant change in scenery. The road is always turning, always some big rock appears ahead as if to block the passage. North of La Farge I came upon a stone bluff, so stern and composed that I fancied it to be the tower of David. It was imposing enough in appearance to bear the honor gracefully. Then followed a succession of bluffs almost uniform—little brothers linked hand in hand.

Strong personal characteristics are exhibited by some. I passed one dressed all in green with oak and spotted with poplar that invited a stay for a picnic. Another sat on a squatty, solid base, sullen with dignity, its top thinned and bare with age. At times the bluffs on opposite sides of the river crowd close as pirates to exact a toll for passage, only to widen out for little farms after we have passed through the narrow gate.

At every turn was a voice of welcome. It was not the bizarre sign-posts that point the way to distant hill attractions. It was the sharp explosive call of the "Bob Whites." This is their habitat. I saw more of them on a thirty-five mile trip down the river course to Gays Mills than I had seen before in as many years of travel. The green woodlands and the brush piles on the heights make the gorge a paradise for wild life. The zigzagging road made the way interesting; openings in the trees gave views of the distant valley rim, and the sunlight which played in the foliage flecked the route we traveled.

For the first time I noticed north of Viola that a railroad traversed the valley. The tracks were so hidden with weeds and so shaded with low hanging tree branches that I might not have detected its right of way had it not been for the mouth of a little tunnel. It was like the doorway to a cool nook and I cannot bring myself to believe that it is ever dark and smelling of gas. People along the way told me interesting things. After heavy rains, when the valley becomes suddenly flooded, the tracks are inundated and days may pass without a train.

"People who travel this way are never in much of a hurry," ventured one of my informants.

By a freak of nature, residents on the Lawton farm, three miles north of Viola, are able to check the accuracy of their calendars twice each year. Due westward across the valley from the farm is a high precipice of rock, the base of which has been pierced by an opening about four feet in diameter.

"Early in December and again early in January, when the sun crosses the line and swings back, it appears at the opening, flooding our farm windows with light after it has disappeared below the horizon," explained Ray Lawton. "After a few days the sun edges its way beyond the opening and the phenomenon has then passed for another year. Annually we await it and it always comes and is always gone on the same day every year."

Under the protecting shadows of Mount Nebo, we enter Viola. The heat has increased because the valley walls check the breezes. A keen desire to find the natural Pantheon described by a geologist hastened our departure to Readstown. Fortunately, I had with me a picture of the rock temple.

Several townsmen were lounging in the shade of the little park. They shook their heads when shown the likeness,—all but one farmer.

"I saw something like that on the Lerum farm two miles out of town," he announced and gave directions.

Uncertain of the way at a crossroads a mile out of town, I stopped at a soft drink parlor for further information. The place was crowded with a hilarious local ball team and their boosters. Picture in hand, I approached the bar.

"Let me see that photograph," asked one of the ball nine, after I had made known my mission. They crowded around me. Some stood on chairs at my back and all were asking questions.

"When the game is over, let's go and see this stone," interjected one of the ball players. Of probably thirty, only one had ever seen the strange sculptured aerial throne.

The Pantheon of the Kickapoo Valley is reached by a sharp, steep climb up a long embankment. Great pillars have been sculptured by Nature to uphold its heavy roof. I crept close to the entrance way to listen for some command of the spirits. At the doorway between cone-tapered columns, I felt that I was in a palace of Nature's art. The temple is much larger than I had anticipated. Inside is a seat that may have been the throne of some woodland goddess of these beautiful surroundings. Sunlight flooding through the openings between the pillars gave a hypnotic reality to my half-haunted dreams as I lingered.

"That dark cloud is coming closer," warned my companion. At the base of the hill I turned back for a final look. Leaving, I took the wrong road and found I had mounted the valley hills and had come to the town of Sylvan.

"Luck is with us all the same," I explained. "For the state geologist of Wisconsin told me this was one of the finest picnic grounds in the state and I intend to see it before returning to the valley."

A perpendicular wall, nearly one hundred feet high, is hid in the woods. Surrounded by a gentle farming country and known in the local countryside for its caves, the place is a quiet gathering ground. It has scenery as bold as that at Camp Douglas, and its inviting surroundings are such as would make it a clandestine retreat for lovers.

Back in the valley again we learned from enthusiastic signs that Gays Mills is "the Banff of Wisconsin." The comparison is extreme, but the village and its setting are beautiful, nevertheless. Low buildings hug closely the tortuous Kickapoo.

Residents of this valley live in a bowl surrounded by orchard-dotted hills. One main highway leads to Orchard Heights where 1,800 acres of apples, cherries and grapes are under cultivation. Returning, the road winds down a long route into the village but, as one stops on the heights, he will see spread a panorama of one of the most picturesque views in all Wisconsin—the Kickapoo Valley for miles along the river. He will see the green hills in summer. If, by chance, he returns in autumn to look over the amphitheatre again he will see the leaves in a myriad of all the rainbow colors—the golds, reds, yellows, browns, vermillions and oranges, painted by the brush of Nature.

South of Gays Mills, the valley becomes narrower and the river itself more crooked. As little streams join the main channel, the bluffs recede and in the expanse fine farms have been established.

Approaching the mouth of the river we met the first spatters of rain. I looked back through the "pillared shade." I found it difficult to realize that this was the end of the journey. No familiarity with the quaint villages, the green slopes, the long sunstreaked bluffs can solve the valley's mystery. Frequent visits cannot blur the memory of its distinctive beauty.

The Kickapoo Valley runs south of Cashton to Wauzeka in the western part of the State. It is outside the glacial path. Visitors should travel Highway 27 from Cashton south through Viroqua and then take County Trunk Highway M down the Kickapoo Valley. Wauzeka is one hundred miles from Madison. Viroqua is one hundred four miles from Madison. It is eighty-three miles from Sparta to Wauzeka.

A TYPICAL CHEESE FACTORY IN WISCONSIN'S SWISS AREA.

STIRRING CURD AT A SWISS CHEESE FACTORY IN THE MONROE AREA.

CHEESE VATS IN ONE OF THE WORLD'S LARGEST SWISS CHEESE FACTORIES AT MONROE.

UGH MILK TO FLOAT
BATTLESHIP GOES
WISCONSIN'S SWISS
ESE FACTORIES
EVERY DAY.

WISCONSIN PUTS AN OFFICIAL STATE BRAND ON ALL HER CHEESE.

LIFTING A 200-POUND WHEEL OF SWISS CHEESE IN THE CURING ROOM OF A MONROE FACTORY

STAND ROCK, ONE OF MANY FANTASTIC SCENES IN THE WISCONSIN DELLS REGION.

HEADWATERS OF THE WISCONSIN RIVER AT LAKE VIEUX DESERT.

LOWER JAWS OF THE WISCONSIN DELLS.

HORNET'S NEST OF ROCK AT THE WISCONSIN DELLS.

ALLIGATOR'S HEAD NOSES ITS WAY INTO WATERS AT THE DELLS.

SWALLOWS MAKE THEIR NESTS IN THE SANDSTONE BANKS OF THE WISCONSIN DELLS.

TRANSPLANTED SWITZERLAND

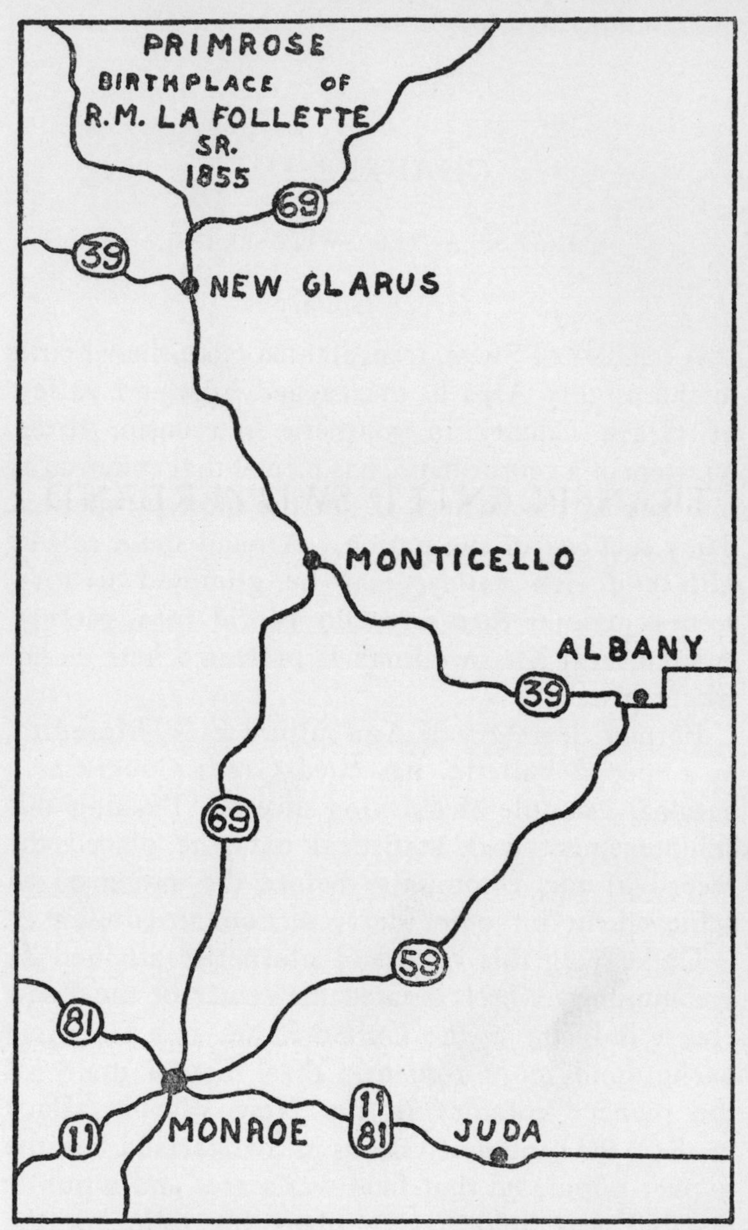

Chaper IX

TRANSPLANTED SWITZERLAND
GREEN COUNTY

CHAPTER IX

TRANSPLANTED SWITZERLAND

Green County

A COLONY of Swiss, transplanted from their homes in the mighty Alps to the rugged hills and valleys of Green County in southern Wisconsin, three-quarters of a century ago, has turned that community into one of the richest, if not the most prosperous, dairy sections in the nation. Around these rolling hills and rich valleys may be glimpsed pastoral scenes quainter than any Old World farm picture. Agricultural life in climax is presented here as no-where else.

Former Secretary of Agriculture E. T. Meredith, in a special bulletin, has cited Green County as a national example of dairying success. Backing this announcement with statistical data, he placed the record of this community before the nation as an achievement for other dairy sections to emulate.

Underlying this record of prosperity attained by a community which created the center of the Swiss cheese industry of the United States, is a historical background more romantic than that of many of the pioneer colonies in the New World. Back in 1845, the canton of Glarus in Switzerland became so over-populated that food was scarce and a public meeting was held to lay plans for relieving the economic pressure by sending some of the members to seek a new home in the United States. Two agents were dispatched to look for suitable lands, which in topography would resemble the mountainous scenery of the native land.

On a rainy day in April, 1845, the men, women, and children gathered on the banks of the Linth Canal to begin the long journey. There were nearly 200 persons, and arrangements had been made for only 140. Two leaders and two spokesmen were chosen and the colonists pledged them their implicit obedience. Hardships were experienced from the start. Packed closely in an open vessel, they were pelted by rain, and a blinding snowstorm added to their discomfort. The vessel was so small and the passengers were so many that there was scarcely room to lie down. After much distress Zurich was reached, and there the women and children were transferred to covered wagons.

"We arrived at Basle on the 18th," says the journal of Mathias Duerst. "The cold rain was falling in streams, and the utter wretchedness and discomfort were enough to chill the ardor of the strongest among the wet, shivering men. The wagons containing our wives and children arrived about the same time, and, although they had been packed in like a lot of goods, we were glad that they had not been exposed to the cold and wet as we had been."

Distress marked the remainder of the journey. Many of the colonists were compelled to sleep on bare boards on the vessel deck on the trip down the

Rhine. On the way from Rotterdam to New Dieppe they encountered a terrible storm and at each stopping place they were compelled to skirmish for provisions. While awaiting the arrival of an ocean vessel at the latter place they camped on the shore in the manner of gypsies.

Finally they embarked on the trip across the ocean. There was much suffering from hunger; and there was misery and distress among the weaker members. Two deaths occurred at sea. It required forty-six days for the sailing vessel to make the voyage which is now accomplished by a luxurious liner in one-eighth the time.

On the forty-ninth day after breaking home-ties, they were landed at Baltimore. They stopped long enough to hold an indignation meeting to condemn the crowded condition and treatment they received on the trip. Then they set out for St. Louis.

"Then we experienced the greatest pleasure of our lives," continues the diary of Mr. Duerst. "None of us had ever before ridden on a railroad. The train took us to the Susquehanna River at Columbus, where we left the cars and loaded our baggage and persons on canal boats, which were to carry us to Pittsburgh. We were packed in, like a herd of sheep. Many could not even sit, but had to stand up the whole night."

There was keen disappointment for the colonists when they arrived in St. Louis. It was here that the two messengers dispatched by the Swiss government to select the lands for the colonists were to meet them. And there were no tidings. Two members were dispatched by the colonists in search of them. These emissaries roamed over the prairies of Illinois and finally into Wisconsin. By chance the prospectors were located. Meantime, the colonists had grown weary of their life in two rented cottages at St. Louis and set out for Galena, Illinois, then the head of immigration for the mining section. On the day of their arrival in Galena, which was later to attain national fame as the home of General U. S. Grant, the leaders met them.

On the fringe of the lead mining section in southwestern Wisconsin, tracts of land had been selected as the new home. After their old canton home, it was named New Glarus. Here the colonists arrived on August 15, 1845, with the pots and kettles they had carried from their Old World home. Rude huts thatched with hay were built, but it was Christmas day before the entire colony was housed. Rules and regulations were adopted for their government, some of them being unique:

"Everyone is obliged to take the land which he draws by lot, and whether it is better or worse, to accept the same without protest.

"The main street from east to west shall be thirty feet wide, but the other streets shall be only fourteen feet wide.

"All creeks, springs and streams shall be the common property of all lot owners.

"The colonists shall be obliged to assist each other in building houses and barns.

"Should mineral be found, then the lots on which it is found shall revert to the society, and the owner shall receive therefor appropriate compensation."

The cantonal authorities in Switzerland bought the land for the colonists. Although all organic relation with the home colony long ago ceased, the colony remained for many years essentially Swiss, speaking the German-Swiss dialect, yodeling the Swiss songs and maintaining the customs of the motherland. The success of the settlers of New Glarus resulted in emigration of more of their countrymen to Wisconsin, so that the neighboring townships of Washington, York, Monroe, Mount Pleasant and Sylvester in Green County are all settled by these frugal, industrious people.

Approaching the village of New Glarus today by cement trunk line highways, one sees large signboards which briefly relate the history of the colony. The Swiss are proud of their progress.

But no one who has heard of the colony need be told when it is reached. The comparison between Swiss farming and that of ordinary Americans is as distinct as the color line in the South. Large red barns with two or three silos and modern farm homes—some brick, others stucco, but all well painted—that would do credit to any city, are the rule. The landscape is undulating, and up the hillside sleek herds of cattle are grazing. Truck-loads of milk rumble over the highways and fields and fence corners are free from weeds.

In the gloaming over the pasture lots is heard the

tinkle of cow-bells as the lowing herds wind slowly to milking barns. Now and then there is the yodel of some Swiss melody, for the young farmer lads have kept up the singing customs of their ancestors.

All of this peace, contentment and prosperity has come as the result of toil and many hardships. For more than twenty years after the coming of the colonists to New Glarus they raised wheat. Untrained in American agriculture, they soon had their lands depleted, and they had no implements for the rapid harvesting of their crops. When the crop was gathered there was no nearby market, and it had to be hauled by horses and oxen over 150 miles to the Milwaukee lake port. Prices were low, and even in the best of years the members did not realize over 35 cents a bushel for their harvest.

With the still further tumble of prices after the Civil War the colonists turned to dairying. The change was imperative. Their exhausted soil would no longer raise a full crop; the ravages of the chinch bugs swept away many of their acres and the development of new lands as wheat fields across the Mississippi river threatened the ruin of their vanishing market.

"Drovers from Ohio had brought cows to Exeter, then known as a mining town," writes Emery A. Odell, the editor of an enterprising daily paper at Monroe, in explaining the transition. "The Swiss excelled in the care of the cow, and now the Switzer turned to his benefactor in the old country. Cows were purchased in sufficient numbers to give each family one. The cost was $12 each and was paid out of an unexpended balance of $1,000 aid that had been sent to them from Switzerland. It was the inauguration of the dairy industry, which was to be the foundation of the prosperity of Green County.

"Fields were seeded to clover; cows obtained; cheese factories built, and in five or six years cheese-making became almost the sole occupation of the farming population. Farms became more productive year by year, buildings better and larger, the homes more comfortable and modern, while bank accounts grew with the natural increase in the value of the land, and made all the earlier dairymen wealthy.

"Cheese no larger than a saucer made in the homes was increased in size until the 200-pound Swiss cheese is today the standard. Cheese was first made for home consumption and later it was found it could be sold for profit in Monroe, the county seat, and in Milwaukee. Afterwards a ready market was found in the large cities of the East, and in time, the cheese moved in carload lots to every state in the Union."

Green County has played no small part in making Wisconsin the leading dairy state in the Union. Wisconsin ranks first in the total production of cheese of all kinds. Approximately two-thirds of all the cheese produced in the United States is made in Wisconsin.

In this dairy achievement record of Wisconsin, Green County stands out pre-eminent. This single county produced two-thirds of all of the Swiss cheese made in the United States. It has become the heart of the foreign cheese industry of the Nation. While two-thirds of the foreign cheese made in the county is Swiss, almost two-thirds of the remainder is Brick and the rest Limburger. A recent report showed there was but one American cheese factory in the county.

Little wonder that this pre-eminence in dairying should lead Wisconsin to establish the first dairy school in America at Madison, the seat of the state university. Nor is it strange that a course should be established to teach the art of foreign cheese-making.

Many curious stories are told about the development of this foreign cheese industry. When the Swiss farmers first began to haul their Limburger cheese to Monroe for shipment to other markets, the first "Yankee" residents of the county seat objected to the odor of the wagon loads. Once it was proposed that an ordinance be adopted that would exclude the fragrant shipments from the main public thoroughfares. But with the large financial returns, a saner judgment prevailed and today Monroe is one of the principal cheese shipping points.

Moreover, there has been a deep sense of gratitude among these Swiss farmers. Every dollar that was loaned by the cantonal government of Glarus in Switzerland for the founding and development of the colony has been repaid with interest. Sixteen years after their coming, a fire swept the city of Glarus in Switzerland, and the 425 residents of New Glarus sent $5,000 in aid. In 1880, when the Swiss town of Elm was overwhelmed by the falling of a mountain, the New Glarus farmers sent a contribution of $20,000. This is the loyalty that has prevailed; this is the spirit of gratefulness and charity that has manifested itself among these people.

With the development of the cheese industry came the improvement of the farms. Herds of high grade Holstein and Brown Swiss cattle took the place of "scrubs." With the erection of the big barns came the silos until today there are nearly 2,000 silos in the county, a larger number than can be found in any other county of the state. It also leads the other counties in the growing of alfalfa, and, on the basis of population, in the number of automobiles owned.

Nor is Green County large in area compared with some of the other counties in Wisconsin. It is only twenty-four miles square. It has a population of 21,870 according to the 1930 census. The number of cattle outnumbers the population three to one. There are approximately 40 head of cattle to every farm. All but five per cent of the farmers are actively engaged in dairying.

"Every night and morning the cattle of the county yield enough milk to float a ship," said Mr. Odell, "and each factory is the scene of great activity in the early hours of the day and following the evening milking until late at night."

Nor has the sturdy, prosperous Swiss farmer forgotten the hard trials of the first generation of immigrants nearly all of whom have passed away. In the public square, on the edge of the old churchyard in New Glarus where the early colonists were buried, a large granite monument has been erected extolling the virtues of the first pioneers.

Cities to be visited are New Glarus, Monticello, and Monroe. Monroe is forty-seven miles from Madison, and New Glarus is twenty-nine miles from Madison. Highway 69 from Verona to Monroe passes through the heart of transplanted Switzerland. New Glarus is thirty-two miles from Mineral Point and fifty-six miles from Janesville.

SCULPTURED GRANDEUR

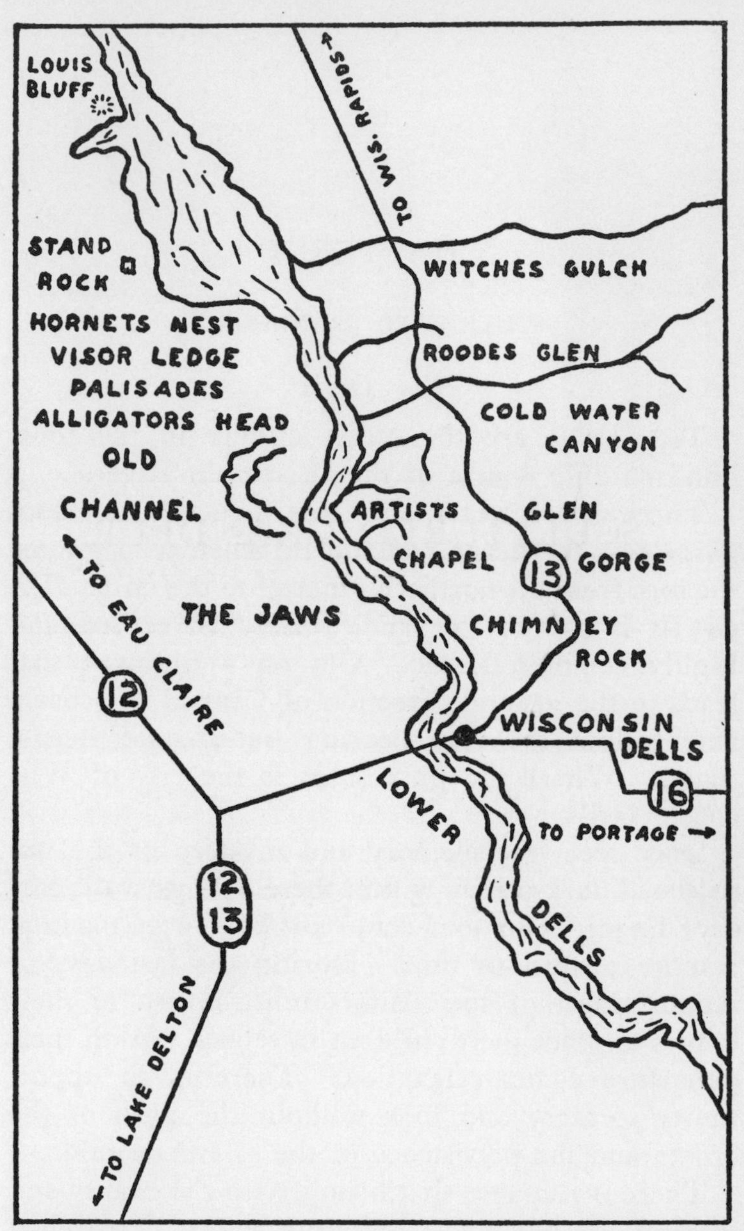

Chapter X

SCULPTURED GRANDEUR
THE DELLS

CHAPTER X

SCULPTURED GRANDEUR

The Dells

THE Dells are the scenic climax in the four-hundred-mile course of the Wisconsin River.

Three score years ago this twisting, tortuous gorge was the despair of the raftsmen who piloted the logs from the northern pineries to the mills. To-day it is a vacation land, widely advertised and highly commercialized. Get on a highway that leads in the general direction of Central Wisconsin and follow the cars bearing out-of-state license plates. Where the pilot stops is the city of Wisconsin Dells.

Once seen, the memory and mystery of the imprisoned dark waters within these narrow walls forever linger. Our tour could not have been made at a more propitious time. During the last days of August most of the visitors must return to their homes to place their children in school. With their departure comes relaxation. There is an opportunity to tarry and look without the push of the crowd and the persistence of the salesman guide.

There is romance that blends with the beauty and song of the old river. Months before, I searched out its source in Lake Vieux Desert on the state's northeast boundary line. There its waters were calm and transparent, with only the motion of soft ripples as the sun, banked behind a cloud, burnished the spangles. Again I watched it from the highway at Eagle River, but it was now a darker hue. The coloring from tamarack and pine needles and the stain of iron were on its soul. On further, as it starts a route cornerwise across the state, the scent of wet fragrance greeted us as we parted the underbrush under a cathedral of pines to reach its waters. It seemed so gentle and so courteous at times, like the spirit of Father Menard, the first white missionary within the state to lose his life on its banks.[17] The site of his martyrdom in 1661, south of Tomahawk, is commemorated. Turning a bend, the river sings a soft, reminiscent refrain to the boisterous Frenchmen and the roistering traders who once sought commerce with the Indians in the heart of this fur-bearing empire. Centuries have little changed its somber wildness.

At Merrill, the river was rejoicing. It had gathered the surplus waters from nearly 1,400 lakes and had taken on strength and volume as it glided by park spaces and between lanes of arched trees that dipped their boughs and admired their reflec-

[17] **The tablet near Bill Cross Rapids on Trunk Highway 91, North of Merrill, reads:**

"IN HONOR OF PERE RENE MENARD. BORN AT PARIS, SEPT. 7TH, 1605; ENTERED THE JESUIT ORDER NOV. 7, 1624; SAILED FOR QUEBEC IN MARCH 1640; LOST HEREABOUTS IN JULY 1661 WHILE ENROUTE TO HURON VILLAGE TO BAPTIZE INDIAN REFUGEES."

PALISADES OF THE WISCONSIN RIVER.

SUGAR BOWL AND INKSTAND ROCKS IN THE LOWER DELLS OF THE WISCONSIN RIVER.

CHIMNEY ROCK AT THE DELLS OF THE WISCONSIN RIVER.

HISTORIC INDIAN AGENCY HOUSE AT PORTAGE.

PHEASANTS GATHERED AROUND A FEEDING STATION, STATE GAME FARM, POYNETTE.

VISOR LEDGE AFFORDS A SPLENDID VIEW OF THE WISCONSIN RIVER.

GORGE AT DURWARD'S GLEN, COLUMBIA COUNTY.

SPRINGTIME AT DURWARD'S GLEN.

RURAL SCENE AT DURWARD'S GLEN.

ST. CAMILLUS NOVITIATE, DURWARD'S GLEN.

VIRGIN OF THE HILLS WATCHING OVER DURWARD'S GLEN.

THE FOUNTAIN AT DURWARD'S GLEN.

tions in the surface. Before the glaciers came to this region, the course of the river was probably nearly a direct line from Stevens Point to the Lower Narrows of the Baraboo River and through the gorge at Devils Lake.

The icy plowshare of the glaciers buried this old channel with a few hundred feet of sand, gravel, and clay, and dammed the river so that it made a great shallow lake that extended from Baraboo to Wisconsin Rapids and from Friendship to Tomah. Its outlet was through the Black River. When the great glaciers melted, the Wisconsin found a new channel at the Dells, and through the ages carved the intricate features now seen. When I saw the river at the Dells it had been turning the wheels of factories; now its spirit was brooding.

"The youngest part of the gorge is about 30,000 years old," the "skipper" told us as we prepared to make the Dells boat trip. Something was said about his having been the guide of governors and ambassadors to his fantastic world of rich scenery, but, in a scramble for a good seat, I did not hear it all.

"This seven-mile rocky gorge has come to be known as the Dells," continued the guide as the boat put off.

The designation is incorrect, however, as the name "Dalles" was applied by the first French traders to this peculiar formation, because the layers of rock resembled "flagstones." But Americans have their own way of pronouncing French names, so the place has come to be known as "The Dells."

Geology has written a history of ages with an indelible pencil along the river wall. Once this region was a sandy plain at the bottom of the sea. When lifted to the light the sand layers hardened, but before the transformation some strata were tilted endwise to fill a depression, and others were warped or twisted like the texture of molasses candy to meet some other defect in structure. Most of the main top layers remained horizontal. As soon as the liquid sand found a place to rest, Nature fastened its mould. Long ages intervened. Then the force of pent-up waters from melting glaciers came to plow a channel through the center of the plain. The incision revealed the contorted rock construction—the crudest work of Nature's masons.

Soon the artistry of wind and weather was at work. A difference in the hardening of the brown sandstone walls resulted in the softer elements yielding to the chisel of sun and frost. Weird freaks and gargoyles appeared to laugh and mock at the passing waters. And the designing never ceases.

The rivermen, with a flair for oddities, gave these strange sights unforgettable names, and the tourist trade has added to the graphic vocabulary. What visitor would not sit up to see such strange objects as:

THE DEVIL'S BATHTUB
WITCHES' GULCH
FAT MAN'S MISERY
RATTLESNAKE ROCK
THE GIANT'S SHIELD
ARTIST'S GLEN
THE NAVY YARD
STURGEON ROCK
THE ALLIGATOR

"Thirty years before Jeff Davis was president of the Southern Confederacy he rafted logs through these Dells," commented the guide as we approached the gateway to the rocky display. "He was a captain at Fort Winnebago on the river below here, and came up with a detail of soldiers to cut timber to erect fort buildings. He was one of the first visitors. That's back in 1830. But Jeff never wrote a line about the scenery."

Early Wisconsin was such a painted wonderland of rivers, trees and shades that other sight-seeing was undreamed of. Few visited the Dells until the river had been deserted by lumbermen. Annually each spring the river brought through the gorge its cargo of sawlogs, piloted by cussing, bizarre-dressed rafts-men. Some stopped for a night at a famous old Dells House, now a vanished hostelry of mirth and song. Each summer Indians in gaudy garb paraded in canoes up and down through the channel. When the trade of the pineries ended in 1890, the glory of the pioneer departed. Then a man with a camera came along to take pictures. Those who saw the views doubted that such scenery existed so near at home. They went out to see. That was the beginning of the annual trek to the Dells.

Within recent years the gorge has been bisected by a power dam which has lifted the waters of the Upper Dells twelve feet, submerging some old landmarks but creating new delights and fresh wonders. The river's width varies from fifty-two to one thousand feet; the depth at the narrowest point reaches one hundred and fifty feet. Below the dam, the rocky banks diverge two thousand feet before a level country is reached. It is at the Upper Dells that most of the grandeur in scenery is on exhibit.

"Those holes in the rock along the water's edge have been drilled in the soft sandstone by thousands of swallows who come here annually to nest," droned the guide, breaking my compilation of figures concerning the power of such a stream. Just then, in front of the boat, several birds dipped gracefully and made haste to their sandstone caverns with provisions for a hungry household. This section has been called "The Swallow's Home."

So intent were we in watching the swoopings of the swallows that the boat had already entered the jaws of the Dells—the threshold to the exhibition. Romance Cliff sits on the left, its crest in a spotlight of golden sunlight; High Rock on the right stands out stolid and stern as the parapet at Quebec. The narrow passageway elbows the river into a fifty-foot lane, and the dark waters in the shadows turn sullen and resentful. The sun-flecked walls look like pieces of tapestry of an ancient pattern. The etched designs are many and fantastic.

Then a picturesque array, imitations of things in Nature, appears. A giant alligator pokes his ugly head from one wall with mouth eager for prey; a chimney built in pioneer's design, from another; the Devil's Elbow, which has forced the river to turn in its course, and the Clam Banks, which rip-rap the shore like a succession of huge shells transformed into rock, hold the river within its course.

"The Great Stone Face on the wall at the right has been named after the Indian Chief, Black Hawk, who was captured near here," the guide explained.

When Black Hawk's invading warriors were annihilated on the banks of the Mississippi in the summer of 1832, the chief escaped and went into hiding in the recesses at the Dells. The soldier who captured him reported to the government:

"Near the Dalles of the Wisconsin I took Black Hawk."

This is probably the first mention of the place in an official document. Soon after this event, visitors at the Dells began to make comment about the weather etching of a face in a stone cliff on the river's wall. Its resemblance has become so characteristic of the chief, Black Hawk, that the promontory now bears his name. Other rocks were shaped or adorned to resemble commonly known objects.

There were so many that bore suggestive names that I did not get them all down in my notebook. There was a Frog's Head; a Giant's Shield that some Achilles must have carried; an exhibit of two rock pillars, called the Twin Sisters; a cool, sequestered cave with a pulpit, styled Chapel Gorge; Sturgeon Rock, shaped like the fish itself, where so many of its kind were speared by the early settlers; a Turtle in stone, ready to nose-dive into the river for an afternoon's swim; Sliding Rock, so designated by rivermen because of the difficulty of standing on its surface; Steamboat Rock, sitting out in mid-stream like a camouflaged boat decked with shrubs and evergreens; and Lover's Lane, an inviting passageway of quiet, shaded waters away from the main channel of the river.

Most unique of all is the Navy Yard display. Huge vessels appear to move forward in battle array, with prows and sides and ribs, so distinctively outlined as to require little imagination to fancy them plowing upstream to some widespread haven for gun practice over the dark waters.

Hidden in receding gorges along the eastern banks are wonders still more alluring. These canyons into the river-bed were cut ages ago when the waters from the melting glaciers found outlet through these walls into the main stream. Artists' Glen, Witches' Gulch, Coldwater Canyon, Glen Eyrie and Roodes Glen piercing the eastern bank of the Upper Dells, and Mirror Lake Gorge and Congress Hall of the Lower Dells are all post-glacial stream channels.[18]

There is a great similarity between Coldwater Canyon and Witches' Gulch. Both have steep sides like Watkins Glen in New York. Witches' Gulch is about one hundred feet wide at its mouth, but at places it narrows to two feet causing "misery for fat men" to pass. So deep and narrow are the gorges, so shaded in summer with trees and vine, fern-breaks and flowers, that the temperature is twenty degrees below that outside. A sickly yellow sunlight

[18] Martin, Lawrence, "Physical Geography of Wisconsin," pp. 325-333.

and a cool dampness penetrate the atmosphere even on the hottest days.

Coldwater Canyon is a never-ending wonder. The Devil's Bath Tub and other singular sights are here. With every visit I have found new charms and attractions. Hemlocks and pines cling precariously to the mossy, chasm walls, sending long roots down the rock crevices to reach nourishment and water. One large tree sits as stolidly as a nesting hen on a level rock, held in place by a maze of uncovered roots. Most of the trees in the gorge grow tall and slender, searching to reach the sunlight.

"That promontory in the distance was named for Louis Dupless, a pioneer raftsman on the river," explained the guide as our boat moved slowly out of Witches' Gulch, by the towering pinnacle rocks of Sunset Point and into the main channel. The river curves around its base making it appear like a hilltop island from the distance. The boat was headed toward the western bank.

"Now you can see the Palisades, not as extensive but as beautiful as those of the Hudson," continued the guide.

I decided to take pictures and forget about my notes. The Palisade walls are rounded and there are sculptured cornices, ornamental capitals and scrolls that rival the skill of the old Greek architects. As the boat docked, I saw in the wall above an enormous Hornet's Nest carved in the rocks. No one need explain to me what that represented. It was as realistic as some I had tried to destroy in boyhood.

The guide pointed out Visor Ledge, a protruding slab of rock extending into a valley amphitheatre; a Toadstool; and a Luncheon Hall under a natural bridge of stone.

From the rocky roof of the hall, vistas up the valley became clear. Close by is the famous rock of the Devil's Anvil, and Stand Rock, a pillar with a spindling base and broad top.

"Stand Rock is the most photographed exhibit of the Dells," remarked the guide. "Sometimes I think it has been photographed more times than Plymouth Rock."

The rude pathway from one marvel to another is deep with the silt that accumulates from the weathering rocks. The walk leads by an ancient council ground of the Indians. Now their descendants gather to amuse a season's tourists. But with them abide the spirit of the wild and treasured legend of a vanishing race. The chief told me that the guide's story of the geological transformation was untrue.

"The Great Spirit in the form of a snake came down from the forests of the North in search of the sea," I was informed. "He was so powerful that trees were brushed aside and the animals of the wilds fled in fear. So heavy was his body that, as it wriggled along, it left a valley into which the waters poured. The splash of its tail formed the thousands of lakes in Northern Wisconsin. When it reached the vicinity of the present Dells it saw an opening in the rock. The twisting of the river through the Dells was made by the struggles of the manitou to get through. The scraping of its sides caused the ridges in the rock. Once out, it sped on more rapidly and turned in the direction of the Mississippi."

"How long ago was this?" I asked.

"Perhaps as many moons as there are sands at our feet," he responded.

I looked down and saw that the beach was deep with beautiful white sand.

"That's longer ago than the geologists prophesy," I suggested, but the Indian chief only smiled and left me.

Looking up the river, I saw the approach of another steamer stirring the dark waters of the Wisconsin. The shadows of tall trees crowning the Palisades fell on the mirror before me. These are details remembered, but the general effect—the silence, the rocks crumbling to sand, the pillars, the deep coves and the innumerable forms—all blend into a beautiful canvas.

Two graves in the Wisconsin Dells cemetery are of interest. Civil War veterans have forgotten the rancor of battle and have marked with like honors the resting places of Belle Boyd, famous Confederate spy, and Salmon Brown, a nephew of John Brown, American abolitionist.

There still remained time for other wanderings. For many years I had read and admired the "Friendship Village" stories by Zona Gale. She had given such nobility to humble life that I could not return without visiting Portage. On the streets walked the people revealed in her books. She, too, loves the Wisconsin River and her beautiful home overlooks a long sweep of its waters.

Near the city outskirts is the historic "Agency House," the setting for "Wau Bun,"[19] one of the earliest stories to be published about Wisconsin. The old home of the Indian Agent's family has been reclaimed as a landmark of those days when Mrs. John H. Kinzie, the first white woman to make her home at Fort Winnebago, was the center of military activities on the border. It is a relic of Indian life that had passed in Wisconsin long before the Civil War.

One more hour before sundown!

Almost midway between Portage and Madison, the State has established, near Poynette, a state game farm of extensive acreage and equipment, where wild life is propagated and distributed just as fish is from the hatcheries. Under the supervision of trained experts, 42 varieties of upland birds are being raised; more than 20,000 pheasants of all varieties are annually distributed. The sight of 7,000 Mongolian pheasants living on the farm in their natural habitat makes a picture of brilliant colors no camera can ever record.

As a distinct adjunct and distant from the game propagation pens, the state has acquired hundreds of acres to be used for the raising of wild animals—mink, skunk, otter, fitch, and coon. An annual dis-

[19] "Wau Bun," Mrs. John H. Kinzie, (Chicago, 1856, first edition).

tribution is made to the State's wooded areas.

The heyday and romance of the fur trade have passed but Wisconsin conservationists insist that the State must remain a hunter's paradise.

The Dells of the Wisconsin are at Wisconsin Dells, which is a city of 1,500 population, fourteen miles north of Baraboo on U. S. Highway No. 12. They may also be reached on Highway 16 from Portage. The Wisconsin Dells are one hundred twenty-two miles from Milwaukee; fifty-six miles from Madison; one hundred sixteen miles from Prairie du Chien; ninety-four miles from La Crosse; one hundred thirty-one miles from Green Bay; two hundred forty miles from St. Paul; and one hundred thirty-five miles from Eau Claire.

LIVING BOTANY

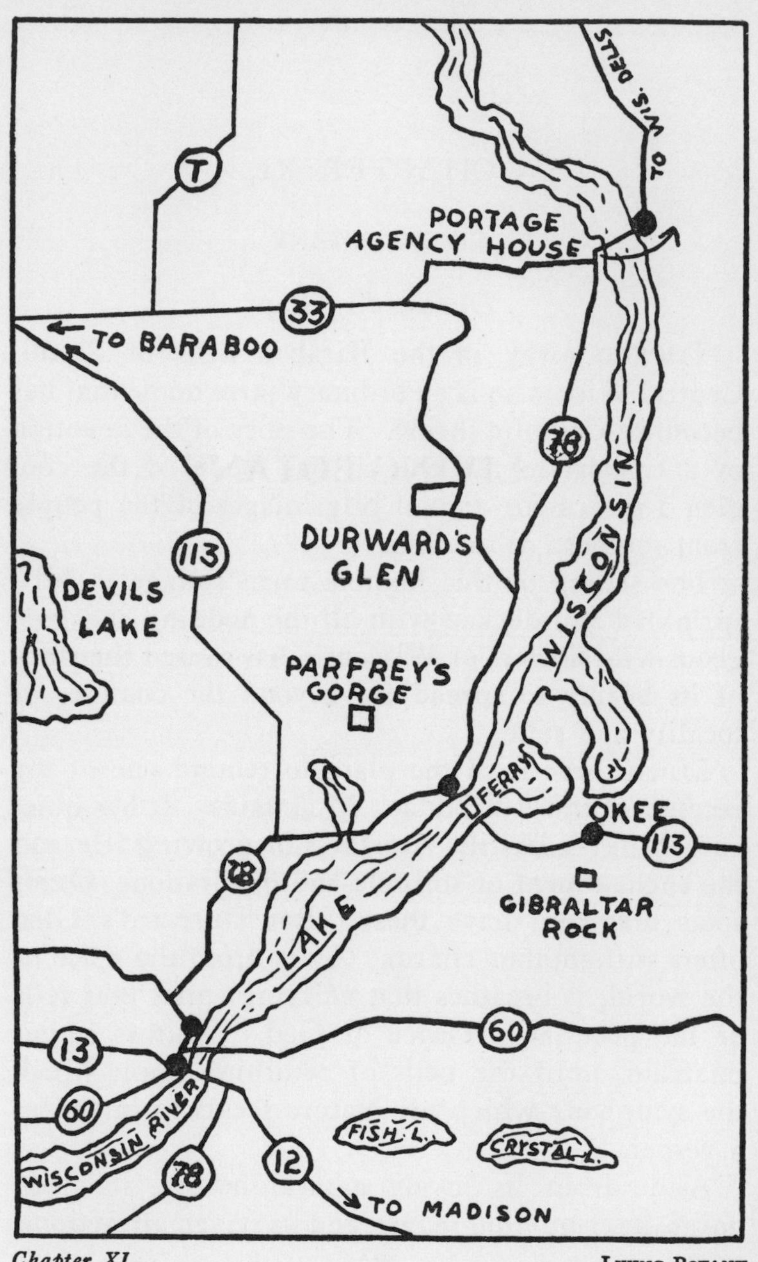

Chapter XI

LIVING BOTANY
DURWARD'S GLEN

CHAPTER XI

LIVING BOTANY

Durward's Glen

TUCKED away in the Baraboo hills of South-Central Wisconsin is an ordinary farm home that has become a Catholic shrine. The story of the devotion of a convert to the church has made of the cool glen a mecca for annual pilgrimages of the people from southern Wisconsin.

The setting of this humble farm cottage in hills sprinkled and decked with all the nodding and gorgeous wild flowers of Wisconsin has caused the story of its beauty to spread far beyond the confines of locality and state.

Much there is of the place to remind one of the recesses of the Adirondack Mountains. It has quiet and shade; it has the sweetness of growing life and the enchantment of solitude and meditation. Other spots may also have these. But Durward's Glen offers still another charm. Away from the noise of the world, it breathes that edifying spirit that tells of the peculiar presence of God. Visitors linger unafraid, until the bells of returning herds break the symphony which all Nature seems to intone as a vesper.

Aside from its lovely natural beauty, its deep gorge, its crumbling ledges, and its sylvan attractions, the Glen has innate religious associations. It was here that Bernard I. Durward—poet, painter, professor—and his wife came, following his conversion, to make the spot their home. From here two of their sons entered the Catholic priesthood. Perched precariously above the gorge on a rock altar is the hill-top church, and nearby the simple little monument to the mother, which bears the inscription, "Mother of Priests." Ancient trees shield the family graves, and through the branches the summer countryside appears incomparably emerald. When over the hilltops the ascending sun breaks into the valley, the whole scene becomes a verdant wonderland—a valley such as poets populate with the good fairies of dreams.

The little chapel, known far and wide as St. Mary's of the Pines, annually attracts many thousands. According to the caretakers of the place, more than 1,000 visit the scenes every Sunday, when the weather permits, and on one Sunday early in June there were 4,000 visitors. Most of these come from all over southern Wisconsin; some from other states.

Little wonder such a home has come to be idealized. Bernard I. Durward, the father of the family, was born in Scotland and came to America in 1845 at the request of Joshua Hathaway of Milwaukee. He was a poet and portrait artist, and some time after his arrival painted Bishop Henni. While engaged in his work he was converted to Catholicism. Life in Milwaukee, already growing into a city, did not

RUSTIC BRIDGE OVER THE STREAM, MOUTH OF DURWARD'S GORGE.

VINES COVER THE ARTISTS' BUILDING AT DURWARD'S GLEN.

ONE OF SEVERAL STATION SHRINES AT DURWARD'S GLEN WHICH WERE PLANTED IN SOIL BROUGHT FROM THE HOLY LAND.

A SHADY PATH THROUGH WILD FLOWER GARDENS AT DURWARD'S GLEN.

THE LITTLE CHAPEL ON THE HILL AT DURWARD'S GLEN.

STATE OPERATED FERRY OVER WISCONSIN RIVER AT MERRIMAC, NEAR DURWARD'S GLEN

LOCKS AT JUNCTION OF FOX RIVER WITH THE CANAL AT PORTAGE.

CANAL LOCKS BETWEEN THE WISCONSIN AND FOX RIVERS AT PORTAGE.

VIEW OF GREEN LAKE FROM THE LAWSONIA ESTATE.

LARGEST IRRIGATION FARM IN WISCONSIN, NEAR MONTELLO.

AN EXCLUSIVE HOTEL ON GREEN LAKE.

WHERE THE FOX RIVER JOINS THE WISCONSIN AT PORTAGE.

appeal to the father, and in 1862 the family started for Central Wisconsin in a one-horse wagon, crossing the Wisconsin River at Portage. The Glen was reached on November 1—All Saints Day. Near the spot where they stopped at the mouth of the famous gorge, on a high rocky ledge, a full-sized statue of the Virgin Mary has been erected. Around its base the pathway leads to the hill-crest, where the family cemetery is located, and on the topmost knoll stands the church.

At the mouth of the gorge, there is a little wooden bridge spanning the cold, fountain-fed stream which comes singing along, flecked by a soft, mysterious light which filters through the towering tree canopy over the high embankments.

The pathway across the stream leads to the fountain, which has been encased in a stone structure, every surface being lettered for some friend of the family. When the father took visitors to this spot he would facetiously remark, if there were young ladies along, "Bathe your brow at the ledge and you will be beautiful." Seldom was the opportunity neglected.

Mary's well at Nazareth could not be more inviting to the tired and thirsty throngs. Four large streams of water rush from the spring's encasement. Above the receiving basin, a part of the stone work covering the gushing waters has been worked into a large white cross on which is inscribed: "Christ said, 'I Thirst.' Brother or Sister, Think of Him and Drink." The Christian and Jewish years are cut in the stones at the base.

At such a refreshing fountain it requires little imagination to transport one to the scenes of the Bible and vision the mothers of Nazareth with their earthen vessels poised on shapely heads, coming to draw water, just as the mother of Jesus must have come many a time with her Divine Boy running beside her.

Further along the pathway, around a clump of trees, is the old family home that is fast becoming a shrine, exemplifying the simplicity and devotion of ideal family life. The cottage is a frame structure of attractive design, with a flower garden in the front yard.

Close to the residence and the apiary is a large stone structure in which are kept the paintings and drawings made by the father and his son, Charles. This was the artist's gallery.

"It is a matter for congratulation," according to the booklet on the Annals of the Glen, "that almost all Charles' creative work has been kept in the family, and with a tendency to be still further treasured in one unique collection on the very soil that knew the artist and his labors. This is what he himself would have desired, and will be appreciated by all his admirers, much as they would have wished during his lifetime to see his productions hung on the line in the metropolitan galleries. But now—now it is different; let the appreciative and the merely curious make the pilgrimage here and see these pictures in their most fitting setting."

Across the stream again and up the hill stands the stone church. The chapel was erected by the family, neighbors and friends in 1866. Two of the sons, James and John, said their first Mass there.

Father John Durward was born in Milwaukee in 1847 and for many years was pastor of St. Joseph's Church at Baraboo. He was the author of a book, "Holy Land and Holy Writ," which had a wide distribution. He died in 1918 and is buried in the family lot at the Glen. His brother, the Rev. James Durward, died in 1933.

"The station shrines were erected in 1889 when Father John returned from Palestine," explained a woman who had come with a bouquet of wild flowers for the graves.

"Are you a member of the family," she was asked. The question was possibly unheard. Anyway, it was not answered. But—

"That year Father John, returning from the Holy Land, brought a little soil from the site of the original stations in the Via Dolorosa at Jerusalem, and this was incorporated with these, making the hilltop a veritable Holy Land."

The deep gorge, with its precipitous out-croppings of rock over seventy feet in height, has its attractions, but the lover of Nature will find much of interest in the birds and the riot of wild flowers, ferns and mosses. Cardinal lobelia, wild rose, and honeysuckle perfume the morning air in June and early summer.

"Our feathered choristers are of rural extraction and abode also," declared one of the Durward brothers in a description of the glen, "but though they often sing together their various songs, there is no discord. I am somewhat puzzled over this, and the only theory or reason I can think of lies in the great altitude of bird tones, and the consequent rapid vibrations, which do not jar on each other so much as slower and lower tones would. A tireless band of songsters, full of quaint humor and musical enthusiasm, these shy sylvan friends are very near to my heart. Some of them make melody through the hours of darkness, an ecstatic, full-voiced chorus greets the dawn, and even the dread heat of the August mid-day is braved by at least one hardy and good humored little musician."

It must have been in the dreams of the discoverer of this idyllic spot that it should ever be devoted to the nobler aspirations of men. Instinctively, the thoughts of the visitor to these picturesque hills and valleys, mantled in spring with flowers, or brown with the parti-colored splendors of early fall, turn to the heavenly home. It was in the autumn of 1934 that the owners decided to turn Durward's Glen over to the Camillian Fathers[20] for a monastery.

It is the only novitiate of that Order in this country and is the only building known to be of its type of construction of any religious order in the United

[20] See article, Capital Times, Madison, Wis., June 9, 1935.

States. The exterior construction is of solid oak logs; the roofing, hand-split shingles; and the porch, fireplace and tower, stone of that locality.

The novitiate provides cloistered seclusion for candidates for brothers of this Order who remain here for one year before going to Milwaukee to complete their training. Formerly, candidates went to Europe for their education as they prepared to carry on the Order's purpose, the care of sick and infirm men of any race and creed.

Reminiscent of the catacombs in old Grecian days when followers of Christ were forbidden to use His name, is the insignia on the tower. It resembles the initials "P-X" as though they were interlapping and forms the Christian sign used in the olden days.

Durward's Glen is in Sauk County off Trunk Highway 78 from Merrimac to Portage. It is twelve miles from Portage; twenty miles from Baraboo; thirty miles from Wisconsin Dells; and forty-three miles from Madison.

WHERE JOHN MUIR LOAFED

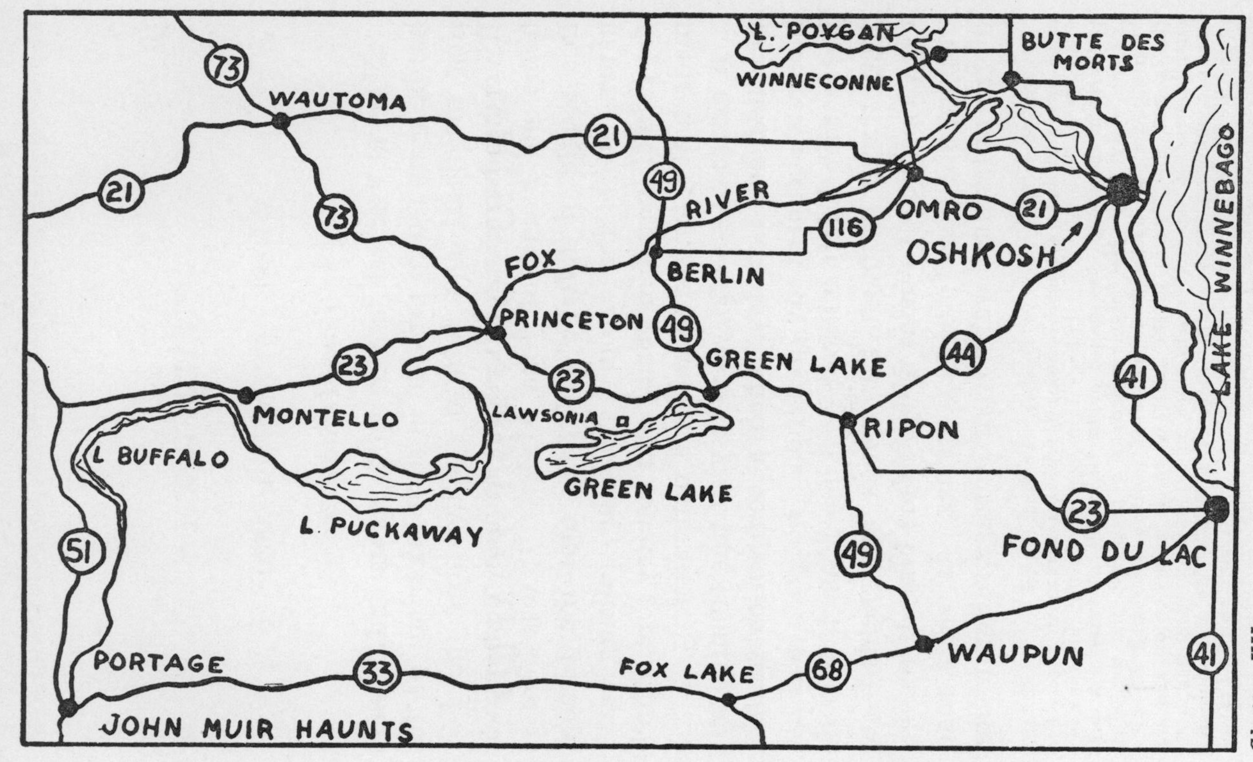

Chapter XII

WHERE JOHN MUIR LOAFED
THE FOX HEADWATERS

CHAPTER XII

WHERE JOHN MUIR LOAFED

The Fox Headwaters

NATURE'S storehouse of wild plants and flowers has been raided to provide in such luxuriant profusion the floral and foliage display near the Fox River headwaters in Wisconsin, around the boyhood home and haunts of John Muir.[21] It was here in this tangle of foliage and trees that the famous naturalist obtained from a budding, pulsing earth the primal lessons in botany and country lore, which made him later renowned as a naturalist.

A desire of several years to visit this country was gratified one hot day, when a companion of like interests accepted my invitation. So great was my hurry that I left without packing a lunch for the long tramp through the woods and fields,—not even a packet of raisins which Muir himself recommended for out-of-door excursions. It was a road of ten miles northward from Portage, close to the

[21] John Muir was born in Dunbar, Scotland, April 21, 1838, and came to Green Lake County, Wisconsin, with his parents in 1849. For a decade he labored on his father's farm, getting during this time but one term of schooling. He studied at the University of Wisconsin during the early 60's. He became noted as a naturalist and geologist. Muir Glacier of Alaska, first discovered in 1879, is named for him. He labored many years in the cause of forest preservation and the establishment of national reservations and parks. Among his best-known books are: "Stickeen, the Story of a Dog," "My First Summer in the Sierras," "The Story of my Boyhood and Youth," and "Travels in Alaska." He died at Los Angeles, December 24, 1914.

twisting Fox River bed, but the country highway was resplendent with the liveries of the season. This was no tourists' route of travel. Conversation was on one subject. Along these paths Muir had trudged many times on his way to town on a mission for supplies. Over this sinuous, sandy trail he had often driven a yoke of oxen, "wise and tame with no other harness than a chain and a crooked piece of wood on their necks."

When Daniel Muir came with his two sons from Scotland to make a home in this wilderness in 1849, before the other family members came, the land was homesteaded by him from the government. Selection of the spot was determined because of a gushing spring from the hillside above which the rude pioneer home was erected. And then began the task of clearing the land, a toil so irksome and grilling under the stern commands of an exacting father that in all the years to follow these labors remained both fresh in John Muir's mind and depressing to his spirit.

"We were all made slaves through the vice of over-industry," he later wrote in his memoirs. "It often seemed to me that our fierce, over-industrious way of getting grain from the ground was too closely connected with grave-digging."

These tiresome, long days of labor to the boy in his teens gave later compensations. During his work in the fields he became familiar with the habits of birds and animals, the characteristics of flowers and trees. The hawk circled overhead to prey on rabbits and gophers. From the withering dry stalks at the grassy edge of the lake which now bears his name the red-winged blackbird pitched his rich, simple strain of "Baumpalee, Baumpalee;" the prairie chickens strolled in family flocks over the freshly plowed ground; the robin in spring sang his "Fear not! Fear not! Cheer Up! Cheer Up!" and when autumn came with its cold, frosty nights the Canadian gray geese, in long trains, flew honking over the little eyelet of water on their journey southward. These were the scenes which lightened the hours of his monotonous days.

As we neared the scenes so vividly described by him in his Nature books and memoirs, there was no need for inquiries. The landmarks were still about us as commanding as a guidepost directing traffic. From the narrow grounds about the little white country schoolhouse, there was a glimpse of a lake. Aside from the meager schooling Muir had obtained in Scotland, he had gone here one winter. The building had since been remodeled but the surroundings were untouched. The door stood ajar. The one room was less than twenty feet long and fifteen feet wide; a steel engraving of Washington hung on one wall and a picture of Longfellow on the other. Later we learned, from an aged resident of the neighborhood who knew Muir, and who looked enough like him in physical appearance to be taken as his brother, that the Washington portrait had been in the school "ever since John attended."

The schoolhouse is set in a hillside clearing; outside there is an ugly brick chimney between the two entrance ways and a huge amber bell hangs in the cupola. Great bunches of painted warrior grow wildly in brilliant exuberance about the yard. When I visited it, there were no beds of domesticated flowers, no out-of-doors apparatus for athletic enjoyments. The building looked worn and tired of educational work. Across the highway was a tangle of trees and shrubs. There had been heavy rainfalls during the spring months and the growth was so abundant as to retard progress through the thicket.

Down the roadway a few rods, we came upon an old, unpainted, weather-beaten, deserted farm house that was fast falling into ruin. Behind it was the glistening lake.

Over sandy, weedy hummocks we rushed to get a full view of the basin of water. This was the Eureka for our trampings. Fountain Lake, as it was called when Muir fished, bathed and paddled its surface, now known as either Ennis or Muir Lake, is about a mile long and half as wide. Its crystal spring waters spangle and shimmer in the sun as of old. The hills about it and the sloping meadows tell the age-long story of its glacial origin. There are neither ridges nor rocks to encumber its shores which are low and boggy from the decaying marsh grasses and which shake like jelly under foot. A few rods out, where the lake deepens, the circumference is rimmed with pads of green, supporting white and yellow water lilies—a scene which the nature vandals have not yet laid to waste.

Pushing through a lush, tangled grass, I came

upon the nest of a red-winged blackbird—and then another. Around about were scores of these songsters deftly balancing themselves on tall, swaying, last year's cat-tails, singing the same notes that were sung when John Muir paused in his labor of clearing the land three-quarters of a century ago to find inspiration in their gleeful music. A thirsty swarm of singing, stinging mosquitoes began to interrupt our musings. While we hesitated I visioned Muir's story when, as a youthful, sinewy lad, he saved himself from drowning in the center of this cool pond; how he, through the ice in winter, skated on clumsy, home-made runners over its smooth surface.

From its still shores came a swishing of waters through the weeds. The muskrat was still busy. What a paradise this must be for his multiplying progeny!

A journey around the end of the lake added to the wonders. The flaming, spotted Turk's cap was in riotous bloom. In the shade of the trees grew sarsaparilla and ginseng; there were unevenly arranged clumps of yellow snapdragon and scores of other blossoming wild plants, which Muir must have communed with intimately—but were strangers to me. But even to the uninitiated, however, there were thrills at this sight of Nature's gay plumage.

A lane bordered on each side by fields of waving, rustling corn led from the lake. In the dooryard of the large farm home at its far end sat an old man, with long, grey beard. Had I now known that John

Muir was dead I would have mistaken the identity. It was Samuel Ennis, 76, his old Scotch-Irish friend.

"My farm of 160 acres was all grubbed out of the wilderness by John Muir," he related. "John was older than I, but I remember him. As a lad, he was always working from early morning until late at night. His father was a hard taskmaster. After John had left the community and lived in the west, he returned two or three times and always came to visit with me."

Together we returned to the lake.

"Here are the foundation stones of the house which Daniel Muir built, when he came in 1849," he said, pushing back the matted grass at the top of a little knoll which overlooked the glacial meadows and the lake. "The house was located on this spot so as to be close to a spring which was a few rods below in the ravine. The fountain is dry now. There are the lilac bushes which John's sister Sarah planted; and here's an oak which John's axe spared."

"Have the lake and its immediate surroundings changed much since John Muir lived here?" I questioned.

"Not much," and the face of the old man brightened. "The gophers still plunder the fresh fields of planted corn; the blackbirds steal the ends of the ears when in the milk; the frogs still hold their evening song festival, and the partridge drums 'boomp! boomp!' from the fence corner. It is as John told the story in his book. Wild life interested him. He was always making some new discoveries in Nature. Once, when he was in California, he wrote to me for a plant that grew in the marsh land by the lake and said he had never found it elsewhere on his travels."

"Were all these farm lands about cleared by the Muirs?"

"Mostly by John and David. John was the older and did much of the work. After eight years of labor, when these fields had been improved, John's father sold the land to David M. Galloway, who had married Sarah Muir. A few years afterwards the property came into our family and we have lived here since. The old buildings burned many years ago and we rebuilt closer to the roadway."

Returning to the highway, my companion and I started in search of the second home of John Muir. It was four miles away and is still known as the "Hickory Hill Farm," a name given by the Muirs because of the groves of hickory trees growing on the long, serpentine hill, where the farm house was located.

Nowhere outside of the unsettled lands of northern Wisconsin will be found such a profusion of trees and flowers as in the vicinity of Muir's boyhood haunts. The meadows and hillsides are gorgeous with colors. Much of the low foliage of the woods has not been trampled under the hoofs of cattle nor suffered the constant snipping by the sheep. The woods remain as gardens of wild nature.

The Hickory Hill 320-acre farm was brought to a high state of cultivation when owned by the Muirs.

Orchards were planted by them, grape vines were started, and some member of the family, with a love for tall, spindling willows, placed them conveniently about the dooryard and near the well.

"I never take a drink of water but I think of John Muir and what an industrious, ingenious young man he must have been," said Thomas Kearns, the present Hickory Hill farm owner. "The well is over ninety feet deep, and all but ten feet of loose earth on the surface was chiseled by John Muir through solid rock before water was reached. It was a task of months. He told us on his last visit many years ago how he would be let down every morning, to chip away at the hard rocks until noon and then return to the same hole for several more hours before he was hoisted up by his father or brother in the evening. John said that he nearly lost his life in digging the well. One day he was overcome with choke-damp, but tumbled unconsciously into the bucket and was brought to the surface."

Many improvements were made after the Muirs sold the farm. A part of the old barn is still standing; a section of the house, now veneered with brick, is there;[22] the basement corner, where John crept every morning at ten o'clock to invent thermometers, early rising machines, clocks and locking devices, is pointed out.[23] From this home, with his bundle of

[22] "The Story of My Boyhood and Youth," John Muir (Houghton-Mifflin Co., 1913), pp. 274-287.

[23] Muir's Clock, which was attached to his mechanical bed to throw him out of bed early, is on display in State Historical Society Museum, Madison, Wis. For story of clock and bed, see The Daily Cardinal, Madison, Wis., Sept. 23, 1932.

FLOCK OF SHEEP GRAZING BESIDE A STREAM IN COLUMBIA COUNTY.

BIRTHPLACE OF THE REPUBLICAN PARTY AT RIPON (1854).

LAKE WINNEBAGO, LARGEST INLAND BODY OF WATER IN WISCONSIN.

BEACH AT LAKE GENEVA.

A SUMMER MOON OVER LAKE GENEVA.

YERKES OBSERVATORY AT LAKE GENEVA

THE SWIRLING WOLF RIVER BREAKS FREE FROM A GORGE ON THE MENOMINEE INDIAN RESERVATION.

HERE THE RACING WOLF RIVER LEAPS THE ROCKS AT BIG EDDY FALLS.

RAINBOW FALLS OF THE WOLF IS AS BEAUTIFUL AS ITS NAME IMPLIES.

HIGHWAY SHADOWED BY DENSE VIRGIN TIMBER ON THE MENOMINEE INDIAN RESERVATION.

KESHENA FALLS IS THE BEST KNOWN WATERFALL ON THE MENOMINEE INDIAN RESERVATION.

THE WOLF RIVER AT "GILMORE'S MISTAKE."

home-whittled inventions, he went to Madison in the early sixties to attend the state fair and exhibit his collection. It was this visit to the outside world that thrilled him and sent him in pursuit of education at the University of Wisconsin—a pursuit which resulted in his matriculation as a life-long scholar in "the University of the Wilderness."

There is inspiration in a tramping trip to the haunts of John Muir. With all the hard work which he had to do in his youth, he found in Nature a love which kindled his heart as his own thrilling words of enthusiasm have rekindled the aspirations of millions who have since read the stories of his strange wanderings. Away from the streets of the world he brooded over Nature in boyhood, and, when a man, became a relentless fighter for national parks and wildlife preservation.

The Fox at its headwaters, around which John Muir learned his nature lessons, is a sluggish stream. Marshes impede the flow. In a course of fifty miles it has a gentle grade until it mingles with the Wolf in historic Lake Butte des Morts and, later, joins the waters of Lake Winnebago—the largest inland lake in Wisconsin. There is less than a six-inch slope to the mile as it widens into two lakes—Buffalo and Puckaway—both meccas for hunters.

Following closely the winding river is a cement highway which passes through Montello, scene of the largest irrigation farm in the state, Princeton, Berlin, Eureka, Omro, and on to Oshkosh. Along the quiet route the scene is one of changing pageantry. Close to the city of Berlin, near the cemetery, is a ridge, the crown of which dominates the valley for miles. To the west spreads verdant Sacramento Valley; to the far south "Democrat Prairie" of boundless rural beauty, rolling on to the heights of Ripon, where on the college grounds still stands the little white school house, birthplace of the Republican party, March 20, 1854. Nestling closer to Berlin on a hillside to the south is the recently discovered long-lost village site of the Mascoutin Indians, visited by all the early explorers from Nicolet to Marquette.[24] From this craggy crest, where so often flashed Indian signal fires, is a panorama of sun-bathed green groves, interspersed with white farm homes, and in the blue rimmed distance twinkles like an eyelet of God, Green Lake, to which Grover Cleveland, while president, came to fish.

> "Beneath the open sky she spreads the feast;
> 'Tis free to all—'tis every day renewed;
> Who scorns it, starves deservedly at home."
>
> (Cowper).

The Fox headwaters are westward from the city of Portage. The old home of John Muir is ten miles east of Portage and seven miles from the old camp site of Fort Winnebago, just on the outskirts of the eastern city limits of Portage.

[24] Wisconsin Historical Proceedings, 1906; Wood, John J., "The Mascoutin Village," p. 167; Jones, Rev. Arthur Edward, S. J., "The Site of the Mascoutin," p. 175. Also article on Copper Crucifix found on site, Milwaukee Journal, Feb. 19, 1934. Also Martin, Lawrence, "Physical Geography of Wisconsin," p. 269.

WELLS OF THE MASTODONS

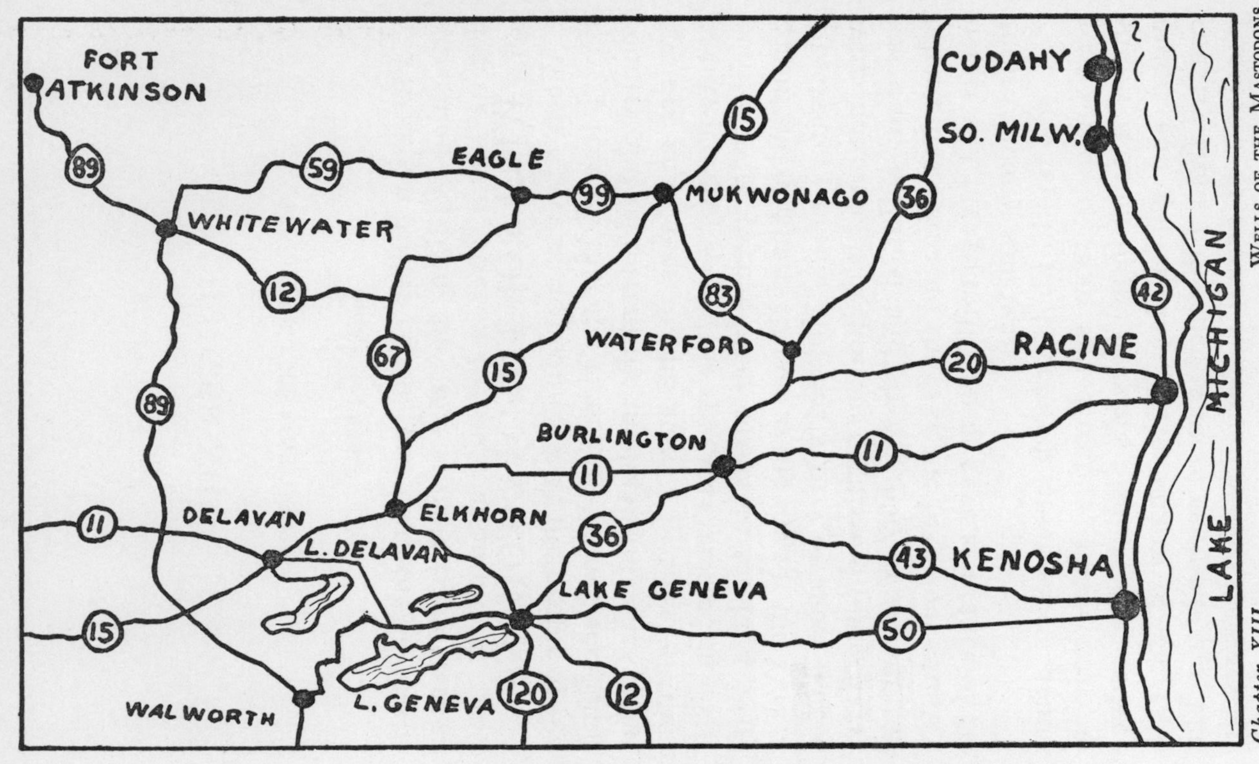

Chapter XIII WELLS OF THE MASTODONS
LAKE GENEVA

CHAPTER XIII

WELLS OF THE MASTODONS

Lake Geneva

THERE is a hilltop on the road from the north approaching Williams Bay that reveals Lake Geneva shining like a jewel in the pure atmosphere. And what a crystalline jewel it is!

When I became acquainted with the people at the Bay, I learned that the clear air distinguishes both country and lake from the thousands of other countrysides and lakes in the state. Because of this, twenty-five years ago, the spot was selected in competition with twenty other places in southern Wisconsin and northern Illinois as the site for the Yerkes Observatory of the University of Chicago. There were inducements of glorious nights and sunny days; less dust, pollution and smoke than in any of the other cities. Around the lake the luxurious country homes of Chicago millionaires gave assurance of no future factory smudge.

A mammoth khaki-colored observatory dome, seen for miles from any direction, stands near its shores to drink in the heaven's display on the silver nights and golden days. The charm of the lake country from a distance is more compelling. The panorama of homes in the valley, the shadowy visions moving from place to place—woods, meadows, gardens, all in vari-colored green—detail a picture of beauty.

Before approaching the lake, we drove around for a view of its well kept shores, its artificial trails, its trimmed trees, its well groomed lawns. In spite of all the civilizing influences, Nature refuses to yield the wild spirit of the lake. So the little city that bears its name has hung out this sign as a lantern over the roadway, welcoming visitors:

LAKE GENEVA

THE WORLD'S WONDER

SPOT

A lake set in such a surrounding of verdure-clad hills leaves an impression upon the mind that the Creator desired in designing this country. Geneva Lake came to its present loveliness only after ages of invasions by two ice sheets. Once it was part of a long channel connecting in one watershed Lakes Delavan, Como, and Geneva. That was after the first aggression. So discernible are its traces that the first settlers called the region "Troy Valley."

There is no exact record of the time when the valley was rearranged a second time. Some think it was 20,000 years ago. Another ice plow moved over the land. It turned a neat furrow that shaped the hillsides that surround Lake Geneva. It nosed before it a pile of gravel and dirt that dammed up the channel and made a hilltop at the lake end from which the astronomers have trained their long-range telescopes on the universe. Another furrow made a pocket for Lake Como. Glaciers do things in a big way.

"About this time the wind or something shifted, for the temperature changed," explained a resident who has spent years gathering every fragment of evidence about the country. "Soon the ice started to melt. It receded first on the hillsides, and the escaping waters that before had fled westward to the Mississippi were now turned by the dam of earth to flow in the opposite direction. All of this resulted in keeping the lake at the depth at which it had been plowed."

"That doesn't seem possible," I interposed. "Wouldn't the waters from the hills carry earth deposits that would fill in the lake and make it shallower than when scooped out by the ice plow?"

"That's just how most people reason," he continued. "The only explanation for the present depth is that the ice in the lake was the last to melt and the hillsides were held in place by the ice block until the land was dry. The dirt washed down, settled on the lake edge, and made the fertile shore lands."

"And, when the land dried, vegetation started?"

"Exactly! Nature shaped the lakes and the hills, and then left the lands to grow trees and raise animals until the country was needed by man."

It must have been a magnificent kingdom for animals. On one of my visits to the Williams Bay country I learned that a dweller digging in his garden had upturned the teeth of a mastodon, a mammoth, elephant-like animal, long extinct.[25] Its discovery led to much speculation. The mastodon roamed exclusively in timbered regions, where it sought shelter, and near valleys for water. No less than a dozen evidences of the presence of the mammoth have been found in southern Wisconsin in recent years. One can not but admire the instinct of a beast that, seeing the Lake Geneva country, should make it a home and use the lake as its watering pool.

Where the mastodons went and why they left Wisconsin I have been unable to learn. Some zoölogists believe that for centuries they tenanted the lush wilds of the Mississippi Valley, finally crossing the isthmus into South America.[26] It is rather disconcerting to confess that they left the Lake Geneva country voluntarily. I would rather believe a sudden change of climate drove them out temporarily, and that, when the warm season returned, they were unable to find their way back to the paradise of the "Troy Valley" and died searching for it.

Even for centuries after Wisconsin had been discovered by white men, Lake Geneva basked in its virgin obscurity known only to the Indians. Around its shores three of their villages were built; on its banks their dead were buried. On one of the spacious lawns in the village of Williams Bay stands a much visited boulder which bears this message:

[25] Jenkins, Paul B., "The Book of Lake Geneva," p. 4.
[26] Chamberlin and Salisbury, Geology III, pp. 496-97.

IN 1836 ON THE CREST OF THIS GROUND WAS BURIED ON A PLATFORM AND DRESSED IN INDIAN FINERY, A WIFE OF BIG FOOT, CHIEF OF THE LAKE GENEVA POTAWATOMI. LATER EARTH BURIAL WAS MADE, PROBABLY BY CAPTAIN ISRAEL WILLIAMS, THE FIRST WHITE SETTLER OF WILLIAMS BAY.

Traders learned of the lake but never came. It was not on the main water routes. But that inconvenience did not keep the Indians at home. Long before the white visitors arrived, Indians were trading their furs at Milwaukee and going to council gatherings at Fort Dearborn.

One day in the summer of 1831 the first white visitors came over the Indian trail from Chicago. They were following a deep rutted route[27]—deep rutted in places even today—which was part of a primitive system of communication from Lake Michigan to the "Four Lake Country" at Madison, and on westward. The family and friends of John H. Kinzie were returning from Fort Dearborn to Fort Winnebago, a military outpost on the outskirts of the present city of Portage. The men traveled on horseback, the women in a "Dearborn wagon," the first luxury of the kind ever seen on the prairie. Two decades later Mrs. Kinzie published a book, "Wau Bun," giving her experiences in Wisconsin, which

[27] Tablet South of lake reads:

"THE OLD INDIAN TRAIL FROM THE FOOT OF LAKE MICHIGAN TO LAKE GENEVA AND ON TO 'THE FOUR LAKES,' AT MADISON, PASSED HERE,—PART OF A PRIMITIVE SYSTEM WHICH PRACTICALLY CROSSED THE CONTINENT. THE FIRST WHITE VISITORS, THE KINZIE FAMILY OF CHICAGO, CAME THIS WAY, MAY, 1831."

has become a valuable historical contribution. So indelible on her mind was the impression of Geneva Lake after a lapse of twenty years that she wrote:

"Soon after mid-day, we descended a long, sloping knoll, and by a sudden turn came in full view of the beautiful sheet of water denominated 'Gros-pied' by the French, 'Maunk-suck' by the natives, and by ourselves, 'Big-Foot,' from the chief, whose village overlooked its waters. Bold, swelling hills jutted forward into the clear blue expanse, or retreated slightly to afford a green, level nook, as a resting-place for the foot of man. On the nearer shore stretched a bright, gravelly beach, through which coursed here and there a pure, sparkling rivulet to join the larger sheet of water.

"On the rising ground, at the foot of one of the bold bluffs in the middle distance, a collection of neat wigwams formed, with their surrounding gardens, no unpleasant feature in the picture.

"A shout of delight thrust involuntarily from the whole party, as this charming landscape met our view. It was like the Hudson, only less bold,—no, it was like the lake of the Forest Cantons, in the picture of the Chapel of William Tell! What could be imagined more enchanting! Oh, if our friends in the East could but enjoy it with us!

"We paused long to admire, then spurred on, skirting the head of the lake, and were soon ascending the broad platform, on which stood the village of Maunk-suck, or Big Foot."

While the first visitor to see Geneva Lake admired its beauty, the second visitor gave it a name. Because the scenery reminded him of his boyhood home in Geneva, New York, John Brink, the government surveyor, gave the waters the name of Lake Geneva on early maps. Little could he have realized that the title should in time have profound significance among the summer resorts of the Nation, and that the beauty of the lake itself would sorely tempt President Coolidge, when serving as Chief Executive, to make it, for a season, the scene of his summer White House.

A century later, on the occasion of a centennial celebration [28] of the first visit, I stood at Glenwood Springs on the spot where the first glimpse of the lake was obtained. The same view was there. The dark blue lake waters sparkled in a basin rimmed by a shoreline of trees in heavy foliage. Across the lake an embankment of green rolls up the hillside and along the valley. As the same feelings which stirred the first visitor surged upon me, I turned to be greeted by a tablet which read:

> "THE OLD INDIAN TRAIL FROM THE FOOT OF LAKE MICHIGAN PASSED A SHORT DISTANCE SOUTH OF THIS POINT. FROM IT THE FIRST WHITE VISITORS, THE KINZIE PARTY FROM CHICAGO, SAW THE LAKE, MAY, 1831."

Within five years of this visit the Indians of the vicinity had ceded their lands and were being removed to a reservation. Big Foot, whose name has come to be associated with the lake, was a Potawa-

[28] June 27-28, 1931.

tomi chieftain, with two villages at the end of the lake, one at Williams Bay, the other at Fontana. Unfriendly to the United States, he and his warriors refused, however, in the summer of 1832 to join Black Hawk in a proposed raid against the white settlements, but in 1833 he joined in a cession to the United States of all Potawatomi lands in Michigan and Wisconsin.[29]

Three years later, following a tragic farewell, he departed for a reservation. After a visit to the old camp site at Williams Bay, he returned to his Fontana lodge. With an arm around the cedar "council pole," he stood a long time drinking in the afternoon rays as they stirred the shifting scenery of the lake. At last his eyes fell to the ground. Slowly he turned away and the next morning he led his dejected followers on their long journey to a western reservation, from which no message from him ever returned.

Almost a century later, Simon Kahquados, the last hereditary chief of the Potawatomi, came from the reservation at Blackwell, in Forest County, Wisconsin, where descendants of Big Foot still live, on a farewell mission to the land where once the authority of his tribe was supreme. After visiting the old Fontana camp and village sites, he went to the "Seven Sacred Springs" on the grounds of the Big Foot Country Club at the west end of the lake. Something in his action warned his hosts not to follow too closely. Beside the overflowing basin on one of

[29] Lake Geneva and Lake Como, the Wisconsin Archeologist, Vol. VII, No. 3, p. 139.

the seven he stood a few moments, talking in an Indian monotone. Out of his pocket he drew a pouch. Scattering tobacco on the waters he returned to his companions, his face in brightness, and informed them he was ready to return to his Northern Wisconsin home. The Indian gods had been appeased.

So impressed were the awed onlookers with the solemnity of the occasion and the sacredness in which the Indians held the springs that on the occasion of the centennial the springs were rededicated. Some touch of their sanctity is suggested in this tablet erected near the fountain head:

THE POTAWATOMI INDIANS
DEEMED THESE SEVEN POOLS THE ABODE OF
SPIRITUAL BEINGS WITH POWER FOR GOOD OR EVIL IN
HUMAN AFFAIRS. NO EXPEDITION OF HUNTING OR WAR
WAS BEGUN WITHOUT HERE ASKING THEIR FAVOR.
SIMON KAHQUADOS, LAST HEREDITARY CHIEF OF
THE WISCONSIN POTAWATOMI, PERFORMED HERE THEIR
TRADITIONAL RITES OF WORSHIP MAY 31, 1929.
JUNE 27, 1931, POTAWATOMI ATTENDING THE
CENTENNIAL DISCOVERY OF THE LAKE BY THE
HEIGHTS, HERE REPEATED THE ANCESTRAL RITES.

The Indians saw beauty in Nature. Where stood their villages are to be found the settlements today of Fontana, Williams Bay and Lake Geneva. Probably, because of the springs at the western end of the lake, the more important Indian councils were there held. Vision Hill, now used as a natural amphitheatre in summer for open air services by religious organizations on the grounds of the Y. M. C. A. property, was an Indian gathering place of scenic beauty. It is still considered an idyllic spot, the exact likeness of which it would be difficult to find, according to Friends of Our Natural Landscape, whose pageants of Nature have been held there.

Geneva Lake owes the crystalline purity of its waters to the many springs that feed it. Fontana had gushing natural wells so ebullient and powerful as to turn the wheels of an early day grist mill. Undiminished in vigor, those same springs are bubbling today. Scores of other fountains feed little streams that lead to the lake.

Geneva Lake is one of the three largest bodies of water in Southern Wisconsin. It is seven miles long and two miles wide at Williams Bay, with a circumference of eighteen miles. Green Lake exceeds it in depth, and both Green Lake and Lake Mendota exceed it in area. Along its banks grow forests of trees—elm, maple, oak, and hickory.

There has been preserved on the north shore an acreage that recalls the life of the country—of wild flowers and trees and scampering little squirrels—as it was before the settlers came. "Wychwood," owned by Charles L. Hutchinson, is a garden, the like of which has never before been maintained outside of a wilderness. There are no artificial beds, no trees foreign to the community. Probably more wild flowers, trees and shrubs of different native varieties flourish here than elsewhere in the State. It is a perennial flower guide, and those who love flowers travel long distances to see it. Sitting beside the water, one finds its attractiveness enhanced.

Neither the size nor the depth of the lake has

brought it popularity. It is the setting and the beauty of its waters—a wilderness untamed. In a storm it tosses in anger; under the morning sun it smiles from its blue depth, charming with each wave ripple. In the light of a new moon its shadows turn the waters into pictures of dreamland and the shoreline buildings are transformed into fairy castles. It has character and individuality.

Down at the end of the lake, when the clouds of evening disperse and the moon and stars appear to bathe in the reflection, a renowned savant formerly took his seat at the lens of one of the world's most powerful telescopes. For more than twenty-five years he explored the heavens so intently that the light of his eyes failed. On one of my visits, he paused to tell what he had learned from long observation. It was a message to soothe those broodings which the hidden mysteries of the lake have stirred.

It was the venerable Edward B. Frost,[30] then director of Yerkes Observatory.

"I have learned much in my lifetime," said Dr. Frost, "and everything has confirmed my belief in a spirit behind the universe. The universe is perpetual—it has no beginning and it will have no end."

Lake Geneva is in southeastern Wisconsin on U. S. Highway 12. It is seventy-five miles from Chicago; thirty-eight miles from Racine; forty-seven miles from Milwaukee; seventy-three miles from Madison; and two hundred sixty-two miles from Eau Claire.

[30] Dr. Frost died May 14, 1935.

THE MENOMINEE INDIANS COPY THE WHITE MAN'S WAYS FOR COLLECTING TOLL.

IN THIS MANNER, TOO, THE INDIANS CAPITALIZE ON THE BEAUTY OF THEIR RESERVATION.

AT ONE TIME THE MENOMINEE INDIANS BELIEVED THAT WHEN THE ROCK CRUMBLED THEIR RACE WOULD BECOME EXTINCT; HENCE THE NAME, SPIRIT ROCK.

PAGAN INDIAN GRAVES ON THE MENOMINEE INDIAN RESERVATION.

INDIAN CABIN BESIDE THE MENOMINEE RESERVATION HIGHWAY.

THE WOLF RIVER OFFERS SOME OF THE MOST THRILLING FISHING IN WISCONSIN.

POETS CAN DREAM OF NO MORE BEAUTIFUL SPOT THAN BEASLEY CREEK, CHAIN O' LAKES, WAUPACA.

INDIAN CROSSING, WHERE THE BEAUTY OF THE WAUPACA CHAIN O' LAKES SEEMS TO CONVERGE.

CANOEING UP EMMONS CREEK, CHAIN O' LAKES, WAUPACA.

SHADOW LAKE AT WAUPACA

CHINESE WATERWHEEL USED TO BACK WATER INTO BASS REARING POND NEAR WAUPACA.

HERE IS THE POND MADE BY THE CHINESE WATERWHEEL.

SHOTGUN EDDY

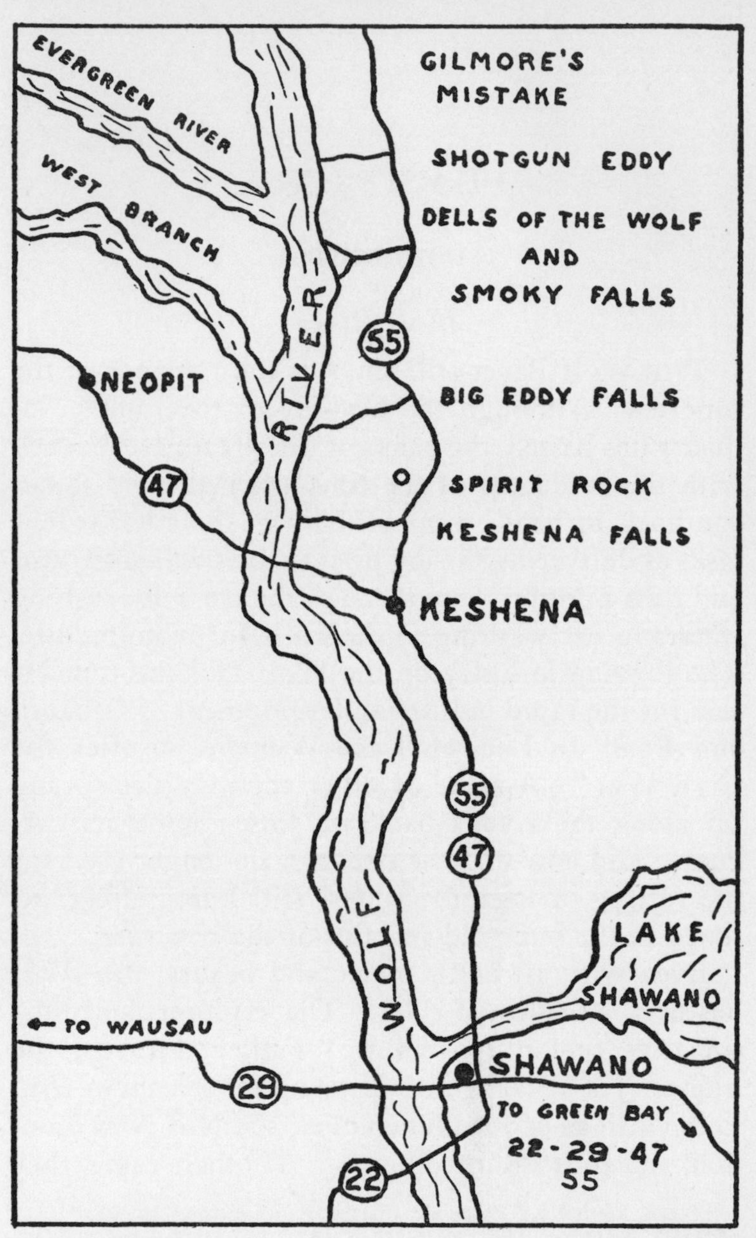

Chapter XIV

SHOTGUN EDDY
WOLF RIVER

CHAPTER XIV

SHOTGUN EDDY

Wolf River

THE Wolf River still sings of the romance of the pineries. Although the hey-day of the lumber industry has passed, the banks of the stream are marked with the evidences of the time when the red-shirts, canthook in hand, went blithely to their hazardous tasks of delivering the log piles to the swollen streams and then piloting them through the ice-cold, rushing waters in early spring to the mills for manufacture. The logging industry on the Wolf laid the foundation for the rapid industrial development of Oshkosh and Fond du Lac, on Lake Winnebago, after the Civil War.[31] A score of other communities sprang up along the river's banks to fatten upon its cargoes. And now that the stream is no longer used for the rafting of logs, the waters still hurry along, attuned to the same old refrains of the rivermen.

Even with all of its music and beauty, the Wolf has been a neglected river. The explorers and missionaries seldom visited it. Father Allouez, the pioneer Jesuit evangelist, came up the stream in 1670 to the village of the Outagamies, south of New London, and then returned home.[32] If others came, they

[31] Merk, Frederick, "Economic History of Wisconsin," p. 127.
[32] Gary, George, "The Fox River Valley," pp. 33-45.

have left no record. Because of its 150-mile length and the volume of water furnished, it should be known as the Upper Fox, but a sluggish stream, 110 miles long, making a connecting route by a portage with the Wisconsin River, gained that title. When the white settlers crowded into Eastern Wisconsin, three successive treaties were made with the Menominee Indians who claimed the lands. This tribe, generally at peace with the whites, derived from "meno" good, "min," a grain, the Chippewa name for wild rice. They were first found at the mouth of the Menominee River, about 1634, their settlements then or afterward extending south along the west shore of Green Bay as far as the Fox River. By the agreement at Lake Poygan in October, 1848, the year Wisconsin became a State, they consented to retire to a reservation.[33]

The old chiefs knew well their geography, for the lands selected by them along the Wolf River in Shawano County have become one of the beauty spots in the State. The most seductive scenery of the entire watercourse is there on display. Within the reservation's borders is enough undeveloped water-power to light half of northern Wisconsin. It is a hunting ground dotted with a hundred lakes. The Indian removal occurred in 1852. The new reservation, now populated by 1,600 Indians who own the lands in tribal ownership, consists of ten townships containing 360 square miles or about 230,400 acres.

[33] Wisconsin Historical Collections, Vol. VIII, pp. 227, 407; Wisconsin Blue Book, 1923, p. 68.

It is located about thirty-five miles northwest of Green Bay and five miles north of Shawano.

Nowhere in the State is there such a combination of lakes and streams in untamed wildness; so much virgin timber remaining uncut upon the lands occupied by an Indian tribe not far removed in civilization from that of their ancestors of three centuries ago. And no beauty spot in Wisconsin is so completely marked as are the scenic wonders of the Wolf from Shotgun Eddy thirty miles down. The Indians have done just enough work on roads and trails to put Nature on dress parade.

Three times I had promised a lumberjack friend that I would follow the Wolf with him. His suggestions of places to be seen and tales of woodman events of long ago made the invitations alluring. Still stirred with the spirit of the forests, he wanted me to go as a companion on a revisit to the old haunts. Three times I was forced to decline. The fourth request I accepted. I saw so much in a single day that I became bewildered. Within a month I had to go back to review the woodsman's lesson. Far into northern Wisconsin we drove, along the banks of the stream. Returning, every opportunity to approach the waters was taken. My companion had cruised timber, chopped trees, and scaled logs along the Wolf. So as we retreated downstream and the cool scent of the hardwoods and pines stirred his blood, the old days returned for him, and again he spoke the language of the pineries.

"This highway was authorized as a military road

when Abraham Lincoln was President of the United States," he announced as we approached the reservation from the North. Later we came upon a marker which recorded that the road from Shawano through the Indian reservation was approved by act of Congress, March 3, 1863.

"The lumber industry north of the reservation used this road to haul logs and to bring supplies," he continued. "Up to about 1924 all improvements and repairs were made by the companies using it. Now that it has been taken over and improved by the State as a part of State Highway 55, it would be difficult anywhere to find a more pleasant route to travel."

Along the highway which threads its way close to the tree-shaded river, various stations and taverns were erected in the early seventies for the accommodation of the workers in the woods. Many of these are still standing. Gauthier's and Otter Slide were noted stopping places on the Wolf at the north end of the reservation; Beauprie's and Mag Lawe's were a day's team drive nearer to Shawano.

At one spot on the road the teamsters, going and coming, always planned to meet. Among the drivers a glacier-polished boulder beside the road was known as "Communion Rock." The spirit of the former occasions has been preserved by a tablet erected beside the stone:

DEMOCRAT PLATFORM
HERE ON THIS ROCK THE EARLY
TOTE TEAMSTERS PLEDGED ANEW
THEIR FAITH AND DRANK TO THE
SUCCESS OF THE PARTY.

About a mile from the north reservation line, the road and the Wolf River approach, at Log Cabin, built by Crist Hill in 1874. The waters flowing in a fever of white foam waves over a flooring of solid rocks are dashed through crashing rapids. Huge boulders stand beside the stream determined that neither ice nor water shall budge them. There is rhythm in the restless stream.

For a long time we watched the turbulent waters without a word. The opposite shore-line was dark with forest and underbrush.

"They call this 'Gilmore's Mistake,' " he finally said, turning his face upstream.

"Why Gilmore's Mistake?" I asked, looking about to see what disaster might have occurred.

"A man named Gilmore came up this way a long time ago," he responded. "The country was a mass of trees and brush. No white man has ventured this far before. It was all such an overgrown tangle at this point that he thought the waters came out of the ground. So he reported this place as the source of the Wolf River. It was his mistake. The beginning of the Wolf was afterwards located in a series of small lakes about forty miles north of here, near Hiles Junction."

Upon entering the reservation we enjoyed hours of delightful scenery. Descriptive names used by lumbermen still identify many of the places. Burnt Shanty Rips is a slide in the river course that sends the waters dashing, and Shotgun Eddy cannons them onward with tremendous velocity.

Not only is the road winding through the reservation but at places the tall pines have been preserved by boulevarding in the center. "The Three Pines," "Pine Row," and similar signs have been posted to call attention to the approaching spectacles. After a few miles of slow driving the scenery and shaded way so captivate the visitor that all hurry is forgotten.

Kamawon Way, a delightful section of the main highway, recalls the name of an old Indian doctor who had a wide reputation for cures with herbs and roots. So many came to see him that the name of the river landing place near his vanished tepee is still retained in memory of him.

Smoky Falls and the Dells are reached by a little roadway maintained by the Indians. Smoky Falls is a little Niagara—a lovely place to stop for an hour or more. The green waters are tossed into a mist which the sun changes into rainbows. Leading the way to the Falls is a narrow boardwalk suspended upon logs, some marked WXI and others marked .˙. W .˙.. Only after inquiry did I learn the meaning of the hieroglyphics.

"Several lumbermen would be using the river at one time to float their logs," my companion explained, "so each individual owner had a brand which was stamped on his own logs. This made it possible to segregate the property of each with the same certainty that branded horses are separated in the West. WXI, called the W Cross Notch, was the brand used by the Morgan Lumber Company, and

.˙. W .˙., meaning Rabbit Track W Rabbit Track, was the log insignia of Hollister's. Both were Oshkosh concerns. These logs were undoubtedly lost in rafting downstream."

Over the passageway to the Falls was a sign, unique in Indian spelling and printing, reading:

We Made the Road from 55.
We Worke Hard for you White
Peobles So Please Pay Toll
10¢ Each.

BIG SMOKY FALLS OF THE WOLF RIVER.

MANY YEARS AGO BEFORE 1925 THERE WAS NO ROAD WITH WHICH PEOPLE COULD GET INTO THIS PLACE AND IN ORDER THAT TOURISTS COULD SEE THESE WONDERFUL WATERFALLS WE WORKED HARD TO BUILD THIS ROAD SO THAT YOU CAN COME HERE AND VIEW THE FALLS AND ALSO THE BEAUTIFUL SCENERY THAT SURROUNDS IT. THIS IS WHY I CHARGE TEN CENT ADMISSION FEE. WE THANK YOU. CALL AGAIN.

JOS. F. CORN. A MENOMINEE TRIBESMAN.

Two milcs up stream are the Dells of the Wolf. They are shorter in length and with passage much more restricted than the famous Dells of the Wisconsin. The sixty-foot walls are dark and covered with moss and lichens. The waters roar through the narrow rock chasm, which at one place cannot be more than thirty feet across. A pine tree clinging to a ledge of rock close to the water's edge has sustained itself there for a century.

"We used to think that some raft of logs caught in the Dells would sweep this tree away," my fellow traveler remarked. "One of the reasons I wanted to come back was to see if this old tree still survived."

There is enough bewitching scenery at the Dells

to satisfy the appetite of the most fastidious. Pathways lead to the waters. There are no hidden recesses. But I would as soon run a canoe through these headlong waters as down the La Chine Rapids of the St. Lawrence. Below the high rock walls the river widens and the waters go their way in peace.

Back again on the main highway and a few miles South stands the old log house of John Corn, a Menominee tribesman who operated a logging house for lumbermen from 1870 to 1900. Relatives of the same John Corn still live there. Soon the river spreads itself over a wide stretch of land, passing "Five Islands in Mid-Stream."

Turning off the main highway one mile, the traveler comes to Big Eddy Falls. Back of the falls is an expanding bay, where in the spring season the log rafts accumulated during the day. Into it the waters rush, sending the stream into an eddying swirl.

"At sundown every night the bay would be so full of logs that it would automatically empty its accumulations within an hour," my raftsman companion went on. "I cannot explain why it should wait until sundown. All I know is what happened many times."

My interest reached its high pitch at Spirit Rock. Learning that Keshena Falls was but a mile further on, I was hastening along the densely shaded way when I noticed several persons gathered around a spot with a protection of white posts. Fancying it might be the grave of a noted Indian chief, I stopped the car. I was in a mood to pay proper respect to one who had preserved a spot in my state as it was about the time Charles de Langlade in 1764, near Green Bay, laid out the first farm in Wisconsin. Imagine my surprise to find a brown crumbling rock of large proportions sprinkled with tobacco. Below the picture of an Indian head was this legend:

PRESERVE
OUR
TRADITIONS

SPIRIT ROCK

TO THIS ROCK THE MENOMINEE TRIBE BROUGHT THEIR GIFTS TO THE GREAT SPIRIT. THE INDIANS BELIEVED THAT THE CRUMBLING OF THE ROCK FORETELLS THE PASSING OF THE RACE AND THAT UPON COMPLETE DISINTEGRATION THE RACE WILL BE EXTINCT.

At Keshena Falls State Trunk Highway 47 leads northwards to Antigo by way of Neopit, the metropolis of the Indian reservation. There the Indians under Agency supervision operate a tribally-owned saw-mill. The Agency maintained at Keshena consists of Government offices, large Government and parochial schools, attended by about 250 Indian children, stores, hotels, and dwellings. Seventy per cent of the Indians on the reservation are Christians; the others still cling to their original religion and ceremonies, and on the reservation are known as "pagans."

The so-called "pagan" Indians are an interesting

people. They are known as strictly honest. They maintain all their old religious customs, hold their dances at various seasons of the year, and live as did their ancestors. They still cling to their burial customs. After the dead are interred, a small hut is usually built over the grave. In it are placed food and tobacco for the use of the dead. The Indian burying grounds are among the show places where all tourists are taken. But the time of the "pagan" is probably short.

There is compulsory school attendance on the reservation and the younger generation is growing up with different ideals than those of the older folk. Most of the young men and women turn Christian. But, Christian or "pagan," there is one common characteristic of the Menominee Indians: They love the waters of the Wolf.

It was springtime when I made my first visit. The woods were flushed with green; the young oaks by the roadside were unfolding buds of velvety pink; under the trees there were acres of nodding white trilliums—the lily of the forests. The Wolf was running at full stream.

The paradise which the fleeting riverman saw in rafting the logs was there for a few days. When I came back in summer, the river sang softer, but the gorgeous picture was smothered in a raiment of dark green.

The Menominee Indian Reservation is in Shawano County, five miles north of the city of Shawano. State Trunk Highways 55 and 47 pass through the Reservation. The Reservation is fifteen miles from Antigo; forty-five miles from Green Bay; one hundred fifty miles from Milwaukee; one hundred forty-eight miles from Madison; and one hundred seventy-six miles from Eau Claire.

CHAIN O' LAKES

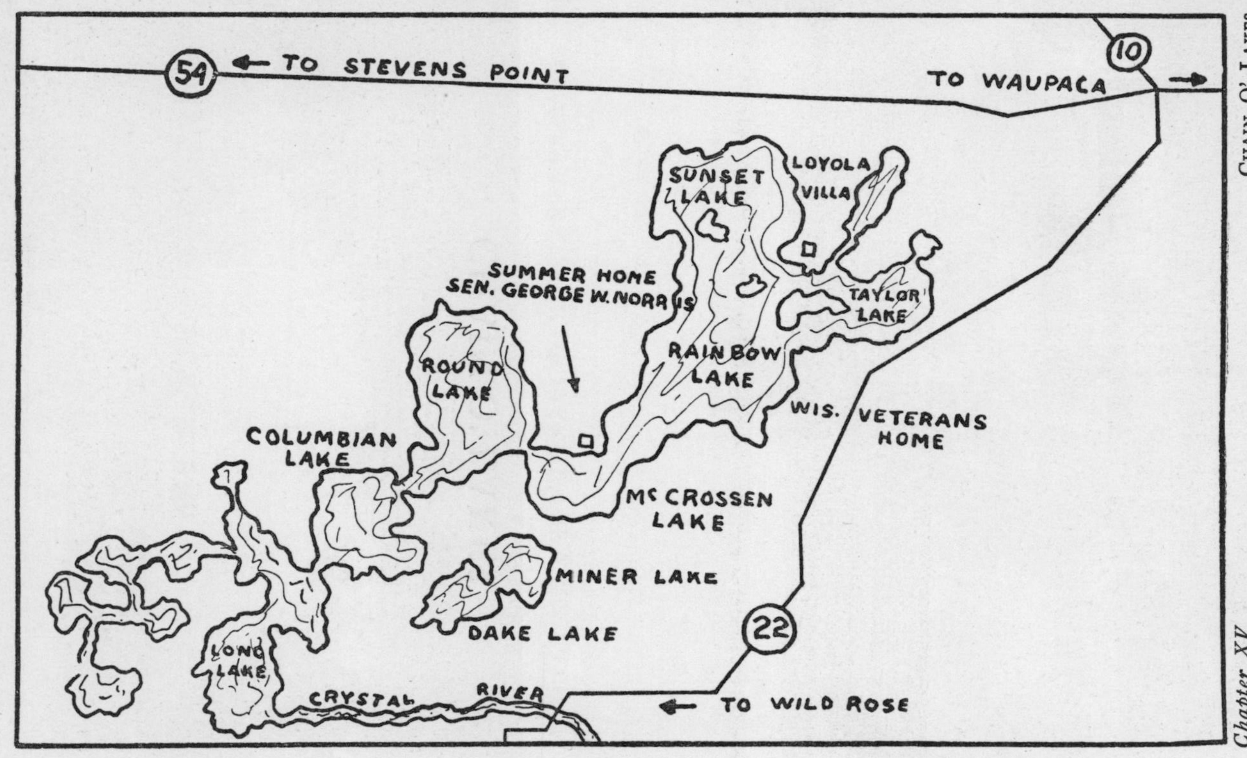

CHAIN O' LAKES
WAUPACA

Chapter XV

BEASLEY AND COLUMBIAN LAKES OF THE WAUPACA CHAIN.

BRYANT HALL, VETERANS' HOME ON RAINBOW LAKE.

ENTRANCE TO THE CHAIN AT TAYLOR LAKE, WAUPACA COUNTY.

LAKES LIKE THIS BODY OF WATER, NEAR WAUPACA, ARE SOMETIMES REFERRED TO AS THE KILLARNEYS OF AMERICA.

IN THE SUN, SILVER LAKE AT WAUTOMA RESEMBLES A SHEET OF SILVER.

RUSTIC BRIDGE OF CRYSTAL RIVER, OUTLET OF WAUPACA CHAIN.

—*Milwaukee Journal Photo*

JACKSON HARBOR AT THE NORTHERN END OF WASHINGTON ISLAND.

ELEMENTARY SCHOOL AND MONUMENT TO WORLD WAR VETERANS ON WASHINGTON ISLAND.

STONE FENCE AND BIRCHES ENCIRCLING A CORN FIELD ON WASHINGTON ISLAND.

SAILING ALONG THE SHORES OF TERRY ANDRAE STATE PARK, SHEBOYGAN COUNTY.

CEDAR LAKE, WASHINGTON COUNTY, IN THE HEART OF THE KETTLE MORAINE DISTRICT.

GRAVEL HILLS DEVELOPED BY GLACIERS IN THE KETTLE MORAINE COUNTRY.

CHAPTER XV

CHAIN O' LAKES

Waupaca

THE Chain o' Lakes lies waiting and watching the coming of the sun, whose radiance transforms the clear waters into a spiritual green, as beautiful in its hues as the Canadian Lake Louise. Like two strings of pearls—thirteen in the larger chain and eight in the smaller—these lakes in Southern Waupaca County so stirred the admiration of early pioneers that they called them the "Killarneys of America."

It was only when I went to look at their animated waters that I realized my neglect in passing them unnoticed for ten years. At a distance they appear like other lakes. Close by they are emeralds of captivating beauty. Their bottoms of marl reflect every prism of light, changing the blue waters into green mirrors that record every evanescent mood of wind and sun.

A visit to the Veterans' Home, a state institution on the banks of Rainbow Lake, gave me my first introduction to the chain. Afterwards I went back again and again, until I came to know the crooked little roadways and deserted Indian trails along their banks, and finally I came to understand parts of the story which these proud lakes repeated to me each day, when I would sit down and listen to their murmurs. They have a confiding way of talking about their affairs. The two chains are less than four miles long and one mile wide, their arrangement suggesting "so many flags or garments on a line, all fluttering and flapping in the summer breezes."

The glaciers made these lakes—some shallow and others one hundred feet deep—some so small as to be called lakelets. Great ice blocks melted after the ground about had become firm and left these pools for water. A whitish substance, known as marl, was deposited for bottoms. This fertilizer, now much sought for depleted farm lands, stimulates in the waters the plant life which feeds the many varieties of fish. If the basins of these lakes were to be robbed of their wealth, the lands of the whole county could be enriched. But such vandalism would displease the sun. These lakes are among its delightful hand-mirrors. By sending its rays into the deeps, the sun enables the waters to take on a variety of pleasing colors, similar to the action of the sunshine on the volcanic ash basin of Lake Louise.

At the head of the "Big Chain" is Taylor Lake, so closely joined with Sunset, George, and Rainbow that on a map they look like one. Around the high banks and wooded slopes the Menominee Indians made their home for centuries.[34] The lake region was a trail crossing from the wild rice fields of Lake Poygan to the Wisconsin River and from Portage

[34] Brown, Charles E., "Indian History Survey, Chain o' Lakes, Waupaca," p. 14.

to Lake Shawano. Investigations in the region show that no less than three principal trails meet at the shallow ford between Round and Columbian Lakes, which to this day is known as "Indian Crossing."

Recently, residents about the lakes induced Charles E. Brown, a noted archaeologist, to make a survey of the region. He told me that he found numerous Indian campsites and hearthstones and scores of mounds.

"The Chain o' Lakes country was an attractive place for the Indians because of the good fishing and plentiful game," said Mr. Brown. "The existence of seventy-two mound sites has been established. Of this number all but three were on or near the shores of the lakes of the 'Big Chain.' The greatest concentration of these mortuary monuments was on and near the shores of Taylor Lake, where there was a total of fifty-two. Of the rest, four were once located on the shore of Rainbow Lake, and indications of three remain on the shores of Sunset Lake. There was one mound on the shore of McCrossen Lake, and one on the shore of Columbian Lake. Three formerly existed at Ottman Lake and six in the vicinity of Emmons Lake.

"The only mounds known to have existed on the shores of the lakes of the 'Little Chain' were a single mound near Bass Lake and two near Knight Lake. Of the total number of 72 mounds, 52 were round or oval, 12 were linear, and 8 were effigy mounds. A few others were on the shores of the small lakes east and north of the Chain. Of the mounds formerly located on the shores of the Chain o' Lakes, 15 remain, the remainder having been destroyed in the cultivation of farm fields, in gravel pit excavations, and in highway improvement.

"Other records of the Indian history survey show the location of 6 village sites, 43 camp sites, 11 groups of pits, several burials in ordinary graves, 2 corn planting grounds, 3 plots of garden beds, one sugar camp, 2 caches or hoards of flint implements, 10 refuse heaps and pits, a possible pottery kiln, and numbers of former flint workshop sites. Of the village sites some were occupied both in prehistoric and in recent times."

The Indians and the fur traders knew the lakes long before the lakes found their location on state maps in 1852. Rummaging through the records of Waupaca County in the State Historical Library at Madison, after one of my visits to the lakes, I came upon a letter of Dorchester Jones. He claimed that his father, Granville Jones, coming there in the fall of 1849, was the first to lay out a homestead on the lakes, and that he, himself, was "the first white boy to set foot on its frozen surface." When he wrote his letter from his home in Missouri, he had been away from the lakes for more than fifty years,[35] but he spoke of familiar scenes as if he had made his visit but yesterday. The attraction of the lakes had been his life's remembrance.

"I also assisted my father in building the first

[35] Jones, Dorchester, letter printed in Waupaca Republican, Nov. 10, 1905.

white man's boat ever floated in their beautiful waters," wrote Mr. Jones. "Not a cranny or nook of the entire coast line of the Chain o' Lakes have I not visited time and again in this selfsame boat, sometimes with boon companions, but more frequently by myself."

Once on the waters of these lakes, one sees their beauty unfold like the petals of a rose. Boats go through the entire chain. Canoes carry the Nature-lover into little nooks and recesses of sylvan loveliness. One day, passing Government Island at the doorway of Rainbow and Taylor Lakes, I stopped for an inspection. It is a tangle of underbrush—goose, huckleberry, snowberry, and sumac, and there are evidences that its maple trees were once used by the Indians for sugar-making. Near the center of the thirteen-acre tract is a hogback from which there are impressive glimpses of Rainbow Lake through the trees. Leaving the island and circling Taylor Lake, one gains a fine view of its sloping shores and the dense greenery that comes down to the water's edge.

On a high promontory north of the island that overlooks Sunset Lake is Loyola Villa, a summer home for priests of the Jesuit order. The house is embowered in pine trees and there are long walks that invite quiet and meditation. Those who live in such a secluded spot must be at peace with all the world.

On the way down the chain, two other islands in Sunset Lake are passed. Onaway Island is used as a camp ground for Boy Scouts, while Crescent is only a third-acre strip and is seldom visited. Near the main shore before Nessling Lake is reached, a long pine towers fifty feet above its hardwood neighbors. It is a singular sight.

"Formerly there were three tall pines there," the guide explained, "but the lightning has shattered the other two."

At the entrance of Nessling Lake on a little peninsula is the summer home of Mr. George W. Norris, United States Senator from Nebraska. Further on is McCrossen Lake, named for a pioneer farmer. Outlined on the maps it looks like a hammock. On the south shore is Greenwood Forest, the summer home of former Congressman E. E. Browne, of Wisconsin. The mainland is a mixed stand of native trees and shrubbery, so dense as to conceal all evidences of habitation.

"The frenzy into which the wind is able to whip the lake caused the Indians to believe that it was the summer home of the water monster," continued the guide. "This giant fish, according to their legends, was able to snag swimmers, overturn boats and drag the victims to the bottom of the lake to be devoured. The Indians had a legend that the leader of their tribe was asked to destroy the monster. Equipping himself with knives and other implements, the chief sought out the lair and was quickly caught and devoured by the monster. Within the body of the fish he found his brothers—the bear, the deer, the porcupine, the raven, and the pine squirrel.

All had been caught for destruction. Immediately the Indian began to sing a war dance and was joined by the animal kingdom. As they capered around in the body of the monster, the fish began to reel, and finally the chief stuck his knife through the heart. Then he cut his way out of captivity and escaped to his wigwam.

"Indians say that in the old days the hiding place for this fish was in McCrossen Lake and, because of the turbulence of the entrance channel during stormy periods, they believed that the spirit of the evil water monster was still about."

Columbian and Round Lakes are connected by a shallow ford dredged so that smaller boats may pass. This is Indian Crossing, a spot where all the beauty of the lakes seems to converge into a single entrance. The shaded shore lines narrow down; the boat goes bumping along over muck and stones, but soon the crossing has been made, the Columbian waters expand before us, and in the distance is Long Lake.

Beasley Lake, a little bay at the north of Long Lake, is the beginning of the "Little Chain." The creek that connects it with the lakelets, Bass and Orlando, is one of the most scenic of water courses. It is crossed by a narrow bridge but the whole is always in forest shadows. This lake, more than forty feet deep, has a darker water coloring. Its bottom contains a large percentage of weedy material, shutting the sunlight away from the marl places. Were it not for their depth and the beauty of the high banks, the lakes of the Little Chain would be but ponds. Some day the artist will search them out and make them famous on canvas. The lakelets—Bass, Youngs, Orlando, Knight, Manomin, Pope, and Marl—can be reached only by canoe, but they have a seclusion found nowhere else in either chain.

Each time I leave the Chain o' Lakes after a day in the hot sun through the sandy potato belt of Wisconsin it is with plans already made for the next visit. And the plans are always the same. The next time I shall follow that creek with the green-shaded banks which the lovers take when they canoe to Otter Lake. It will be evening and I shall pause at times to listen to the vesper song festival of the birds that faintly come to me when I pass the bank of ferns hiding the stream's entrance. Then in the morning, on Columbian Lake, I shall have the guide row me by Camp Cleghorn, a summer assembly established by the order of Good Templars, and still maintained along Chautauqua lines. Nearby we shall find the canal that will take us to Dake and Miner Lakes. The day will be spent exploring the banks which always look so refreshing from the roadway. And on the next I shall go to the tamarack swamp on Long Lake and follow those currents of spring water moving so slowly by lily pads that their yellow blossoms are always upright. Maybe the day will be long and we will follow the Crystal River through the farm lands to the Wolf, and then the Fox, all the way to Oshkosh, where other tribes of the Menominee made their home on Lake Winnebago, the largest inland body of water wholly within the borders of a single state. These pleasures we have planned for the next visit.

But today we shall remain under the pine three centuries old on Rainbow Lake and watch the green waters. The magic of changing colors in the lakes will not release us.

The Chain o' Lakes is three miles southwest of Waupaca. It is on State Trunk Highway 22 and near U. S. Highway 10 from Green Bay westward across the state. The Chain o' Lakes at Waupaca is in the vicinity of the Wisconsin Veterans' Home. The lakes are fifty miles from Oshkosh; sixty miles from Fond du Lac; fifty-two miles from Green Bay; one hundred twenty-five miles from Milwaukee; one hundred fifteen miles from Madison; thirty-five miles from Wisconsin Rapids; sixty miles from Wausau; and one hundred fifty-five miles from Eau Claire.

VIKING SURVIVALS

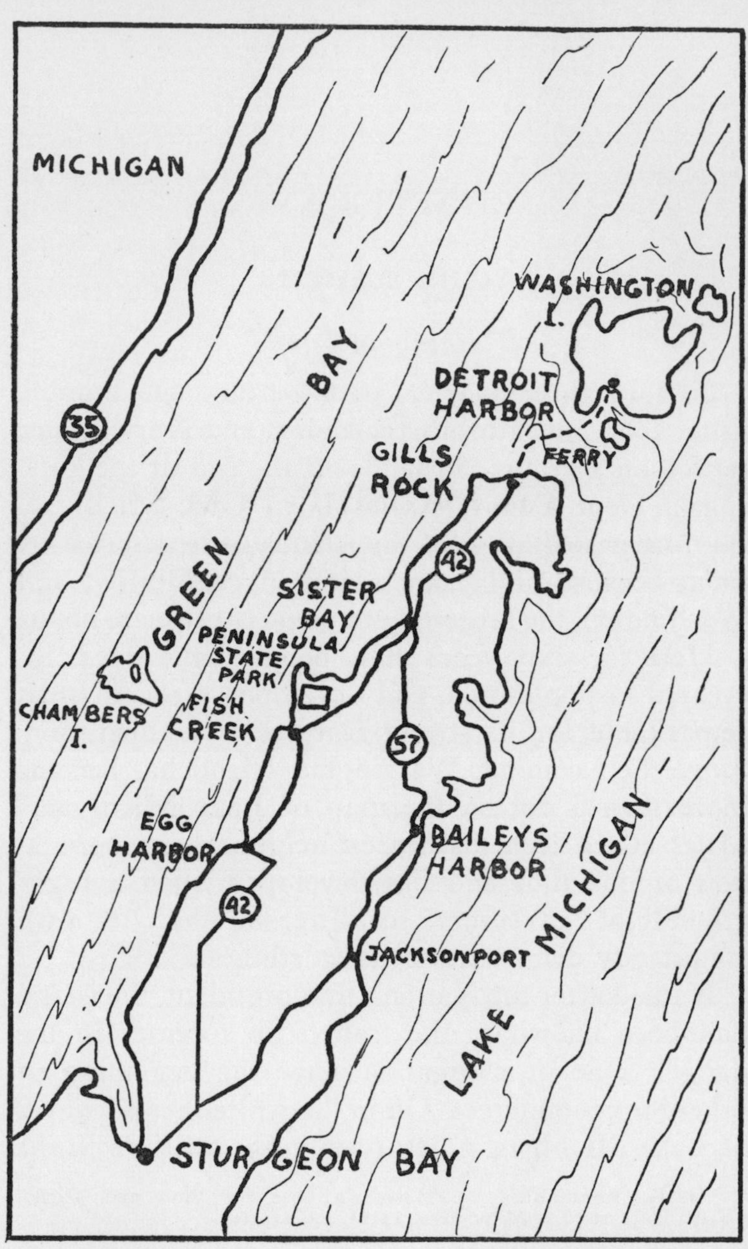

Chapter XVI

VIKING SURVIVALS
WASHINGTON ISLAND

CHAPTER XVI

VIKING SURVIVALS

Washington Island

NEARLY three-quarters of a century ago humble fisher folk, adventurous Icelanders and Norwegians, settled on a group of islands off the end of the Wisconsin Door County peninsula in Lake Michigan. As time passed, most of the islands were deserted by them because of bleakness and inaccessibility, and Washington, the largest, became their ultimate home.

Here for sixty years these people have lived, increased in population, and developed a social spirit remarkable for its strong features of co-operation. Since their coming, Washington Island has become more than a dot on the map of Lake Michigan.[36] Miles at sea from its nearest neighbors, its population of one thousand has developed upon a background of adventure so different that its own singularity demonstrates its worthiness.

Named after the Nation's first president, the island had been known to the traders as a center in the danger zone of navigation since the beginning of inland sea commerce. Off in the white-crested waves of Lake Michigan it lies, twenty-five miles from the

[36] Davis, Susan Burdick, "Wisconsin Lore for Boys and Girls," (E. M. Hale and Co. Milwaukee, 1931), pp. 219-237.

mainland of northern Michigan and twelve miles from Door County peninsula in Wisconsin.

Around it the currents toss and flow, now smiling and quiet; now angry and turbulent. In summer the cool breezes come in from the restless waters—clean, fresh, and invigorating—but in mornings when the horizon is murky, the sun bolts out of the eastern sky in a cloud as gray as dust, gliding swiftly like a charioted ball of fire over the zinc-colored surface. Even the fishermen, tugging at their nets, pause and gaze in the solemnity of such a moment.

Morning is day's gem with these fisher folk. They go about their tasks early, retiring to their homes in the afternoons for agricultural pursuits. Far away the world of affairs is noisy and busy but they do not invite its disturbance.

Washington Island is a governmental township about six miles square and with a shore line of twenty-six miles.[37] Its northern sides are high and precipitous with castellated limestone caverns reaching to the water's edge, two hundred feet below its peaks. Fantastic figures, fashioned and sculptured by the winds and storms of the ages, have been wrought in the stony surfaces. Over it all the clinging cedars have woven a drapery of green to hide its bald outlines. Detroit Harbor on the southern crest is its most important commercial port.

Inland, second-growth timber is now foresting the

[37] Holand, H. R., "Old Pioneer Days" (Menasha, Wis., 1931), pp. 85-104.

uncultivated places. On top of the high ridges and cliffs are heavy growths of hardwood, birch and maple; small oak and spruce and arbor vitae go down to the water's edge. Cords upon cords of flat pieces of limestone have been gathered by patient labor from the fields and utilized in the building of strong fences or walls. In some clearings the open fields are rugged with great rock out-crops and in others the ground is deep and the earth tillable. Such has been the home and environment of these immigrant Nordics.

Those Vikings of Norway who landed on Iceland in the Ninth Century found it a barren and rock-strewn waste of desolation. Today it supports a population of more than 75,000 people with farming and stock raising, with extensive fishing and industries. The tenets of democracy flourish; education is general and the people have turned the ugly landscape into good homes and busy cities.

The settlers on Washington Island planned in like manner. Their rock-spattered fields have been cleared; their homes have been made comfortable and their lives are devoted, quiet and peaceful. Three school buildings have come with their progress; roads have been built out of crushed stone from their rock-piled hedge-rows; harbors have been improved; agriculture has been fostered, and each year about forty thousand bushels of seed potatoes are exported. Purebred Holstein cattle have been imported, and it is the dream of the fisher folk farmers that Washington Island may some day have a reputation for purebreds such as is now enjoyed by Guernsey Island off the coast of England.

Isolation affords certain opportunities for shelter and development, which some people seek. Long before the coming of the white settlers, Washington Island was a well-known Indian meeting ground and about it many fascinating legends still are told. Early in the sixteenth century, it was a haven of refuge for warring tribes; later it was the home of nomadic Winnebagoes. While recorded history does not tell of the many Indian exploits, there is tangible evidence of occupancy and progress everywhere. The water's edge is strewn with camp sites, workshops and cornfields. In the interior are the mounds of the Indian cemeteries. It must have been long the home of red men.

When the first white traders came in their canoe visits through the Mackinac passage, the place was peopled. For unknown reasons, it was deserted before the time of our Revolutionary War. After the departure of the Indians, Washington Island was left to its dreams and its memories until about the middle of the past century. When wood was the only article of fuel, the expanding cities of Chicago and Milwaukee obtained a part of their supply from this vicinity. Barges were brought here and loaded and the commercial world knew the island only as a cordwood emporium.

Fisher folk were the first permanent settlers. Their early landings were at Rock Island, a little mountain of limestone about a mile across at the

ːY HILL, SOUTH OF HART-
ːD, IS THE HIGHEST
NT IN THE KETTLE MO-
RAINE REGION.

TYPICAL WISCONSIN FOX FARM IN WASHINGTON COUNTY.

STIFF WINDS OFF LAKE MICHIGAN SHIFT THE SAND DUNES AT TERRY ANDRAE STATE PARK.

CARFERRY ENTERING HARBOR AT MANITOWOC.

LAKE MICHIGAN SHORELINE AT PORT WASHINGTON.

SAND, CLOUDS, AND A COOL DAY AT TERRY ANDRAE STATE PARK.

—Photo by courtesy of A. F. Toepfer, Milwauk

AERIAL VIEW OF MILWAUKEE, ONE OF THE NATION'S GREATEST INDUSTRIAL CITIES.

LOOKING DO
MILWAUKE
FAMOUS W
CONSIN AVEN

THE ALLIS-CHALMERS PLANT, ONE OF THE REASONS WHY MILWAUKEE LEADS THE NATION IN DIVERSIFICATION OF INDUSTRY.

PLEASURE CRAFTS FILL THE HARBOR OF THE MILWAUKEE YACHT CLUB.

WINDPOINT LIGHTHOUSE IS ONE OF THE SHOWPLACES AT RACINE.

PEWAUKEE LAKE, ONE OF THE MOST FAMOUS SAILING LAKES IN WISCONSIN.

North. The place was soon deserted, however, because of its barrenness, and Washington Island became the common home for the fishermen. So many had gathered by 1850 that a township was organized before there was a county to which it might claim membership. It was not until the settlements of the Icelanders were established that the agricultural progress of the island started.

The coming of the Icelanders dates back over fifty years when William F. Wickman of Milwaukee, who had spent some years in Iceland for the Danish government, encouraged a group of Icelanders to emigrate and selected Washington Island as a suitable home for them. It is the oldest Icelandic settlement in America, and with it have been associated men later prominent in the larger settlements in Minnesota and Manitoba as both scholars and writers. These early Icelanders started the fishing trade and developed the soil. The reports back home of their progress resulted in the coming of more of their kinsmen to the Mississippi Valley and it is estimated that there are now more than thirty thousand Icelanders and their descendants in Canada and more than ten thousand in the United States.

Inviting as this fishermen's empire may seem upon a visit, it can only be reached by crossing a treacherous strait so dangerous that its bed is strewn with the wrecks of boats. For the inhabitants this menace of angry waters has been no discouragement. Spanning the narrow distance of twelve miles is a passage called the "Port des Morts"—the Door of Death—

so named by early French voyagers and traders because currents and strong winds drove sailing vessels into the danger-fraught by-way. Near here, according to tradition, La Salle's "Griffin," first sailing vessel to ply the Great Lakes, while laden with a cargo of furs, was wrecked in 1679, and since then scores of passing boats have come to their doom. In the summer of 1871 almost a hundred vessels suffered shipwreck. Treacherous as the straits are in summer, they are even more so in winter. The ice forms late and disappears early. Owing to the strong undercurrents brought inland by shifting winds, the ice breaks up and a surface frozen solid in the morning may be wave-rippled by evening.

The story of how the mail is carried daily through "Death's Door" to the island settlers is a narrative of hardship which rivals any which has come out of the lands of dog teams and mountain passes. Through conditions so dangerous that they tax any except fiction-fed imaginations, the mail sack at Ellison Bay post-office on the mainland is carried in one way or another, depending on winds, to the Detroit post-office on the island. During the winter the task is particularly hazardous. The "Door" is filled with treacherous ice which is constantly moving, and at a moment's notice open water may be encountered. The ice is so thin in places that for miles it cracks under the weight of the carrier and his sack. Heavy snowstorms and blizzards add to the dangers, so blinding the carrier that he often loses his way.

For many years, this mail was carried by Captain Pete Anderson, a character known all along the Lake Michigan shore. Oftentimes he has laid on his stomach on the thin ice, in order to distribute his weight more evenly, and wiggled across. The veteran performed his duty as calmly as the ordinary person would sit down to dinner. Two or three times in the last few years the mail carrier has been carried out into Lake Michigan by powerful moving ice floes. Always his rescue has been accomplished by the heroic assistance of the brave lighthouse guards at Plum Island.

In 1926 Anderson with a single horse and sleigh was caught on a field of moving ice, which was being broken up. Soon it was barely large enough to float the carrier, sleigh and horse. A stiff wind was carrying him out into the lake, and his position was a most precarious one. Watchers at the lighthouse station on Plum Island spread the alarm. Starting to the rescue in their small boat, they had great difficulty in fighting the ice floes, and it was only through what seemed superhuman effort that they forced their way close enough to the ice cake that was supporting him to throw him a line, but not until he was almost out into Lake Michigan, with the mammoth waves nearly washing over the ice ferry that supported him. The horse and sleigh were saved by towing the ice cake back to calmer waters.

Although Washington Island has a population of one thousand people, there is not a village on the island. A gathering of a few houses, a store, ice cream parlor for summer only, and four or five residences makes the nearest approach to a settlement. One drives along the smooth, open road and suddenly finds himself before a solitary building, which he recognizes as a store. It stands as alone as a farmhouse and looks much the same.

Insular life tends to the growth of community spirit if not to congested building. The people of the island are like one big family, law-abiding, kindly, God-fearing. There is a blending of races. Icelanders have married Danes, and Danes have married Norwegians in many cases.

With this genuine community mingling has come progress. There has been a steady improvement in agricultural development within the past few years. Fields have been fenced and the little white cottages have been repainted. There are picturesque homes. Many of the frame buildings are of low setting, mostly of Norse design, much like the country houses of distant Norway and Iceland. Some have blinds with dark-green trimmings. Surrounding the cottages are flower beds and fruit trees, showing a home life artistic and domestic. Pear, apple and plum trees are found on each farm.

These fisher folk of Washington Island are a patriotic people. Of the one thousand inhabitants, forty-three of them fought in the World War, and four of these gave their lives. The township went over the top in every war drive.

Washington Island is off the tip of the Green Bay Peninsula. It is reached by boat from the terminus of County Trunk B. State Highways 57 and 42 reach the Sturgeon Bay and Door County Peninsula. Washington Island is ninety-three miles from Green Bay; one hundred thirteen miles from Manitowoc; two hundred miles from Milwaukee; two hundred twenty-eight miles from Madison; and three hundred miles from Eau Claire.

NATURE'S POTS AND PANS

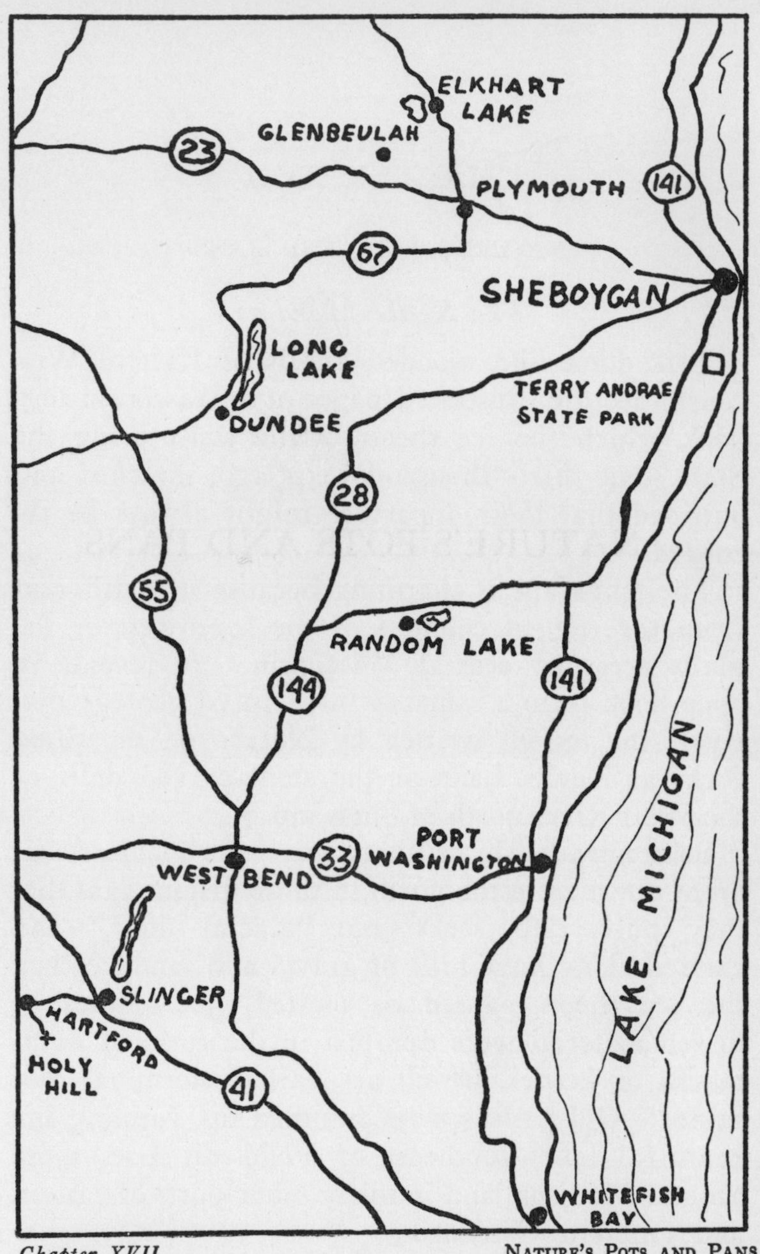

Chapter XVII

NATURE'S POTS AND PANS
THE KETTLE MORAINE

CHAPTER XVII

NATURE'S POTS AND PANS

The Kettle Moraine

THE dome-like, wooded knolls of Eastern Wisconsin are the illustrated pages of a Wisconsin log-book which the ice sheets, while sculpturing the State some thirty thousand years ago, sketched and outlined that their departure might always be recorded.

The landscape is charming because it is different from the rugged counties of the southwest or the plain areas of central Wisconsin. It reveals in open book form a romance in pictured geology that rivals the lessons written by Nature on the tilted rocks at Devils Lake or the stone-carved dells of the Wolf River north of Shawano.

So tremendously crushing were the glaciers that crept down from the north in those distant ages that they pulverized rocks into "glacial flour," and carried along huge hills of gravel and sand. When the ice sheets paused or melted, great piles of mixed material were dumped in the form of hummocks or kettles, which are called "terminal moraine." Old valleys were dammed up, forming the beautiful lakes southeast of Fond du Lac, those around Madison, and in many other parts of eastern and southern Wisconsin.

The "kettles" in Fond du Lac, Sheboygan, and Waukesha Counties are the cast-off burdens of the retreating ice plow. They are the camp equipment which the vandal-glaciers discarded in beating a return under a hot sun. Departing, they left borrowed scenery from the lands of everywhere. Green and picturesque in summer, these knolls in winter appear more like heaps and drifts of snow thrown together by a fickle December wind.

When we went on our visit to the "kettles," another bit of scenery first caught our attention. For a whole morning we sat on a beach of sand dunes south of Sheboygan watching Lake Michigan roll in great whitecaps at our feet. About us drifted currents of white sand. Terry Andrae State Park is a bit of the Indiana sand dune country transferred to Wisconsin. Its outlook on Lake Michigan is most beautiful. Its eastern horizon melts into the blue lake. Its shore is a wonderful strip of clean sand. On the high land there is much virgin timber. In early days, the tract was a favorite spot of the Potawatomi Indians who made this their summer home.

The insistent melody of the waves as they beat on the lonely silver shores is as soothing as a drug. Back under the dark pines where the song is pitched in low undertones, the music and cool lake breezes become more seductive, submerging one's landmarks of resolution and lulling all ambition and sense of duty.

Those great heaps of sand along the shores record

the forgotten stories of storms and shipwrecks. A sparse, coarse grass attempts to conceal parts of the hulks of a broken vessel. Long strands of tattered rope and the remnants of cargoes which the waters washed ashore are partly buried. Over these emblems of tragedy the white sands sift a coverlet, blotting out the tragedy of the destruction.

Even the sands are restless. Some days a hurricane of a wind moves the top dressing from acres, eating the heart out of some dune that had been there long enough to be a landmark. Close to the earth these moving grains strike up a union of song sweeter than the measured roll of the waves. Another wind shifts the scenery back.

When the weather calms for a few days, the sands begin to record the events of night. Footprints of animals show the way to little burrows. Tracks of thousands of gulls who follow the shore seeking food are imprinted. The tragedy of the killing of a luckless animal by a hawk is revealed. These records are ephemeral. The next wind to arise wipes away the stains.

Regretfully we left the park to visit the "kettles" where the print of ages is permanent. No finer examples of glacier landscaping can be found than along the network of country roads between Plymouth and Kewaskum. The countryside is done in billows and valleys. Within this area the Izaak Walton League maintains around Moon Lake a wild life preserve of national beauty and significance.

"There is sufficient gravel in these knolls to make

the foundations for all the roads Wisconsin will need for centuries," commented the State Conservation official who directed our visit.

"That old glacier which scooped out the bed for the waters of Lake Winnebago must have carted all the gravel found along the way and dumped it here," I suggested.

"Yes," he rejoined, "and the gravel from thousands of miles away."

Some farms in the area, where the top soil was worn away, had to be abandoned. The gravel was so near the surface at places that it was no longer possible to use the land for agricultural purposes. The country is such a characteristic example of varied geology and topography, however, that efforts have been made to have it included in the state park system.

Within the vicinity are several pretty glacial lakes, the shorelines of which are being rapidly acquired for private enterprises. Elkhart and Crystal Lakes are already developed. Resorts are being established on Forest, Crooked, Round and Long Lakes. The waters of these basins are as clear as artesian flowage.

If Wisconsin in the days of its wilderness ever teemed with as many varieties of wild life as are now found around Moon Lake, there was never an occasion for a pioneer to starve. Under government protection, duck, geese, pheasants, and quail have again become plentiful. These birds sense their security. The ducks sail away a short distance when the visitors come to the lake and the grouse hide in the brush on one's approach. A movie man set up his camera and took pictures of wild life for an hour without creating any disturbance or flights. It is worth going miles to see primitive Wisconsin in the days of the fur trader—muskrat along the banks and the lakes surface dotted with aquatic fowl.

Because of its proximity to industrial centers this region is more often visited by southern Wisconsin residents than are some of the more widely advertised natural attractions. The winding roads around the hills and lakes give the landscape a pleasing effect of changing vistas.

Between the hills are these bowl-like valleys—the rounded glacial kettles—which imprison the rainfall until it seeps away. From the crests of the moraine, these unruffled pools, the pots and pans of Nature, appear dark at heart and mysterious of soul. The lakes are the larger manifestation of the same landscaping done on an extensive scale. Most of the farmers use the hills for pasturage and the valleys for crops. Often in the depths between ridges tall and spindling trees struggle to reach the sunlight.

"So let us pause right here and consider what we have in the way of scenery that no one else has," said Charles D. Stewart, an inspired acolyte of Nature who has his home under the shadow of one of the moraine's hills.

"Since the days when Rome was in her grandeur, the advanced nations of the world have spent vast sums in building amphitheatres—big bowl-like places, either built up of stone or wood or excavated to suit the purposes of public entertainment. Whether it is the Yale Bowl or a Roman Coliseum or a modern stadium, or even a city theatre with its rising tiers of seats, they follow the same pattern—the inside of a bowl wherein people can arrange themselves and see all that is going on. Here in this unique kettle range—so called because its valleys are like the inside of a kettle—we have amphitheatres "to burn." Each of them might have cost hundreds of thousands of dollars—they would if you built them—but happily Nature put them in place.

"And there is no other place in this country where this peculiarity of glacial scenery is carried to such an extent by Nature. In no other terminal moraine have the hills been set down so thickly that they virtually run together at the bottom to produce enough valleys of this nature that it could be called a kettle range. There is one place in Scotland that compares with it and that is all."

By slow journeying we had followed the kettle ranges southward, searching on the horizon for Holy Hill, the daylight North Star for the immigrant who came pioneering into this region. It is an eminence long since endowed with respect and reverence in the country-side because it is now the home of the Carmelite Fathers.

Nearing Hartford—there it was. Above a bank of woods that curved skyward loomed the church spires on the summit. As we approached it, the Cross on Calvary could not have been more conspicuous than the towers on the tip of the high summit.

Closer by is a deep woods of slender trees that hide the topmost edifice from the roadway while the ascent is made.[38] By another path the pilgrims on foot climb from the dark valley slowly into the sunlight, dropping, perhaps, at each station of repose some burden of sin. No place could be more alluring for meditation; none so elevating in the wholesome aspirations of life. The glacier which had dropped this load upon the landscape left for the generations a natural setting for the delivery of the Sermon on the Mount.

Perhaps, the praying hermit who made his home on the height at the close of the Civil War found here the consolation which the hundreds of thousands who have since followed are seeking. When the farmers went to their work in the morning they would see the hermit praying at a cross on the summit. Something of the hill's spirit entered into the souls of the country-folk, and they climbed the hill to offer aid to one who was in trouble. They built a little log house, which they called "The Hermitage," in the hope that he would occupy it. When the "hill" had softened his heart, he confessed a story of great soul suffering and bitterness toward man.

Gone is the hermit; forgotten the names of the farmers who aided him, but the hill remains to call the faithful to lift up their eyes to the heavens.

From its doors the whole of southern Wisconsin spreads out like a fan. The church appears as if it

[38] Stewart, Charles D., "Essays on the Spot," p. 85.

were on the citadel of the world, with the valleys of doubt and trouble discarded in the green slopes at its feet.

Far away are glistening lakes, green fields, the smoke of Milwaukee. Since the days of the hermit, the rampart of this terminal moraine has been dedicated to the love of God. From its elevated altars the amphitheatre of a beautiful world stretches far, —an unending vineyard for the labors of the disciples who minister in God's name.

The Kettle Moraine Country lies westward and southward from Sheboygan. Terry Andrae Park is three miles south of Sheboygan. Moon Lake, eighty miles east of Madison, is in the heart of the Kettle Moraine Country. Holy Hill is at the southern end. This country is twenty miles from Fond du Lac; fifty miles from Milwaukee; eighty-five miles from Madison.

MILWAUKEE'S WASHINGTON PARK ZOO IS ONE OF THE LARGEST IN THE COUNTRY.

—*Photo by J. Harry Taylor, Milwau*

MILWAUKEE HUNT CLUB IN ACTION, NORTH OF CITY; HOLY HILL IN BACKGROUND.

BEAUTIFULLY LANDSCAPED LAWNS GRACE THE SHORES OF LAC LA BELLE, WAUKESHA COUNTY.

TABLET AT MITCHELL PARK WHICH ATTESTS THE BUSINESS JUDGMENT OF THE FIRST MILWAUKEE SETTLER.

RQUETTE UNIVERSITY DENTAL COLLEGE, KNOWN THROUGHOUT THE NATION.

Artist—Hans Figura
Courtesy F. H. Bresler Co., M

MORE ETCHINGS ARE MADE OF ST. JOHN'S CATHOLIC CATHEDRAL THAN OF ANY OTHER BUILDING IN MILWAUKEE.

TROUT LAKE, VILAS COUNTY, THE CENTER OF STATE GOVERNMENT EXPERIMENTS IN CONSERVATION.

STATE CONSERVATION HEADQUARTERS AT TROUT LAKE.

LOGGING CAMP NAMED AFTER PAUL BUNYAN, AT CARSON PARK, EAU CLAIRE.

FISHERMEN FROM EVERYWHERE HAVE HEARD OF THE FLAMBEAU RIVER.

AN EXAMPLE OF BEAVER ENGINEERING IN NORTHERN WISCONSIN.

HUNDREDS OF SMALL LAKES LIKE THIS IN NORTHERN WISCONSIN HAVE NEVER BEEN NAMED.

A METROPOLIS WITH MEMORIES

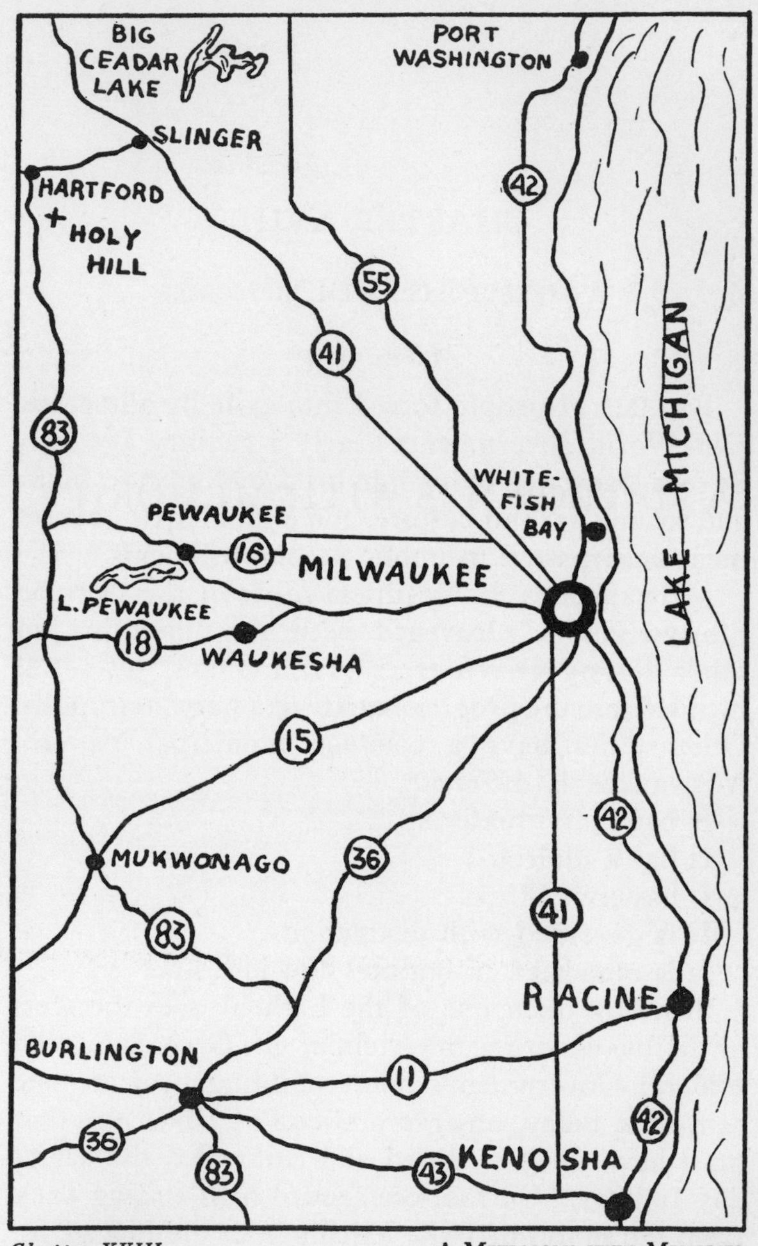

Chapter XVIII

A METROPOLIS WITH MEMORIES
MILWAUKEE

CHAPTER XVIII

A METROPOLIS WITH MEMORIES

Milwaukee

DREAMS of people forced into exile by autocratic Old World governments nearly a century ago may be seen translated today into brick and mortar, home and school, art and culture, and a municipal government unsurpassed in public accomplishments.

Milwaukee is the deathless spirit of the German "forty-eighters," leavened with the liberalism of other destiny driven races—Irish, Poles, Jews—all blended into the progressive life of a busy metropolis. Other cities have a common municipal pattern. Milwaukee is different.

It has individualism.

It has a dialect.

It has civic ideals.

It is governed with distinction.

It is renowned in business and industry.

Standing upon one of the high hills to the west of Milwaukee, in the vicinity of Greendale—the Federal Government's home building project—one can, even today, observe a sweep of landscape that must have daily charmed and enthralled the early-day Indians. On that crescent of hills rolling back from the shores of Lake Michigan at the foot of St.

Francis Seminary, to the south of Milwaukee Bay, northward over the grounds of the National Soldiers' Home again to meet the lake at Fox Point, once stood the wigwams and blazed the council fires of Potawatomi, Menominees, Chippewas, Sacs, Kickapoos, and Winnebagoes. It was a tribal gathering place, beautiful to the eye, a hunting ground with game and fish so abundant that the Indians called it Milwacky—"Place of Good Earth."

It is still a place of beauty. Travelers lodging for a night in downtown hotels catch glimpses in early morning of the blue bay, of commerce, of belching smokestacks, and hear the dull, rasping whistle of a ship ready to dock and discharge its cargo. Old World visitors have since the early days compared the vista of water in front of Milwaukee, surrounded by the hills, as rivaling, and, many say, exceeding the beauty of the centuries-famed Bay of Naples.

The Bay of Milwaukee gives to the city a ten-million-dollar harbor development unsurpassed for depth and availability. It is the leading port on Lake Michigan, and the second on the Great Lakes in point of arrivals and departures. If you remain a while at your hotel window in summer, you may see these giant freighters discharge a cargo of coal, reload with grain, and start off again for the Straits of Mackinac, as silent as the blue waters, leaving only a long, thin trail of smoke on the horizon to mark their course.

Milwaukee's strategic commercial location has

made possible the city's rapid development as, today, the twelfth most populous city in the United States. Her harbor facilities are unique in their adequacy for cargoes of large draft. If the St. Lawrence Waterway is ever an accomplished fact, Milwaukee will challenge Chicago for commercial supremacy. As if by design, Nature must utilize this splendid port for inland markets.

All about this harbor a strange, busy life has developed. Explorer, trader and missionary came early. The place was visited by La Salle in 1679; the Sulpitan Father, Saint-Cosme, brought his faith to the Indians on its hills in 1699, and Jacques Vieau established his trading post in 1795.

"Fields of wild rice, where you now see factory buildings in the Menomonee valley, greeted him upon his arrival, and among the wild rice fields were thousands of wild ducks." So spoke K. K. Kennan, vice-president of the Old Settlers Club, born in Milwaukee in 1844, addressing an audience gathered at Mitchell Park in the autumn of 1925 to dedicate a marker on the site of the first home.[39] He said that the present City Hall site was then a tangled swamp.

On the brow of the hill in Mitchell Park, embedded in a huge boulder, may be seen a tablet which attests the business judgment of the first Milwaukee trader in picking this site for his post:

[39] Dedication of Vieau marker completely reported in Milwaukee Journal, October 25, 1925. State Historical Publications give Vieau's first name as Jacques. Monument spelling omits the final "s."

ON THIS SITE THE FIRST PERMANENT FUR TRADER
JACQUE VIEAU IN 1795
BUILT HIS CABIN, THE FIRST HOUSE IN MILWAUKEE
HERE ALSO WAS THE CROSSING OF THE
GREEN BAY—CHICAGO TRAIL

Three streams of water, emptying into the now renowned bay of Milwaukee, gave to the meeting place commercial importance and developed a keen business rivalry during the romantic days of the fur trade. Rising to the north in Washington County and flowing south, was the Milwaukee River. From the west came the Menomonee, emptying into the Milwaukee River about three-quarters of a mile to the west of where the Milwaukee joins with Lake Michigan. Out of the hills at the southwest of the city came the Kinnickinnic, mingling its waters with the Milwaukee River at the beginning of the straight cut which constitutes the harbor entrance.

These rivers divided early Milwaukee into three rival sections—East Side, West Side, and South Side. Milwaukee, where Solomon Juneau, son-in-law of Jacques Vieau, settled, was the East Side; Kilbourn town, named after Byron Kilbourn, its moving spirit in business, was on the West Side, and South of the Menomonee and Milwaukee Rivers was Walker town, bearing the name of Colonel George H. Walker, a tower of commercial enterprise in that locality. By an Indian treaty signed at Chicago in 1833, the way was opened for white settlers to acquire lands.

Promised removal of the Indians to the West was the signal for an influx of settlers. New York and

New England States furnished the first arrivals. Increase A. Lapham, Wisconsin's first recognized scientist and the originator of the weather bureau, visited Milwaukee during this period. Writing to his brother in the East on July 27, 1836, he said:[40]

"Milwaukee is on the site of an Indian town, and the wigwams are still to be seen. The Indians found around here belong principally to the Menominees, or Wild Rice Eaters, and are said to be much less savage and quarrelsome than most other Indians. They are certainly better looking men and much whiter than we usually see. The land in the neighborhood has not yet been brought into market, so very few families have settled here as yet, and the town is far in advance of the country and every kind of farm produce is very high. Our town is improving as rapidly as the supply of lumber will allow, and many buildings are waiting for lumber to finish. Lumber is $50 a thousand."

Within ten years, however, the migration from over the ocean had set in. Political disturbances in Germany and Ireland, along with the low price of land and the liberal citizenship laws of Wisconsin, attracted thousands. Other large groups of Poles, Bohemians, Hollanders and Scandinavians followed. Whole communities of Old World neighbors were transplanted to the fertile soil of Wisconsin.[41] Mil-

[40] Gregory, John G., "History of Milwaukee" (Chicago, 1931), Vol. II, p. 1241. The visit of the author of "Alluring Wisconsin" to gather data for this chapter was made in the autumn of 1936, one hundred years after Lapham's letter was written.

[41] Legler, Henry E., "Leading Events in Wisconsin History" (Milwaukee, 1898), p. 297.

waukee soon became known as "The German Athens of America."

Carl Schurz, distinguished German scholar, who was to become an early day German-American national political figure, visited his old neighbors in Milwaukee in the autumn of 1855. The word picture he wrote that first evening to his wife, describing the charms of Milwaukee, is a true one today: [42]

"Just as darkness fell, I came to the height above the lake where stands the white lighthouse tower which can be seen from afar and suddenly I stood upon the steep declivity of the hill, which revealed, outspread before me, the light green sail-covered water plane. The impression of the lake is not very different from that of the sea, only the colors are not so darkly somber. The wish to live here arose strongly within me." [43]

The energetic elements of population which settled in Milwaukee account in a very large measure for its achievements. The wide-awake young men and women from all oppressed countries came, full of life, vigor and determination, to give a flavor and an Old World tang that time cannot erase. They grasped at the opportunity to build full and rich and strong. It is this distinctiveness of life and

[42] Gregory, Ibid, Vol. II, p. 1317.

[43] Carl Schurz spent his first years after coming to Wisconsin at Watertown. While a resident there he was a candidate for Lieutenant Governor and later for Governor, but both times was defeated. He was appointed Minister to Spain and never returned to Wisconsin. His wife founded the Kindergarten system of education while living at Watertown. The Schurz home site at Watertown is appropriately marked.

character that makes Milwaukee different from other cities.

Just as the French people have impressed their image of life upon Old Quebec, the culture and customs of Germany have been stamped upon Milwaukee. And yet Milwaukee is essentially an American city. In 1900, with a city population of 285,315, there were 53,854 who had been born in Germany and 151,045 who had one or both parents of German birth, or a total of seventy-two per cent who were either German by birth or of the first generation.

Everywhere the sturdy thrift of the German element is conspicuous. This gives to Milwaukee a distinctive charm, at once novel and worth while. The early homes of the German pioneer settlers on Prospect Avenue, overlooking Lake Michigan, attest a business frugality that is not found in the community settlements of other nationalities.

Nor has time wiped out social traditions and worn Milwaukee life down to American sameness. On a Sunday afternoon, families of friends still follow the custom of gathering after church for a Sunday meal and then of spending a part of the afternoon in singing and social diversions. The home itself has a quaint touch. Always there are flowers. In summer the lawns are kept green. During August of 1936 a prolonged drought struck Wisconsin. It seared the pasture lands, browned the gardens, and killed thousands of trees. In that period a traveling man who visited a score of cities in other states reported that Milwaukee was the only city he saw with fresh lawns. Every night Milwaukee home lovers were busy sprinkling lawns and gardens.

The Germans' love of culture is written in art institutes, schools of music and libraries. Their enjoyment of paintings, altar statuary, wood carvings, and stained glass is noticeable in the adornments of their homes and public places. From the Germans have come many of the inviting dishes of our diet. Sauerkraut, Cole Slaw, Zwieback, Schnecken, Pretzels, Apfel-Kuchen, and many other palatable foods are of their cuisine. The Germans also introduced the delicatessen stores.[44]

A quarter of a century ago Edna Ferber, novelist, wrote her first winning book of fiction with Milwaukee life as her theme. She selected a German coffee house as the scene for "Dawn O'Hara." The flavor revealed in that story still gives tone to the few remaining old fashioned German restaurants—Fritz Gust's, Old Heidelberg, Mader's, Deutsche Kuchen, and others. There is nothing pretentious about the entrances to these places, but there is food aplenty on their tables—food flavored with the delicate taste of onion—and vegetable soup fit for a king.

Out of this blending of races and cultures has come a dialect as distinctively Milwaukeean as soft words are characteristic of peoples from the South. A year was spent by a University of Wisconsin woman student in compiling words and inverse

[44] A German word for delicious "eats."

phrases of this colorful language. She reached this conclusion:[45]

"People know Milwaukeeans speak a bit differently than the ordinary mode of speech. In a recent New York music review, the master of ceremonies composed a song which he handed to the pianist to read to the audience. The pianist read the composition after which he said, 'Is this ever good!' Whereupon, the leader remarked: 'Say, where do you think you are—in Milwaukee?'"

A day was spent in the company of a county official visiting old homes of citizens of renown and the more than twenty parks scattered at convenient places all around Milwaukee County. My guide pointed out the former residences of General Charles King, famous soldier and novelist; Charles K. Harris, composer of "After the Ball;" Joseph Clauder, bandmaster; Governor George W. Peck, author of "Peck's Bad Boy;" F. W. Heine, Richard Lorenz, and George Peter, famous panorama artists; Nicholas Senn, surgeon; and Henry E. Legler, historian; the site of the Brockway Fair Grounds where, in September, 1859, Abraham Lincoln delivered a famous address on agriculture; the monument in Forest Home Cemetery over the grave of Latham C. Sholes, inventor of the typewriter; and the residences and resting places of a score of others whose names I neglected to write in my notebook.

[45] Jacobson, Hannah, "Milwaukee Dialect," Thesis for B. A. Degree, University of Wisconsin, 1931, p. 1. To be found in the State Historical Library, Madison, Wis.

Aside from the National capital, there are probably more memorials to famous men and works of art to be found in Milwaukee's parks and playgrounds than anywhere else in the United States. Overlooking the Milwaukee Bay in Juneau Park is a statue to Solomon Juneau, first mayor, which gives a sort of foreign distinction to an open place. Out in the parks and gathering places are to be found statues to leaders, poets, musicians, and statesmen, of all ages; Leif Ericsson, Robert Burns, Goethe, Schiller, Latham C. Sholes, Kosciusko, Increase A. Lapham, Washington, von Steuben, Lincoln, and many others. More etchings have been made of the tower of St. John's Catholic Cathedral—a symphony in architecture—than of any other Milwaukee building.

Milwaukee has residential sections of rare distinction. There are gardens within the suburbs of Shorewood and Whitefish Bay that rival for beauty the historic gardens found on the old Virginia plantations. So lavish are the homes and settings that these communities are commonly called the "Gold Coast." Milwaukee has at least two streets, the Lincoln drive north along the bay, and the Menomonee River drive, on the west side, which, I doubt, are excelled anywhere in the United States. When completed, the Kilbourn esplanade which is wiping away old buildings in the heart of the business district between the Kilbourn bridge and the new ten million dollar Court House, widening the whole into a mall, will add another Old World touch. Many will recall, upon viewing the development, scenes of Berlin's Unter den Linden.

Milwaukee's schools of higher learning offer exceptional opportunities. Among these are:

Marquette University, founded and operated by Jesuit fathers, but non-sectarian as to students and faculty; nine professional colleges, a graduate school, college of liberal arts, high school, fifteen buildings, 425 professors and instructors, 5,000 students, coeducational.

Milwaukee Downer College, founded 1851, faculty of fifty-six, college enrollment, 500; seminary, 225; campus of fifty acres, woods and athletic fields.

University of Wisconsin Extension School, new $350,000 building; 3,000 students, day and night classes, two-year college course and special work.

Wisconsin State Teachers' College (formerly Normal School), established 1885, teachers' training and academic college courses, 1,300 students.

Concordia College, Lutheran, 500 students, fifty-two instructors, B. A. and B. S. degrees.

St. Francis Seminary, Catholic, founded 1856, twenty-two instructors, 300 students, high school, college, and four years of theology; library valued at $50,000.

Mount Mary College, for women, built to replace Notre Dame College of Prairie du Chien, $2,000,000 in buildings, 74-acre campus on Menomonee River, and parkway.

Lutheran Theological Seminary, forty student pastors.

Educators from all parts of our country come to observe the methods practiced in Milwaukee vocational schools, whose most recent enrollment was 13,044 in the day school and 17,301 in the evening school. It is reputed to be the largest vocational school in the world. Milwaukee has 106 public schools, including 6 senior high schools, 4 junior-senior high schools, 2 senior "tech" high schools, 4 junior "tech" high schools, and 86 parochial schools. The number of pupils in these schools is: Public, 90,455; parochial, 34,038. The number of teachers in public schools is 2,483; in parochial schools, 963. The value of public school property is $31,537,084.

An entire morning was spent on a tour of the parks within the county, more than twenty in number. More than 3,000 acres of land have been acquired and utilized largely under the inspirational leadership of C. B. Whitnall. To rid the county of stream pollution, a parkway system has been developed. Lands along water courses have been turned into parklands; many hundreds of thousands of dollars have been expended to erect bridges, widen roads, level the grounds, plant trees, and turn the whole into a pleasing picture.

"Milwaukee County has done the logical thing in

dealing with these streams," explained E. A. Howard, Supervising Engineer of the Regional Planning Department. "Streams have to take care not only of the normal flow from the land, but also of flood waters. The logical thing is to take the low lands—lands that are subject to flood—lands that are otherwise not valuable—and utilize them for park and parkway purposes. By doing that, you turn a potential liability into an actual asset. This can be done only by the municipality; it is a municipal problem and it requires a large municipality to handle it."

Oddly enough, the depression has done much to develop the parks of Milwaukee City and County. Thousands of idle hands have been put to work, cutting stone, grading, filling in low places. At times as many as 4,000 of these workers have been employed. The city has five public bathing beaches, eleven country clubs, seven public golf courses, forty-one tennis courts, and a yacht club. Within the last four years the park program has been advanced ten years. No visitor will regret a day touring its more than one hundred miles of park highways. The Milwaukee park system ranks with the great municipal parks of the Nation—the Los Angeles, the Westchester, and the Cook County systems.

Water within the parks is put to a variety of uses. Some years ago it was found that the Greenfield Park was seldom visited. It lacked bathing facilities. On one of the ridges a well was drilled that produced a large flow. Campers were able to catch the cool waters for drinking and cooking purposes. All unused waters flow through two warming basins and finally into a swimming pool. From the pool it is released into a lagoon used for boating. Excess lagoon waters are later transferred to a bog garden where aquatic plants are grown. From the bog garden the water is again pumped to sprinkle the lawns.

"By that time the water is all worn out," remarked the park attendant.

Washington Park has one of the largest zoos in the country. Each animal is provided with surroundings similar to its natural habitat. Mitchell Park Conservatory is renowned for its beautiful flowers. Lake Park has 125 acres of scenic woodlands and hills that brought to me memories of Valley Forge State Park in Pennsylvania. The Milwaukee Museum is reputed to be the largest and best municipally-owned museum in the United States. It is especially famous for its early American characterization and African exhibits.

And now to stimulate further the pride of Milwaukee, the city has been selected, along with Cincinnati and Washington, D. C., by the Resettlement Administration of the Federal Government for extensive experiments in urban and interurban housing. Parklawn, a forty-acre tract on the North Side, is an urban housing experiment, and Greendale is a 3,500-acre interurban plat on the South Side where homes for six hundred families are under construc-

OLD LOG ROAD OVER THE FLAMBEAU.

AN ALLURING ROAD THROUGH THE AROMATIC FORESTS OF FLORENCE COUNTY.

RAPIDS OF THE CHIPPEWA RIVER AT JIM FALLS.

SMALL SECTION OF PULPWOOD SUPPLIES AT A RHINELANDER PAPER MILL.

ONE OF THE LARGEST PAPER MILLS IN THE WORLD, AT ROTHSCHILD.

A YELLOW BIRCH TREE DIVIDES A ROAD IN THE WILDERNESS OF VILAS COUNTY.

ONCE NORTHERN WISCONSIN WAS AN UNBROKEN FOREST OF PINES LIKE THESE AT BRADLEY PARK, TOMAHAWK.

PAPER MAKING IS A LEADING WISCONSIN INDUSTRY. HERE IS A HUGE MILL AT WISCONSIN RAPIDS.

SCENES SUCH AS THIS ARE COMMON THROUGHOUT THE NORTHERN WISCONSIN RIVER VALLEY.

WILD CAT LAKE, VILAS COUNTY, REFLECTS EVERY MOOD OF THE MOON AND SUN.

A YOUNG MONARCH OF THE LAND O' LAKES.

WHAT GREATER ADVEN
TURE THAN A CANO
TRIP ON THE LAKES AN
RIVERS OF NORTHER
WISCONSIN!

tion to be rented to earners of modest incomes. The monthly family charge will be about $27.50. It is the Government's first extensive attempt to solve the national housing program. If the experiment works satisfactorily, it may be extended to other cities.

Equally arresting has been the progress made by the city government. Twenty-five years ago, Milwaukee surprised the Nation by electing a Socialist mayor. Old party leaders were not only shocked; they were horrified. Ever since, the same man, Daniel Webster Hoan, has held the office. The people believe so heartily in good government that traditional party lines are quite generally disregarded. Through the recent years there has ever been present a community spirit which has refused to permit the city government to be used for the selfish purposes of those who might temporarily control it. Always there has been in the public mind a purpose to make the government serve all the people.

Milwaukee's reputation as one of the most orderly of American cities has been won by a high community consciousness. The criminal and the underworld, by whom other great cities have all too often been harassed, have been exterminated by the deep-rooted concepts of political honesty. Milwaukee was one of the earliest American cities to divorce its police and fire departments from politics. It is the only city in the world to establish a plan of ultimate debt extinction.

Because of this good municipal housekeeping,

when the whole country suffered from the effects of "wild cat" banking and unwise municipal financing, Milwaukee was one of the few large cities in the United States which did not repudiate any part of their debt—principal or interest.

But in the marts of trade and business, Milwaukee wears other laurels. In value of production the metal trades industry ranks first. Next in order are malt beverages, followed closely by food, shoes and leather goods. Excavating machines made in Milwaukee dug the Panama Canal; automobiles used throughout the world are built on frames made in Milwaukee; the largest steam and water turbines ever placed in operation were built in Milwaukee. Within one of Milwaukee's factories was constructed the largest hydro-electric unit ever attempted, converting formerly wasted waters of Niagara Falls into 37,500 horsepower of producing energy, lighting homes and operating many factories. The city is the second largest candy-making center in the United States. The manufacturing plants have an annual normal product valued at over $1,000,000,000.

It is not figures that give me memories of Milwaukee. It is flashes of scenes along the way—churches, fine residences, thousands of well-kept homes, Old World settings for buildings, the green parks, and the tree-protected water courses. Of these I was thinking when I drove out National Avenue, past the State Fair Grounds, and into the country.

At a county road crossing, a gathering of members of the Hunt Club—men and women richly dressed in brilliant red coats, white jodhpurs, black hats and boots, mounted on sleek, nervous, chestnut-colored horses, accompanied by baying dogs—halted my progress. I paused to watch the chase begin. The pageantry of the autumn setting, the poise and grace of the anxious pursuit over the hills, the evidences of wealth and leisure fascinated me for the moment. There is a famous English painting of "The Hunt," done in gorgeous, flaming colors, which portrays what I saw there better than anything I can write. After all, a city that clings to Old World traditions will always offer many fantastic dramas.

Milwaukee is just different, that's all! It makes progress but it also lives with its rich and glorious memories. You'll enjoy your visit there. Gemütlichkeit—the friendly spirit of hospitality—greets you in store, and shop, and street. It bids you pause at this gateway to a vacation paradise which leads away over many roads. Perhaps, you will want to go to the Capitol at Madison, the trout streams of the Bunyan country, or the Land o' Lakes.

Out of Milwaukee the railroads and highways of commerce and pleasure radiate, fanlike, everywhere.

Into the heart of Milwaukee all avenues of Wisconsin life converge.

Milwaukee is on Lake Michigan in the southeastern part of the state. Highways of cement radiate in all directions except eastward. Milwaukee is eighty miles from Madison; two hundred fifteen miles from La Crosse; four hundred fourteen miles from Superior; one hundred nineteen miles from Wisconsin Dells; one hundred fourteen miles from Green Bay, and eighty-five miles from Chicago.

THE LAND O' LAKES

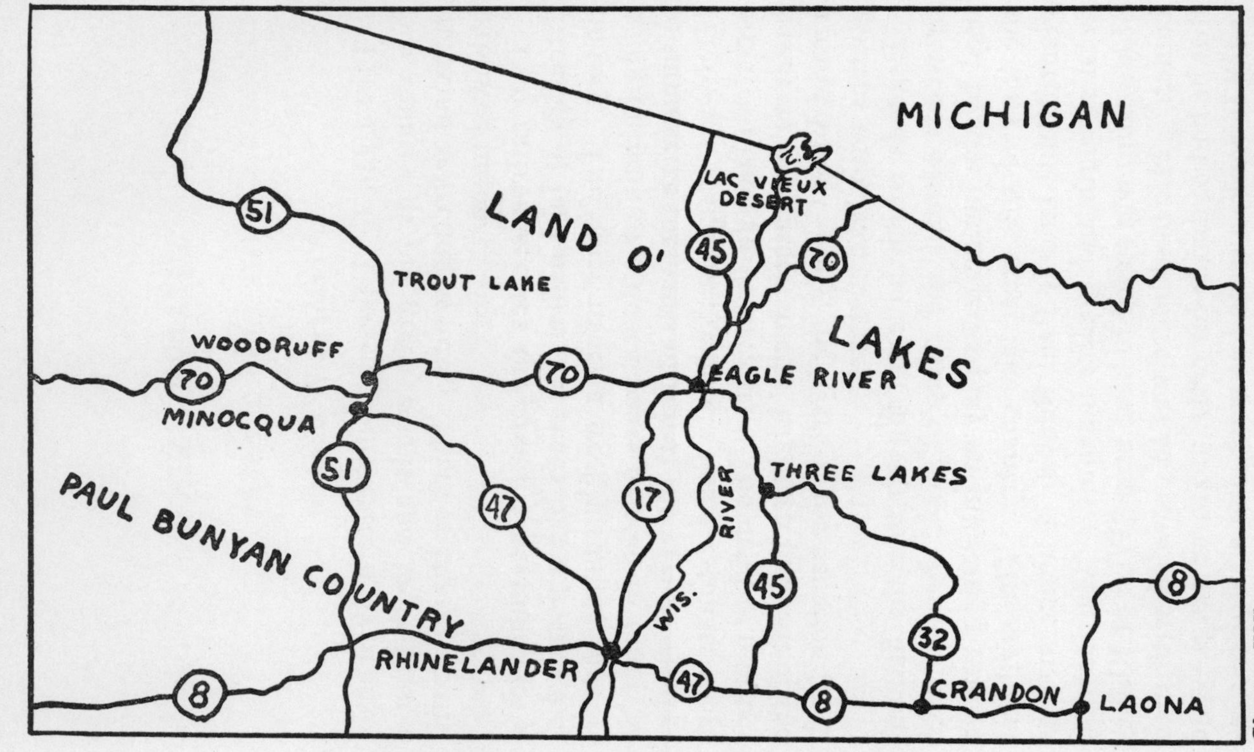

Chapter XIX

THE LAND O' LAKES
NORTHERN WISCONSIN

CHAPTER XIX

THE LAND O' LAKES

Northern Wisconsin

THE Land O' Lakes in Northeastern Wisconsin is a country of big green woods and more than a thousand reflecting waters. There is charm in this hallowed union.

Two railroads enter the area. One publishes a directory of lake names that reads like a pocket dictionary. The other issues a weekly summer advertising bulletin of a dozen pages printed in fine type to summarize the hauls of fish at the various resorts. Highways reach everywhere. Some estimate there are 1,500 lakes in this region. The definite number has never been ascertained. Eighteen per cent of the area of Vilas County, the heart of the vacation land, glistens with lake surfaces.

Legends which have sprung up like the flaming fireweeds around the ruins of cook shanties once used by the lumberjacks play an interesting role in the story of this great lake country. The mythical giant of this land is Paul Bunyan, a lumberman of great strength and greater ingenuity. The location of his camp was stated to have been "West of Rhinelander." His bunkhouse was so crowded with men that he had to divide his crew into three gangs,—one going to work, a second at work, and a third returning from work. But even with this crew, so the stories are told, Bunyan would never have been able to complete his lumbering operations without a huge blue ox, "Babe," an animal with the strength of nine horses, and the weight of 10,000 pounds.

"With the ox Paul dragged a whole house up a hill, then he dragged the cellar up after it," writes Charles E. Brown in his collection of folk tales about Paul Bunyan.[46] "Sometimes the ox slipped in behind the crew, drank the water in the river and left the drive high and dry. Some of the lakes in Wisconsin and Minnesota are in holes made by his feet."

Diligent inquiries and researches of old legends fail to disclose that Paul Bunyan ever attended the University of Wisconsin at Madison. However, a room in the new Memorial Union building has been reserved and dedicated to his memory. Its walls are adorned with maps of the Bunyan logging country of Northern Wisconsin, an enlarged colored representation of the "Blue Ox," and fantastic paintings depicting renowned achievements of the mythical hero. A descendant of one of Paul's "flunkies" acts as waiter, guide, and room attendant. For tourist attention it closely rivals the "throne room" in the State Capitol.

Other legends still repeated by the old lumberjacks, who have since retired to the clearings to become farmers in northern Wisconsin, have become so fantastic as to attribute this myriad of lakes to

[46] Brown, Charles E., "Paul Bunyan Tales," Madison. Wis., 1927. Published by the University of Wisconsin.

splashes made from the Wisconsin River when Paul Bunyan drove the Blue Ox out of the country for lumber operations farther west. And over the door of many a home and resort hangs a huge iron shoe which the owner claims was worn by "Babe" and found when clearing the land after Paul Bunyan's ox had departed.

Once the lumberman's Eden, this rich upland is now teeming with fine farms. An authentic four-man logging camp, named after Paul Bunyan, has been erected in Carson Park on Half Moon Lake at Eau Claire, Wisconsin, to house a museum collection of relics of early lumbering days. Mythical implements used by the fabled lumberman are exhibited. The camp, constructed of white and Norway pine logs, includes cook shanty, bunkhouse, stable, and blacksmith shop. Bunyan's rollicking hospitality abounds.

Westward of the lake region is the beautiful upland between the sources of the Wisconsin and the Chippewa Rivers, where the waters of the state gather power momentum. Near Chippewa Falls is the famous Wissota dam, an outstanding engineering achievement. It supplies electricity to two states.

One story of this section lives on through the generations. Within this region, on the upper Flambeau, "Old Abe," Wisconsin's famous Civil War eagle, was captured by an Indian. The bird's feats of heroism makc a bedtime story for children worth repeating. After capture, it was sold at Jim Falls to an Eau Claire soldier, then helping to organize the Eighth Wisconsin Infantry, later known as the Eagle Regiment. "Old Abe" was carried through seventeen Southern battles. Screaming, he flew over the Confederate lines. After the War the bird was exhibited at all reunions. The sale of pictures brought in a revenue of $16,000.00. P. T. Barnum offered $25,000.00 for the regimental mascot to exhibit with Jumbo. There has probably been no more celebrated bird in history.[47] A monument to the eagle is planned at Island Lake, near where the capture occurred.

Four large rivers—the Flambeau, Manitowish, Tomahawk and Wisconsin—with a score of smaller streams derive in the Land o' Lakes their source of water supply.[48] Traffic officials estimate more than four million tourists come to Wisconsin annually and that the great majority of these are bent on a visit to the lake country.

Some groups of lakes appear on the map like blotches of scattered blue—the Three Lakes waters, near Three Lakes; the Eagle River Chain, near Eagle River; the Turtle waters, near Winchester; and the Manitowish waters, near Manitowish. It is hazardous to mention lake names, when there are so many. But some have such individuality—Tomahawk, Trout, Fence, Spider, Wild Cat, Star, Crawl-

[47] "Old Abe" became an attraction at the State Capitol, where death occurred in 1881. As a little girl, Jane Addams of Hull House fame made a trip from her home near Freeport, Illinois, to Madison, to see the bird. Addams, Jane, "Twenty Years at Hull House," pp. 27-29.

[48] Veatch, Byron E., "My River," a classic description of the Flambeau and of the lake region.

ing Stone, Big St. Germain, Plum, Crab, Presque Isle, Lake Katherine—"Queen of Waters," Minocqua, Arbor Vitae—I wish I could call the whole roll.

In this land of silence and shade, of blue waters and green pines, two distinct civilizations flourish together. Bits of yesterday still survive. The Lac du Flambeau Indian Reservation lies south of the Manitowish waters. On the shores of Lake Vieux Desert,[49] a little Indian village stands on ground deeded by the United States Government to the chief of the Chippewas. Seven reservations, five in the northern section, give Wisconsin an Indian population of 10,000, the largest number in a single state east of the Mississippi. South of the lake country, near Gresham, are a few descendants of a tribe made famous in literature by James Fennimore Cooper in "The Last of the Mohicans."[50] Most of the Indians in the Land o' Lakes are members of the Chippewa bands. They make their living in summer picking blueberries, which flourish in the lowlands, and in winter by hunting and trapping in the labyrinths of the deep forests.

Sixty miles above Wausau on our way to the glacier-plowed lake country we turned off the main highway to visit the tuberculosis convalescent camp of the State of Wisconsin and the American Legion Park and Forest Preserve on Tomahawk Lake. Each

[49] "Katakitakon," Wis. Historical Collections, Vol. XIX, p. 187.
[50] Milwaukee Journal, June 24, 1929; See Chapter 4, "The Last of the Mohicans," Schafer, Joseph, "The Winnebago-Horicon Marsh," (Madison, Wis., 1937), pp. 58-76.

is located on state-owned lands in a sylvan wilderness.

Tomahawk Lake State Camp is the only institution of its peculiar kind in the world. Astonishing results in rehabilitation have been attained, measured by its history of service and treatment. Subsequent breakdowns have been held to a minimum and the life span of former tuberculosis patients lengthened. Ninety-one and six-tenths per cent of its graduates are living, and able to work at their former occupations. When one sees the charming environment under which tuberculosis patients and suffering service men live, there is little wonder that the proportion of successful recoveries has been so large. The wilderness, rough and harsh, pungent and exhilarating, has a charm more potent in healing influence than the smelly halls of imposing hospitals.

The American Legion area contains approximately 36,000 acres and is primarily valuable as a forest. Trails are being cut through the tangle of vine and thicket to connect with Northern Forest Park in Vilas County. Nature-lovers go here for a chance to camp in the woods and on lakes seldom visited. From an observation tower a view of several lakes and a billow of gorgeous verdure greet the onlooker—woods and waters everywhere. It is a cup of sylvan sweetness with no bitter dregs in the last sip.

Not knowing where our road to adventure might lead, except that it went northward, we came across this welcome sign:

TO
MINOCQUA, ISLAND CITY, HUB OF THE LAND O' LAKES

In this direction we turned our car.

Autumn had arrived. A curtain of hazy blue hung over the landscape and draped thinly the distant forest. The woodlands were daubed in a variety of colors. Jack Frost had dipped his paint brush in the sere and mellow tints of early fall and transformed the hardwoods into a marvel of hues. The lemon and gold of the maples blended with the russet and the deep scarlet of the oaks. When this setting is found with a few somber green pines standing out as a background, a picture is presented worthy of the artistry of God.

Minocqua! What a charm of a small city! The road that winds its way about Lake Kewaguesaga is unforgettable. The city is an outfitter's emporium—boats, canoes, fishing tackle. Men of wealth in khaki hustle about the streets anxious to get somewhere. There are long lines of empty sleepers on the railroad siding. It is but a night's trip from Chicago. Today was one of the last of the tourist's season. Next week when the gusts of cold wind come down from the north and the leaves begin to fall, the streets will be nearly deserted.

"Where shall we go now?" asked my companion.

"You name the place and I will take you," I responded. "Which shall it be—Boulder Junction, Hazelhurst, Sayner, Star Lake, Arbor Vitae, Manitowish, Three Lakes, Rhinelander, Mercer, Eagle River, Trout Lake—?"

"Aren't you out of breath?" he interrupted, looking up from a map, bewildered by the names. And then,—

"What about Trout Lake?"

"That's the headquarters for both the State's forestry service and of Northern Forest State Park, a timbered area of 100,000 acres."

"Let's go there first," came the request; "all the other places afterwards."

So we drove up a sandy road that took us far into the deep woods. Other shaded roads went to other places.

Trout Lake, centrally located in Northern Forest State Park, is one of the deepest waters in the State. On its north shore are the forestry headquarters. The state forest lands are chiefly in Vilas, Oneida, and Iron counties, where they are fairly well blocked, facilitating their protection and administration. The headquarters is the center of a telephone network spread over the area to detect fires. Men in steel lookout towers erected on high points watch all day and report any suspicious smoke with its location. A ranger and his crew are notified to take care of the fire.

Within this vast area, the state in 1925 set apart as a park an area of state-owned lands sixteen miles long and nine miles wide. Singularly enough, some of the lands were set aside for park purposes in 1878, but the legislature 29 years later repealed the law. Then after the big pines had been cut the state purchased back the denuded lands. A second crop of trees now covers the area.

The State of Minnesota has a park of 33,000 acres composed of similar country at Lake Itasca, the headwaters of the Mississippi River. The Wisconsin area, with forty-two lakes within its borders, is the center of the "Land o' Lakes."

Unusual interest is attached to this region because the state game refuge and the state forestry nursery are both located within the park confines.

Through the establishment of the state forestry nursery on Trout Lake, where the headquarters lodges are located, Wisconsin has demonstrated the feasibility of planting forests of trees. This nursery, established in 1911, contains seven acres of land on which tree seeds are planted and the seedlings transplanted after three or four years of growth. At a distance the beds of growing trees resemble an onion garden. More than 3,000 acres within the proposed park area have been planted to these seedlings. Several million seedlings are produced and planted by this nursery each spring and fall. A large tract of land at Nelson Dewey Park, at the confluence of the Wisconsin and Mississippi Rivers in Grant County, also was planted to these trees. So successful has been the experiment that the state now utilizes prison labor in camps in northern Wisconsin to carry forward reforestation on an extensive scale.

Game is especially plentiful within the Northern Forest park area. Deer, beaver, partridge, prairie chickens, ducks and all other forms of wild life common to northern Wisconsin, are to be found there. The lake teems with bass, pike, muskellunge, trout, and many other kinds of fish. Two branches of the Manitowish River cross the park borders. Some of the best tracts of virgin timber in northern Wisconsin are to be found on this land.

In the waters of Trout Lake, Dr. E. A. Birge, president emeritus of the University of Wisconsin, with other faculty co-workers is carrying on experiments in the feeding of fish that have attracted the attention of scientists of France, Germany and England. An eminent zoölogist from Germany was at Trout Lake at the time of our visit.

"Some years ago agricultural chemists made studies of the state's soils to determine their suitability for raising certain crops," said Dr. Birge. "We are doing much the same thing with the lakes. We hope to be able to determine how many fish and of what kind a lake with certain feeding grounds should raise. If we are able to answer this question the propagation of fish for all the lakes will be accomplished much earlier than can be done by present methods."

There are few farms along the roads in the Land o' Lakes. At almost every turn a lake is to be seen, its shining face peeping between the trees and under the canopy of heavy foliage like the trailing arbutus from under the last banks of snow in early spring. Under the trees and in secluded places the luscious blueberry is plentiful in mid-summer.

PINE-FRINGED LAKE NEBAGAMON IN DOUGLAS COUNTY.

CITY DWELLERS DREAM OF RETREATS LIKE THIS CABIN IN WISCONSIN'S NORTH WOODS.

FROM THE DIVIDE IN ASHLAND COUNTY, WATERS FLOW TO THE MISSISSIPPI AND THE ST. LAWRENCE RIVERS.

'IDS OF THE BAD RIVER,
.BOVE COPPER FALLS.

COPPER FALLS HAS OFTEN BEEN COMPARED TO THE WORLD FAMOUS TIVOLI, NEAR ROME, ITALY.

WHERE THE FALLS OF GITCHEE MONIDO, PATTISON PARK, LEAP 165 FEET TO BREAK IN A RAINBOW SPRAY.

THE GORGE BELOW COPPER FALLS, NEAR MELLEN.

THE IRON ORE DOCKS AT SUPERIOR ARE THE LARGEST IN THE WORLD.

BLACK GABBRO FROM THIS QUARRY NEAR MELLEN IS USED TO ADORN PUBLIC BUILDINGS THROUGHOUT THE COUNTRY.

TYLER FALLS, ONE OF THE TWIN FALLS NEAR MELLEN.

CEDAR LODGE, THE BUNGALOW ON THE BRULE RIVER WHERE PRESIDENT COOLIDGE SPENT A SUMMER.

THE MONTREAL RIVER, WHICH EMPTIES INTO LAKE SUPERIOR, IS A NATURAL BOUNDARY BETWEEN WISCONSIN AND THE UPPER PENINSULA OF MICHIGAN.

Under environment like this, days were spent in the lake country. The wind over waters breathes a peculiar freshness. Each lake has a temperament and a character of its own. Its mood changes with the seasons. Some lakes are smiling, others frown deep and sullen. With a dance of light on the surfaces, all are merry. The lakes of northern Wisconsin are as capricious as the clouds above.

Already the beavers were at their harvest. These little animals of the north woods fall great trees in the direction desired with the precision of a seasoned lumberjack. They trim the trees of their branches, build their houses on the edge of the stream, and sink the green brush under water for a winter's food supply. The log itself is cut into short lengths and then rolled or pushed into the water where transportation becomes easy.

Sometimes the beavers become such a menace, flooding roads and railroad tracks, that their homes must be blasted by conservation wardens. But it will be a day of disappointment to lovers of the stream if the animal is ever exterminated. The houses of brush and log they build are models of architecture and their housekeeping immaculate.

Once while we were waiting for the beaver to appear, a deer bounded across the clearing. Scenting our presence, he gave a snort as clarion as the horn of an English huntsman. A flash of white tail was all that we saw. When the woods become quiet, other animals show their faces. Nature requires time and patience of those who would learn her lessons. The forest teems with new wonders each day. One visit to the Land o' Lakes is contagious. The same vacationers return year after year. Landing fields welcome wealthy Chicagoans flying their own planes. Vacationers remember the long tramp in the Big Woods, the gamey fight it took to land the muskellunge, the tender breezes and cool shades of summer, the firelight comforts of the log cabin, and the balsam-scented atmosphere that settles down upon this land of forest when the night is still.

Perhaps, if they awake and listen they will hear the laugh of the loon on some nearby lake, the lonely hoot of the owl, or the mournful call of the whip-poor-will. For wild life makes its home in this land of trees and waters.

The seasons advance with determination in northern Wisconsin. As we started for home, a gust of wind blew shrivelled leaves across the road. A white birch shook its thin garment in the breeze. The dark pine tree sang a dirge to the departed summer. Soon the Land o' Lakes will be locked in the security of ice and snow to await a glorious springtime.

Minocqua in northern Wisconsin is the hub of the Land O' Lakes Country. The southern terminus is in the vicinity of Rhinelander, the northern terminus at Lac Vieux Desert, and the western terminus at Hurley. Minocqua is one hundred seventy-four miles from Superior, one hundred four miles from Ashland, two hundred thirty miles from St. Paul, eighty miles from Wausau, one hundred twenty-eight miles from Wisconsin Rapids, two hundred twenty-five miles from Madison, two hundred seventy miles from Milwaukee, one hundred fifty-five miles from Green Bay. U. S. Highway 51 passes through the Land O' Lakes Country.

FALLING WATERS

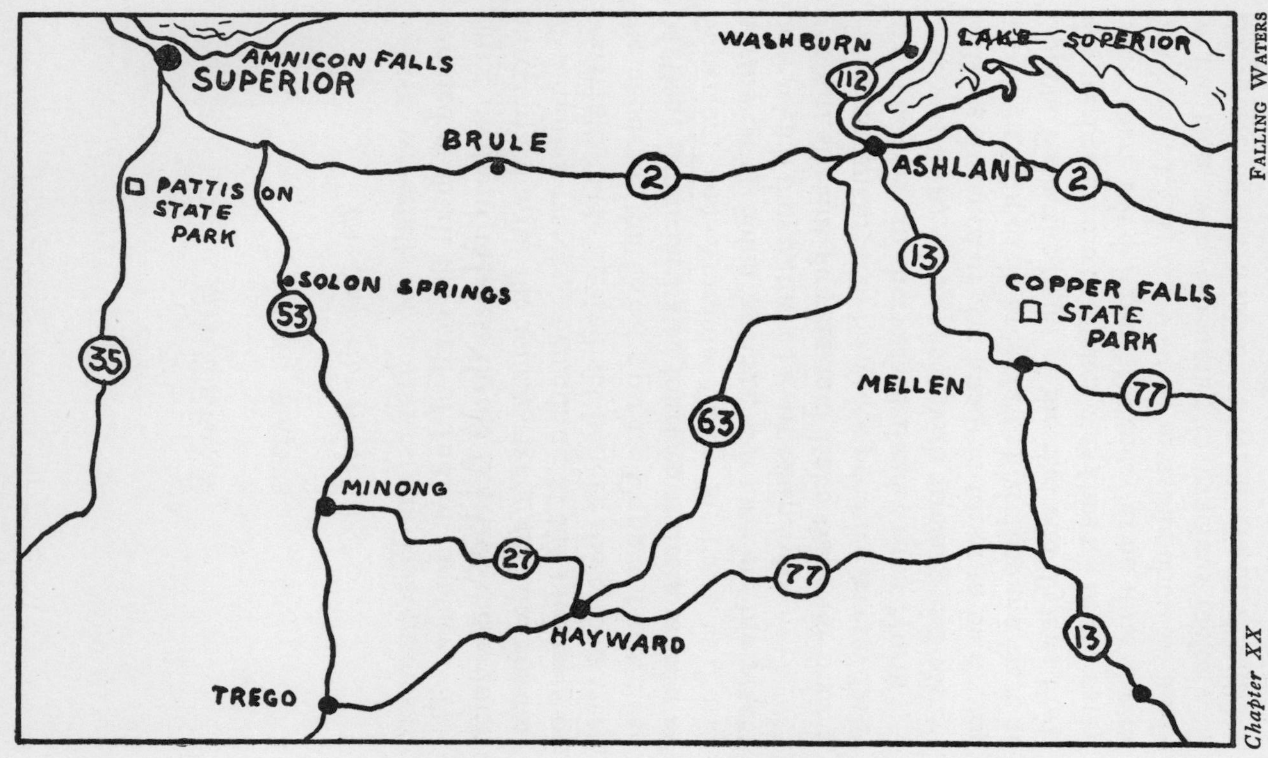

Chapter XX

FALLING WATERS
THE SUPERIOR WATERSHED

CHAPTER XX

FALLING WATERS

The Superior Watershed

THE waterfalls of northwestern Wisconsin are haunted with all the spell of Indian romance. The spirit of the wilderness in the heart of the redman harmonized with the lonely rivers and the rhythm of tumbling waters. Something in the solemnity of waterfalls made the Indians believe these spots were the abode of the Great Spirit. Copper Falls, near Mellen; Amnicon Falls, fourteen miles southeast of Superior; and Manitou Falls, in Pattison Park, northwest of Solon Springs, were among the places near which they gathered to worship.

Short streams flowing into Lake Superior over a sharp embankment of trap rock produce several dashing spectacles in the vacationland of the North.

It was to be a day spent with streams and waterfalls—a distance of one hundred miles to be driven—so we ate an early breakfast at Mellen and were at Copper Falls, the twins of the Bad and Tyler's Fork Rivers, before the caretaker was about. In the early hours there are delights of scenery at no time else to be observed. At our visit an invisible choir of birds in the trees was responding in gracious melody to the music of the waters. A freshness of the air, a subdued light which fell upon the fretting waters, and the peace of seclusion were there.

What a rest and happiness come when one sits down to watch these rolling, tumbling waters for an hour!

Finally the tramp of other visitors broke the spell. A narrow path leads up a steep embankment, and, as the ascent was made, the roar of the falls became more and more distinct.

Copper Falls on the Bad River plunges forty feet over an escarpment. Down a few rods coming from another direction is Tyler's Falls, the waters from its cascades joining at the base. Tyler's Falls has a thirty-foot plunge.

The stream-cut gorges between the two falls and below the juncture, formed in post-glacial time, are deep and steep-sided. At places the lower gorge is two hundred feet high, and in the noon day the sun lights up the dark places in hues of red and green. Then the waters appear visible in eddies of foam.

The twin falls are well named. The water is a deep coppery color and flows over jagged Keweenawan trap rock surfaces. Dense growths of trees—pine, aspen and ironwood—on the high embankments seem to hem in the sound until the visitor is close. Then, as the eminences on the bank are reached, the noise bursts lustily upon the air. There is such tremendous force back of the waters at either of the falls that the whole valley is tossed with spray. The beauty of the Copper Falls scenery has often been compared to the world famous Tivoli, near Rome. Some who have seen the two prefer the grandeur of the Wisconsin offering.

At the junction of the two rivers, on an island of stone, two pine trees have held root, probably for a century, as if defending a fort. They tower high above the other trees, doubtless due to the abundance of water for the roots. This is a spectacle of imposing distinction.

Copper Falls must have been a favorite meeting place for the Indians during the decades. Flint arrow-heads and pieces of fashioned copper have been found in the immediate vicinity. For years hydro-electric interests desired to harness the falls. In the autumn of 1929, however, the state purchased 520 acres of the surrounding property and has turned it into a park.

Before leaving the falls I found that it possessed advantages other than beauty. Black gabbro has been brought to the surface. This beautiful granite, previously found only in the depths of the Swiss Alps, was discovered some years ago by a Swiss stoneworker, Julius Effenberger, while on a visit. The wearing away of the pre-historic mountains of Wisconsin into the Penokee hills of the present day has exposed this molten ledge. Gabbro is an Italian word applied to igneous rock. The rock is very dense, weighing about 210 pounds to the cubic foot, or about fifty pounds more than ordinary granite. It is coal black except for occasional patches of white quartz which serve to enhance the beauty of the polished stone. The rock is so hard that it resists the erosion of wind and water. This Wisconsin product has been used to adorn many public buildings throughout the country.

"We have such an early start, can we not stop at the Brule for a visit to Cedar Lodge where President and Mrs. Calvin Coolidge spent the summer of 1928?" urged my companion.

Secretly I had planned for this stop but wanted it for a surprise. I had been there first in the summer of 1923 when its owner, the late Henry Clay Pierce, the millionaire oil man of St. Louis, had moved a whole retinue of employes, cooks, telegraph operators and physicians, to Winnebayou. He had brought them along to make it possible to have the pleasures of a northern Wisconsin vacation and still be in touch with Wall Street. I remained silent, hoping that I could drive into the estate without making any promise.

"It's only sixty miles and we can be there in another hour," was urged when I gave no answer.

"What shall we do, fish trout in the incomparable Brule and give up the remainder of the trip?"

"No! No! It will only be for an hour. We can see it all."

So I consented.

There are pioneer scenes along the highway. Only in recent years has northern Wisconsin been invaded by the settler. There are little clearings; acres of pine stumps that stand as cemeteries to a forest wasted by lumber barons, and an effort at farming and dairying that makes one feel proud of the courage and persistence of the homesteader.

Turning off the highway from Brule, we traveled a country road for four miles, then three miles down a narrow lumber road into the Brule valley to the entrance of the Pierce estate. The way was barren and bleak. Some of the hillsides had been denuded by axe, others had been ravaged by forest fires.

All was different inside the gates, opened for us only by special permission. Virgin timber now stalks the roadway. The brush has been touched only in the lodge clearing. Within the heart of the forest is a retreat with seventeen buildings of log, bark and stone blended into the green margin of the forest.

The estate comprises thousands of acres and embraces seven miles of the Brule. The main lodge is octagonal in design and covered with cedar bark. This was the home of the President and his immediate family. It occupies an acre island reached by a rustic footbridge. The dining halls are on the banks of the river opposite.

Broad cushioned walks of pine needles on a gravel base with a border of cedar logs wind all about the inhabited portion of the estate. They pass century-old trees—two and three feet in diameter—scarred by the hatchets of Indians, who by that means obtained pitch to calk their canoes. Bears and deer, and an abundance of other wild life, roam the forested region.

The Brule River's history dates back to 1680 when Daniel Greysolon Sieur du Lhut came along the shores of Lake Superior, seeking a water route to the Mississippi Valley.[51] Du Lhut poled his boats up the Brule River, along what was afterwards the President's vacation lands, and abandoned them in the swamplands at its source. Crossing over-land, he reached Upper St. Croix Lake caressing beautiful Crownhart Island opposite the present Solon Springs, and then followed the St. Croix River to the Mississippi—a discovery that wrote his name in history. School children raised funds to erect this tablet where U. S. Highway 2 crosses the Brule River near the Town of Brule:

IN JUNE AND JULY 1680
DANIEL GREYSOLON SIEUR DULHUT
"GENTLEMAN OF THE KING'S GUARD"
SOLDIER, EXPLORER, TRADER, AND GOVERNOR
ACCOMPANIED BY FOUR FRENCHMEN
LAMAITRE, BELLEGRADE, MASSON, AND PEPIN,
PASSED UP THE BRULE RIVER, CROSSED BY
PORTAGE TO THE ST. CROIX RIVER THEN
DOWN TO THE MISSISSIPPI.
THESE WERE THE FIRST WHITE MEN TO USE
THE BRULE-ST. CROIX ROUTE, WHICH WAS
THEN FORTIFIED AND AFTERWARDS USED BY
THE FRENCH FOR MANY YEARS.

A CONTEMPORARY SAID OF DULHUT, "HE FEARED NOT DEATH, ONLY COWARDICE AND DISHONOR."

It happens that this country is also the fabled land of Hiawatha and Old Nokomis, whose wigwam is supposed to have stood on the shores of Gitchee Gumee—Lake Superior—near where the present Brule enters.[52]

[51] Legler, Henry, "Leading Events in Wisconsin History," p. 79; Parkman, Francis, "La Salle and the Discovery of the Great West," pp. 274-277.

[52] Longfellow, Henry W., Works, Vol. VI, p. 197.

"On the shores of Gitchee Gumee,
Of the shining big sea-water,
Stood Nokomis, the old woman,
Pointing with her finger westward,
O'er the water pointing westward,
To the purple clouds of sunset."

"The winds whisper here all the time," remarked my companion as we rested and watched the stream ripple by. The waters are so clear that we could see fish dart and we could count pebbles at a depth.

"It's time to go if we are to have a trout dinner at Brule," he finally observed, and we were off in a jiffy.

Early in the afternoon we came to Amnicon Falls, a beautiful spot now included in James Bardon Park. Down a stairstep carved in living stone, the Amnicon River spills a silvery spray. The volume of water is small, but the sight of the white mist of many hues above a channel of immutable rocks pleases the eye and stirs the imagination.

"As you stand there, speak only to the waters," —for this is a pageant of the geological drama of ages.

So much time had been spent along the way that we were forced to take the shortest route over country roads to see the mysterious Manitou Falls in Pattison Park before nightfall. Approaching from the south we saw first the Little Manitou, a glorious introduction to Gitchee Monido—"Falls of the Great Spirit"—the chief attraction. Big Manitou has a sheer drop of 165 feet and resembles the milky falls along the Columbia Highway out of Portland.

Out of the thundering waters came the voices which held the Indians in superstitious awe. No altar of Nature could have a more artful setting to inspire its visitors with veneration. Against the spell cast by such natural wonders the early missionaries among the Indians had to contend. Father Claude Allouez, the first evangelist in this community, recorded his disappointments with their forms of worship.

"There is here," he says, "a false and abominable religion, resembling in many respects the faiths of some of the ancient Pagans. The Savages of these regions recognize no sovereign master of Heaven and Earth, but believe there are many genii—some of which are beneficent, as the Sun, the Moon, the Lake, Rivers, and Woods; others malevolent, as the adder, the dragon, cold and storms. And, in general, whatever seems to them either helpful or hurtful they call a Manitou, and pay it the worship and veneration which we render only to the true God.

"These divinities they invoke whenever they go out hunting, fishing, to war, or on a journey—offering them sacrifice, with ceremonies appropriate only for Sacrificial priests." [53]

Waters of the Black River approaching the falls seem to sense the compelling mystery of the fearful plunge and hurry faster as each step of the precipice

[53] From "The Jesuit Relations of 1666-67," Wisconsin Historical Collections, Vol. XVI., pp. 50-51.

is neared. I edged along the sharp, stony course interested in the nervous eagerness of the stream. On the crest of the brink the waters roll and toss but momentarily are transformed into a white spray that turns more vaporous down the glide. The receiving basin seethes and foams like a boiling caldron.

The gorge below is very narrow for a short distance and the walls are twisted forms indicating volcanic origin.

Extensive reforestation plans are being carried on in the park area. But under the tall pines around the falls, once lighted by the glare of the ghostly, sacrificial fires of the Indians, are favorite places to lounge and listen to the ceaseless voices.

Night came all too soon—dark and menacing. Above the hush of the threatening storm the falls roared defiance to all unbelievers.

The Superior Watershed is in the northwestern part of the state. Copper Falls is at Mellen. Manitou Falls is at Pattison State Park, eighteen miles south of Superior, and Amnicon Falls is ten miles from Superior. Mellen is twenty-seven miles south of Ashland on State Trunk Highway 13. Manitou Falls is on Trunk Highway 35, eighteen miles south of Superior. The Brule where President Coolidge vacationed is on U. S. Highway 2 from Superior to Ashland.

LOST MATTERHORNS

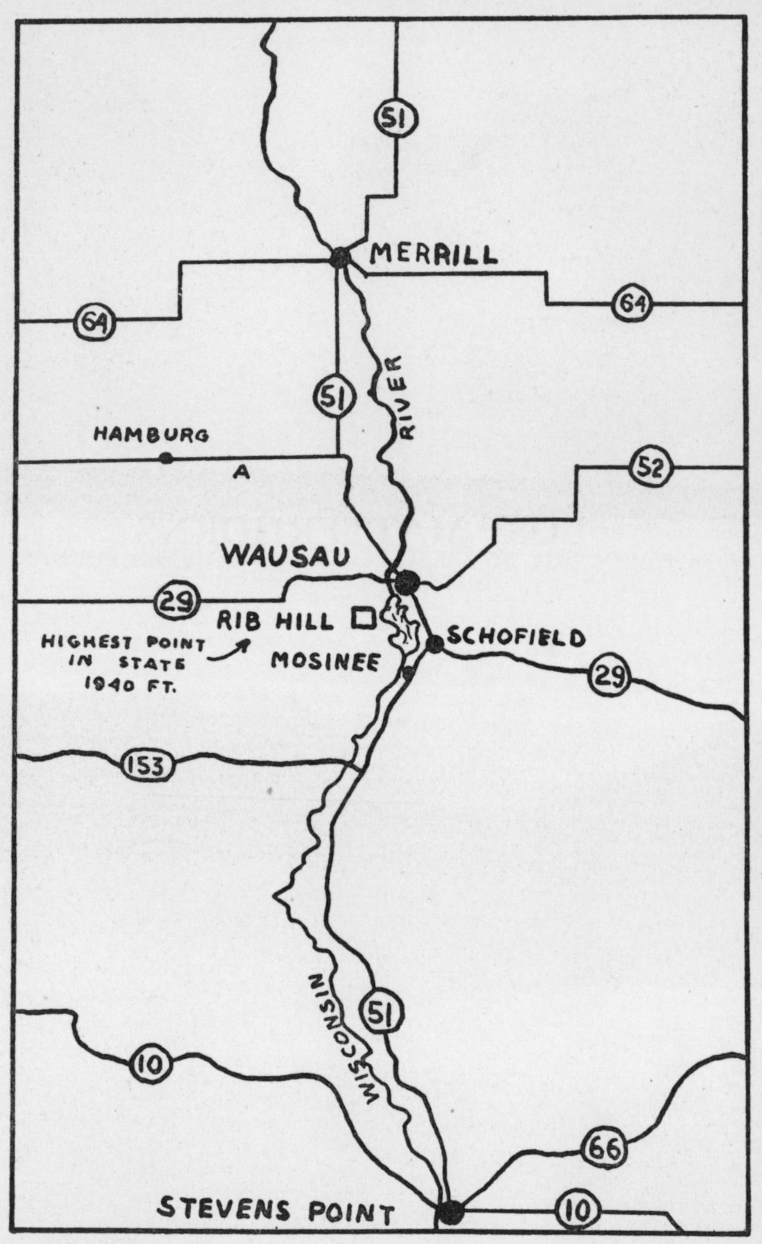

Chapter XXI

LOST MATTERHORNS
WAUSAU HIGHLAND

TO SPORTSMEN, THE NAMEKAGON RIVER, WASHBURN COUNTY, CONNOTES GOOD FISHING.

ANOTHER BECKONING RIVER OF WASHBURN COUNTY IS THE SIOUX.

GORGE OF THE BAD RIVER BELOW TYLER FALLS.

ꞁONG THE TRAIL
ꞁ RIB HILL.

ROCKS HAVE BEEN SHAKEN TO SHARDS ON THE TOP OF RIB HILL.

RIB HILL, WAUSAU, BASKS IN THE AFTERNOON SUNLIGHT.

CAPITOL SET LIKE A DIADEM—FROM ACROSS LAKE MONONA.

UNIVERSITY ARBORETUM IS RAPIDLY DEVELOPING INTO A NATURE WONDERLAND.

PRINCIPAL INDIAN MOUNDS IN THE FOUR LAKES COUNTRY ARE MARKED.

VIEW OF CAPITOL FROM LINCOLN TERRACE.

THE RARE-TINTED LOTUS FLOWER GROWS IN PROFUSION IN UNIVERSITY BAY.

AERIAL VIEW OF GOVERNOR'S ISLAND, LAKE MENDOTA.

CHAPTER XXI

LOST MATTERHORNS

Wausau Highland

RIB HILL lifts its head above the Lake Superior highland, a remnant of the "lost mountains of Wisconsin." Once it was the Matterhorn of a group of peaks similar to those of the Alps.

Now, after a hundred million years of wearing and wasting from wind and rain, followed by centuries of deluge in the sea, Rib Hill emerges still proud as the highest point in the state. Traveling up the Wisconsin River Valley we caught our first glimpse of the hill at Rothschild. Approaching Wausau, the eminence loomed nearby in magnitude.

Before leaving for the three-mile trip to the base of Rib Hill, I took time to consult some geological maps and a geography of Wisconsin which I had brought along. Discovery was soon made that northern Wisconsin is a peneplain—a region which formerly was rugged and mountainous but now worn down to a level. Where once stood sister peaks there stand fragments in the form of the monadnocks of Powers Bluff in Wood County, Mount Thunder and Mount McCalsin in Marinette County, and the Penokee range, near Hurley.

"The wearing down has been accomplished in a long period of time by the erosive action of stream and weather," my book on geography explained. "The topography and rock structures found in northern Wisconsin are exactly the same kind that would be revealed if the Alps or Rocky Mountains were planed across so that their basement portion were exposed."[54]

Upon nearing the road of ascent, one sees enormous blocks of gray rock on the hillside. One begins to feel the spirit of the long past through which this transformation has come. The stony peak, studded with little groves and clumps of shrubbery, is the core of a mountain. Some of the scars on its face are patches where miners once prospected for gold.

"How do people know this was once a great mountain?" asked my companion as we hurried along.

"I can only answer from what I have read in the geography," I responded. "Geologists measure the age of the earth by a study of the folds in rocks, just as the woodsman learns the age of a tree from its annual rings. The study of this part of Wisconsin reveals Rib Hill to be of granite. According to geologists, the existence of this rock pile, stubbornly resisting the elements, indicates that the earth and disintegrated rock which once clung to its sides have been washed down.[55] That took untold ages. Now hard rocks like granite are formed only by deep-seated cooling of molten masses, often beneath the arch of a lofty mountain. That is the principal reason for the belief that this was once a towering peak.

[54] Martin, Lawrence, "Geography of Wisconsin," p. 30.
[55] Martin, Ibid, 347.

"Scientists, moreover, believe this hill to be one of the oldest in the world. Fossils found in the overlying sedimentary rocks show that after it had been wasted away by erosion it was again dipped by some earth convulsion and left for long ages at the bottom of a sea. The time of this last salt water bath is estimated to be fifteen million years ago. Since then Wisconsin has been dry land."

So intent were we on discussing the age of the granite roof, which the glaciers swept around on their southern advance, that, before we were aware of it, we had begun to scale its heights by a new highway, only just completed by the state. Heretofore it had been impossible to reach the top of the hill except by a tedious climb over jagged rocks and precipices. The slopes rise at a ratio of from one thousand feet to one thousand two hundred feet to the mile. Automobiles go up on high.

Rib Hill is now a state park of 160 acres. Donated to the state by the Kiwanis Club of Wausau in the summer of 1924, it was not until six years after that improvements were started to render it accessible to the general public. The crest is 1,950 feet above sea level, 1,360 feet above the level of Lake Michigan, and 800 feet higher than the Wisconsin River at Wausau. It is three miles long and one mile wide, and is the most conspicuous landmark in the state.

Along the wild-wooded way rest old and venerable boulders, tossed topsy-turvy into their places. It is nearly two miles upgrade to one of the three parking places near the Queen's Chair. Short as is this road, its construction was a feat in roadmaking. Rocks had to be blasted to make room for the road. The cost of construction was nearly $30,000.

I must candidly admit that I may have missed some of the scenery on the way up, so great was our hurry to be on the peak at sunset. A large audience of sight-seers had arrived before us to witness one of Wisconsin's sublime spectacles—a sunset from Rib Hill. To those who dislike statistics of places, but appreciate atmosphere and stirring impressions, I recommend this vista.

It were as though the sun had paused a moment to flood the hill with a full mellow light. Then, as it disappeared, the slopes of green trees became darker, revealing below the ledge white birches and silver poplars, hiding the rugged barrenness. In the fall it must be a spot of immense coloring, for the western slope has second growth stands of golden maple, the northeastern ridge bears red oak, and flaming sumac and dogwood are present almost everywhere.

Some of the mammoth boulders on the crest have been shaken to shards, split and cracked as if the universe had been taxed to put them where they are. My companion climbed gracefully to the Queen's Chair, one of the crest's outstanding pinnacles, and took her place at the top of Wisconsin's world with the dignity of an Elizabethan.

Several trails lead from the summit to the deserted gold camps. Many years ago miners prospected these hills and found gold. But the pay dirt was so difficult to mine and of such a poor quality that the sites were abandoned. Visitors who stay on the hill long enough to learn of the placer mining take on a new interest. They search around hoping to find a nugget that will turn the stone ridge into another Sutter's California ranch.

But the pay dirt mined at the foot of this old mountain site today is of another quality. Beneath the rocky surface of this ridge lies one of the largest deposits of pure silicon in the world. The quartz, which is very dense and which shows little evidences of stratification, is loosened by blasting. Afterwards the rock is reduced to fifty-pound blocks and crushed and ground to a powder in abrasive mills at Wausau. Out of this is manufactured every year sandpaper which, if the sheets were placed end to end, would reach half way round the world. Filtration grits, silica cement, and carborundum are also produced.[56] Rib Mountain, or Rib Hill, as many people call it, is responsible for the industry locating in Wausau. The silica blasted out of the hill is ninety-nine per cent pure and requires little refining. The plant, which was built in 1898, is the only one of its kind in Wisconsin, and one of ten similar refineries in the United States.

On the summit of this old mountain we waited for hours to see the shadows fall, the distant places congregate in the gloaming, and the lights come out in a fifty-mile panorama. Far to the northward may

[56] Milwaukee Journal, Feb. 21, 1926, has a full description of the carborundum industry; for Story of Fromm Brothers' Silver Fox Farms, see Saturday Evening Post, Feb. 13, 1937; Readers Digest, July, 1937.

be seen the smoke from the village of Hamburg, where the four Fromm Brothers, largest breeders of silver foxes in the world, conduct their $10,000,000 business. This obscure hamlet is the silver fox capital of America.

The evening was one of peaceful calm, with not a cloud in the sky. The atmosphere, remarkably clear, reflected the site of far places on the skyline. One by one cities lighted up—Marshfield, Mosinee, Wausau, Merrill, and Rothschild. A thousand feet beneath us the meadows and fields had turned black and the hillsides looked gloomy in the approaching darkness. Now and then a flash on the waters reflected the course of the Wisconsin. It was a pleasure full of secret enjoyment and touched by the afterglow of contemplation.

When we left Wausau the next morning Rib Hill was sleeping under a coverlet of blue mist. It looked like a great monster out there across the plain, exciting a feeling of awe. While we watched, the sun touched the farms and dew-pearled foliage along the hill base, quickening the cool of the morning. Soon the whole low countryside shared in the adornment—except Rib Hill, which lay there quietly dreaming of ageless days in the centuries.

Rib Hill, the heart of the Wausau Highland, is three miles west of Wausau. U. S. Highway 51 from the southern state line north to Hurley passes through Wausau. Wausau is ninety-five miles from Green Bay, one hundred eight miles from Oshkosh, one hundred ninety miles from Milwaukee, one hundred fifty miles from Madison, two hundred two miles from St. Paul, and one hundred nine miles from Eau Claire.

FOUR LAKES SERENE AND FULL OF LIGHT

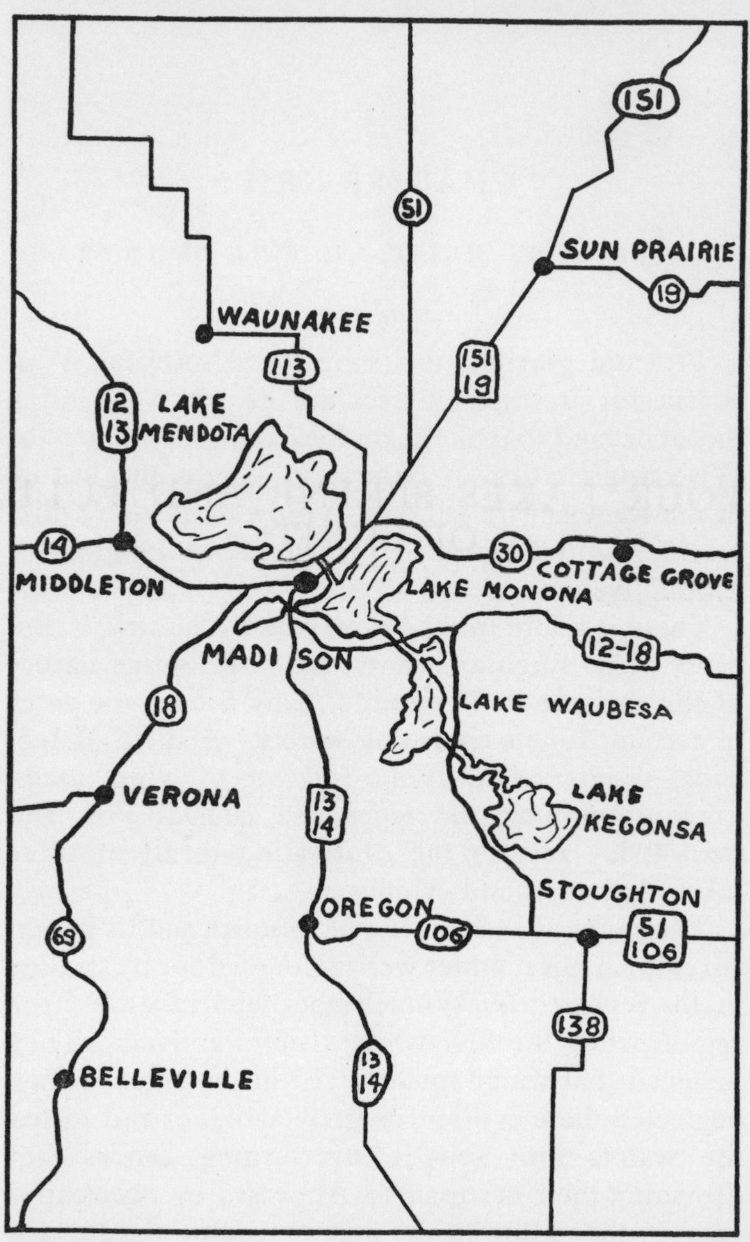

Chapter XXII

FOUR LAKES SERENE AND FULL OF LIGHT
MADISON

CHAPTER XXII

FOUR LAKES SERENE AND FULL OF LIGHT

Madison

THE old glacier must have loved southern Wisconsin for it tossed a necklace of lakes around a throat of land to make a site for Madison, the gem of Wisconsin's cities. Civilization caught the beauty of the scene and raised on this brow of earth a white marble Capitol, set like a diadem above the glory of shining waters.

There is a lure in the "Four Lakes Country." Because of its singular beauty, the imaginative nature of the early Indian conjured many a fantastic story to account for its charming waters. A skein of legends, as interesting as the folklore of white races, grew up around the tepee and council fire, and even today reveals the captivating thrall of these lakes that surround Madison.

The anger of Lake Mendota in storm and its peaceful calm in hot summer were accounted for by strange myths repeated by Winnebagoes who inhabited the region when the first white visitors arrived. They believed that water sprites lived in the lake. When neglected these evil spirits grew arrogant and tossed the waters into squalls, overturning canoes and drowning their occupants. Appeased by reverential respect, they allowed the lake to assume the surface of a mirror. Often the Indians scattered tobacco on the waters as a peace offering to the spirit. Then it was safe to go fishing. Many other legends about this lake exist. They show the myth-making power of a primitive people attempting to account for the bounteous wonders of Nature about them.

Lake Wingra, or Dead Lake, as it is sometimes called, received its pseudonym from the old tale that ancient settlers recount on winter evenings between sly sips of cider. Ordinarily this lake is not included in the chain but is in reality the fifth in the series. The story runs that when the last Indian left the shores of Lake Wingra, driven by the invasion of the white man, he prophesied that the lake would die, and return to the land of its fathers. Strange to tell, during the last half century the lake has, year by year, been slowly drying up. Each year it gets smaller and smaller, and there is now much dry land where once there was high water. It may be that the prophecy of the last Indian is coming to pass.

Back in the dark days when Columbus discovered America, the site of Madison was the home of Indians. Winnebago villages stood on the north shore of Lake Mendota, at Morris Park and Fox Bluff, and on Mendota Hospital grounds, and on Winnequah Heights, across Lake Monona. Upon the University grounds, on the shores of Lake Wingra and in many other park grounds of Madison are to be found some of the most unique Indian mounds in America—conical shaped burial mounds, bird mounds on University Hill; panther mounds on Lake

Mendota shore; ceremonial mounds on the eminence of Lake Wingra. These earth works are the relics of a teeming civilization that has departed.

"I can see fine buildings in many cities, but show me the famous Indian mounds," remarked the late Ambassador James Bryce of England on a visit to Madison. "I want to see the record of a civilization that has passed."

Some mythical spirit must have directed the Indian in scattering these emblems of a primitive art around the country of the four lakes. Through the inspiration of the Wisconsin State Historical Society many of these emblematic mounds have been preserved and now are marked by appropriate tablets of bronze. Two outstanding landmarks are to be found on Observatory Hill. These consist of effigy mounds representing a bird and a turtle.

During summer, the scene of the mounds becomes a lake shrine. From this height there is a commanding view of Lake Mendota, with Picnic Point in the foreground. In the words of Max O'Rell, "All Europe does not possess a spot of greater scenic beauty."

At the foot of the hill an Indian village site was located. One of the mounds of this group represented a turtle with two tails, an unusual item in southern Wisconsin.

Somehow primitive man of the Western world must have been in touch with the stories of the Bible. On the University grounds the fate of Lot's wife is depicted in Indian legend by a singular parallel. Some years ago the "Spirit Stone" of the Potawatomi

Indians was brought to Madison from northern Wisconsin. According to legend, there was an Indian who asked Manapus for a gift of everlasting life and was turned to stone by the Spirit as a punishment for his greed.

"Trail Trees" are still standing at many places in Wisconsin where Indian pathways crossed. Two of these native guide posts may still be seen in Madison,—one on the shores of Lake Wingra and the other, a two-century old hickory at the corner of Van Hise and Chestnut Streets overlooking Lake Mendota. The branches of "Trail Trees" are so bent while young as to indicate the directions of the trails. Their gnarled crooked arms still point the way as they were trained to do by Indians long since dead.

The whole region about Madison—the area of the four lakes—was called by the Indians "Taychopera." Traders and coureurs de bois seeking peltries from them doubtless visited Madison in the early days of the eighteenth century. They left, however, no record of their exploits. The first official notice of a white man to visit the site of Madison was in 1828, four years before the Black Hawk War. Whether the honor should go to Ebenezer Brigham or Jefferson Davis is a question. In 1829 came Jefferson Davis, then an army officer, later president of the Southern confederacy, stationed at Fort Winnebago (Portage). He tells in his memoirs of coming to the site of Madison and of seeing an Indian village on the height across the lake. He claimed to be the first man to visit the site, but a similar claim is made by Brigham.

The next visitors were those who, in the last Indian War east of the Mississippi River, chased Black Hawk westward over the present University campus. Aside from freeing the country from the domination of the red man, the Black Hawk War was not without other permanent results. Soldiers writing home told of the beauty and fertility of the country through which they had passed.

"The Four Lakes country is not fit for any civilized nation to inhabit," wrote an Illinois soldier after having passed that region during the Black Hawk War in 1832. "The lakes are the most beautiful bodies of water I have ever seen, and, if they were anywhere else than in the place they are, they would be considered among the wonders of the world, but it appears the Almighty intended this part of the country for the children of the forest."

Four years later a territorial legislature meeting at Belmont[57] in southern Wisconsin selected Madison, after some rather questionable legislative log-rolling, as the capital of the state. Surveyors in the spring of 1837 located the site of the State House on one hill, and the State University on another—sentinels of law and learning. Then the whole scene was a wilderness. What surveyors believed would be a job for a day or so, turned out to be a tedious

[57] The territorial capitol of 1836 and grounds have been preserved as a state park.

task owing to the isthmus shape of the locality, between Lakes Mendota and Monona. Beginning at the corners of the Capitol Park, an area of almost ten acres—four blocks square—radiating main thoroughfares that suggest Washington, D. C., were laid out with the avenues following the cardinal points of the compass.

The surveyors did more. They named the principal streets after most of the thirty-nine men who dared to sign the United States Constitution. The street parallel to the shore of Lake Mendota the surveyor named Langdon, after the New Hampshire delegate, who with Nicholas Gilman signed for his colony. The next street became Gilman; then Gorham and King of Massachusetts had streets christened in their memory. Southern delegates, Spaight, Pinckney, Rutledge, and Few, were remembered. The main thoroughfare running parallel to the two lakes and midway between them was called after George Washington, president of the Constitutional Convention. And Alexander Hamilton was recognized, with his name given to the main north and south highway through the town.

Few American cities have such a setting. Clasped by three lakes—Mendota, Monona and Wingra—the isthmus of land on which the city has been built poses like a queen on a throne. The Yahara River, a lazy-appearing stream in summer, not unlike the Avon, connects Mendota with Monona, and follows down to gather the waters of Waubesa and Kegonsa before joining the Rock River.

To preserve for posterity a bit of the pristine beauty surrounding Madison from the invasion of civilization, the late Michael B. Olbrich, a regent of the University of Wisconsin, secured the establishment of a nature reservation along the southern shores of Lake Wingra. The 1,000-acre University of Wisconsin Arboretum, Wild Life Refuge, and Forest Experimental Preserve constitutes a living testimonial to his vision and energy. Millions find in this natural landscape joy, happiness, education and recreation. As an outdoor laboratory for students, it is important in the University educational program. When fully developed, it will approach in beauty and usefulness the famous arboretum of Harvard University.

Even the pioneers were proud of the scenery around the four lakes. When the Centennial was held at Philadelphia in 1876, Madison was represented by two lake paintings, the work of the artist Thomas Moran. These gave the conception of beauty which inspired Henry W. Longfellow to write this poem found in all authorized editions of his works:

THE FOUR LAKES OF MADISON

Four limpid lakes, four Naiades
  Or sylvan deities are these,

In flowing robes of azure dressed;
Four lovely handmaids that uphold
Their shining mirrors rimmed with gold,
To the fair city of the West.

By day the coursers of the sun
Drink of these waters as they run
Their swift diurnal round on high;
By night the constellations glow
Far down the hollow deeps below,
And glimmer in another sky.

Fair lakes serene and full of light,
Fair town arrayed in robes of white,
How visionary ye appear!
All like a floating landscape seems
In cloudland or the land of dreams,
Bathed in a golden atmosphere.

Many are the noted visitors who have bestowed praise on the beauty of Madison and the lake country. Clark Howell said that "Nature has done everything possible for Madison," and Horace Greeley, the famous editor of the New York Tribune, pronounced Madison "the most magnificent site of any inland city I ever saw." William H. Allen observed that "Madison's beauty is the best instructor in landscape statesmanship I know," and the late United States Senator Moses E. Clapp of Minnesota remarked, "It is hard to speak of the beauties of Madison without being charged with

WORLD-FAMOUS FEDERAL FOREST PRODUCTS LABORATORY OVERLOOKS MENDOTA.

LEAVING THE UNIVERSITY, ONE PASSES BETWEEN RUSSIAN GOLDEN WILLOWS ON MENDOTA DRIVE.

PICNIC POINT RIVALS THE SCENERY OF NORWAY.

SERENE AS THE AVON, THE YAHARA RIVER LINKS LAKES MENDOTA AND MONONA.

WHITE SAILS ON LAKE MENDOTA.

MOONLIGHT ON MONONA.

exaggeration." John Nolen, an eminent landscape architect, concluded that "Madison has the best opportunity to become a model, modern American city." But the most climactic of all were the words uttered by Sir Edwin Arnold, who announced that "Madison is the most beautiful little city in the world."

Rolling hills and lakes made possible man's municipal beautification of the lake country. "We who love it are always watching to see how well it measures up to its gifts," wrote Zona Gale, famous Wisconsin authoress. Once Amos P. Wilder, a Madison editor, in a burst of poetic enthusiasm headed an editorial with an apt characterization:

"Madison—pearl of shimmering lakes; citadel of learning; temple of power; shrine of law; the residence of thousands of fair young women and stalwart collegians, with homes rippling to the laughter of little children."

The shady walks around Lake Mendota over the University grounds, out toward Middleton and Pheasant Branch, are spacious and intriguing. A good place to start is on top of University Hill where Abraham Lincoln in bronze looks out serenely over the city of Madison, named for another American President. There is the appearance of a dreamer in that sallow face—visions of ideals in government. He seems to be watching the white Capitol dome that pierces the skyline a mile away on another eminence.

One can not sit long beneath the vines of Bascom

Hall without hearing the voices of romance. On yonder knoll John Muir received the lessons in botany under the old locust tree that inspired him to become a naturalist. In that sprawling building of brick Charles A. Lindbergh tinkered with engines, dreamed of aviation, and forgot to study his lessons. And all the time the deep blue sky of which poets write hangs overhead.

Not long ago the Norwegian singers of America gathered early in June for a Sangerfest in Madison in recognition of the eminence of Ole Bull, Norwegian violinist and composer, who lived there after the Civil War. During the festival many visited his old home on the lakeshore, now used as the executive mansion for Wisconsin governors, to inspect the heirlooms of the talented musician.

The climax of their visit came a few days after. One morning a number of the company went to Observatory Hill to witness the sun rise across Lake Mendota in the Tenney Park vicinity. Not one of the assembled had been back to see the hills and fjords of Norway in less than seventeen years. As the sun came coloring the horizon, one after another doffed his little white festival cap as each looked with the deepest awe upon the transpiring miracle. Finally as the golden rim seemed to hesitate on the distant horizon in a kiss of the lake waters, the oldest of the group broke with explosive animation the soft stillness.

"Now I know why Ole Bull loved Madison and lived here!" he exclaimed, his tanned face touched with a welcome-home smile. "This is like old Norway—beautiful Norway!"

The nostalgia of this Viking singer expressed in these words serves as a better description of this bit of indefinable north country than the words or camera pictures of a mere wayfaring journalist.

Leaving the University, one passes between Russian golden willows with views of University Bay that have caught the fancy of many an artist. If it be July, pause to catch the recherche tints from that lake-bed of lotus flowers. Look long and gradually and you will come to understand how the sacred lilies from the Nile were fabled to cause forgetfulness of care and to induce a state of dreamy indolence. Approach, but do not pluck! Their delicate colorings are so rare and fleeting that a state law protects these flowers and punishes those who would break a stem.

This wandering road leads to the base of Picnic Point, past Eagle Heights, and on around Lake Mendota, a distance of twenty-five miles, with panoramic views of lake, wood, and city all the way. Stand, if you will, on the cliffs of Maple Bluff, where stone for the first substantial buildings in Madison was quarried, and watch the afternoon sun run its course. Few artists could put that evanescent scene on canvas with justice to the vista.

There is something magical about this lake country. There are fleecy clouds that marshal in battle array along the western brink toward evening, which the setting sun tints in pinks and deep reds—

a diapason in the sky coloring. Watch those piling mountains of snow and soon you will wish to float away with the downy substance. Listen! The song of birds comes from beneath that canopy of tree tops. The gentle breeze of evening steals in from the lakes. The shadows of a beautiful night hover above.

No scene in the Four Lakes Country compares with Lake Monona in moonlight. A returning world traveler, the late Rev. Charles H. Richards, discovered that "the far famed Bay of Naples is not more lovely." As the dark clouds of evening depart and the red-faced moon ascends into the sky, soaring like a toy balloon, it paves a golden stairway with treads of wave ripples across the lake. If the fabled path to the skies can be as beautiful, it must be a welcome journey for the souls of men.

Madison is the Capital of the state, and the heart of the Four Lakes Country. It is eighty-four miles from Milwaukee, fifty-two miles from Beloit, one hundred three miles from Prairie du Chien, eighty-six miles from Oshkosh, one hundred fifty miles from Wausau, three hundred seventy-five miles from Superior, two hundred eighty miles from St. Paul, and one hundred eighty-nine miles from Eau Claire.

INDEX

X

Y